ART AND THE
CHRISTIAN APOCRYPHA

The Christian canon of scripture, known as the New Testament, excluded many of the church's traditional stories about its origins. These apocrypha included well-known tales such as those of the ox and the ass at the Nativity, the Assumption of the Virgin, and the martyrdoms of St Peter and of St Paul. Although not in the Bible, these popular stories have had a powerful influence on the church's traditions and theology, and a particularly marked effect on visual representations of Christian belief.

This book provides a lucid introduction to the relationship between the apocryphal texts and the paintings, mosaics and sculpture in which they are frequently paralleled, and which have been so significant in transmitting these non-Biblical stories to generations of churchgoers. It reveals the enduring power of the Christian apocrypha in both text and art, and displays the artworks themselves in a new light.

The volume contains more than 100 photographs, and numerous extracts from the apocryphal texts.

David R. Cartlidge is Beeson Professor Emeritus of Religion at Maryville College, Tennessee, USA.

J. Keith Elliott is Professor of New Testament Textual Criticism at the University of Leeds, UK.

ART AND
THE CHRISTIAN
APOCRYPHA

*David R. Cartlidge
and J. Keith Elliott*

London and New York

First published 2001
by Routledge
11 New Fetter Lane, London EC4P 4EE

Simultaneously published in the USA and Canada
by Routledge
29 West 35th Street, New York, NY 10001

Routledge is an imprint of the Taylor & Francis Group

© 2001 David R. Cartlidge and J. Keith Elliott

Typeset in Garamond by
Florence Production Ltd, Stoodleigh, Devon
Printed and bound in Great Britain by
TJ International, Padstow, Cornwall

British Library Cataloguing in Publication Data
A catalogue record for this book is available from the British Library

Library of Congress Cataloging in Publication Data
A catalog record for this book has been requested

ISBN 0–415–23392–5 (pbk)
ISBN 0–415–23391–7 (hbk)

CONTENTS

ILLUSTRATIONS

PERMISSIONS AND ACKNOWLEDGEMENTS

Credits

Texts

Extracts of apocryphal texts are from J. K. Elliott, *The Apocryphal New Testament*, Oxford, The Clarendon Press, 1993, and are reproduced with the permission of Oxford University Press.

Figures

1.1, 1.2, 5.8: Graydon F. Snyder
1.3: The German Institute of Archaeology, negative 41.2665 (detail)
2.1, 6.1: Ekdotike Athenon
2.2, 2.3, 2.4, 2.5, 2.6, 3.6, 4.2, 4.8, 4.9, 4.15, 4.29, 4.31, 5.4, 5.5, 5.7, 5.16, 5.17: Art Resource, NY
2.7: Yale University Art Gallery
2.8, 5.9: after images by Dr Ahmed Fakhry
2.9, 3.2, 4.4, 4.10, 4.12, 4.13, 4.17, 4.19A, 4.19B, 4.22, 4.23, 4.24, 4.25, 4.34, 5.2, 6.4: Cartlidge
2.10: State Hermitage Museum, St Petersburg
2.11, 4.20: Boston Museum of Fine Arts
2.12, 4.5, 4.27, 5.6: The British Library
2.13, 4.33: Herzog August Bibliothek, Wolfenbüttel, Germany
3.1, 4.3, 4.32, 5.3: Reproduced through the courtesy of the Michigan–Princeton–Alexandria Expedition to Mount Sinai
3.3: The Cleveland Museum of Art, 2000, John L. Severance Fund, 1965.241
3.4: Helga Teiwas, photographer, San Xavier Patronato
3.5: Robin M. Jensen
3.7: Research Team for New Testament and Archaeology, Harvard University
3.8, 3.9, 3.10, 6.13: Bibliothèque nationale de Paris
4.1: Monumenti Musei e Gallerie Pontificii, Vatican
4.6: after a photograph supplied by William Stroud
4.7: Austrian National Library
4.11: John Rylands University Library, Manchester
4.14: Nicaraguan Cultural Alliance and Quixote Center/Quest for Peace

xiii

4.16, 4.18, 4.21, 4.26: Peter Heman

4.28, 4.36: Foto Marburg/Art Resource, NY

4.30: Biblioteca nacional, Madrid

4.35: Utrecht University Library

5.1: Soprintendenza archeologica di Pompei

5.10: The Nelson-Atkins Museum of Art (Purchase: Nelson Trust), Kansas City, MO

5.11: The National Gallery of Art, Washington, DC

5.12: The Metropolitan Museum of Art, NY

5.13: Edwin A. Ulrich Museum of Art, Wichita, Kansas

5.14: Cartlidge, after a photograph by P. Styger

5.15: Cartlidge, after a drawing by Le Blant

6.2: By permission of the Société archéologique et historique, Avesnes-sur-Helpe, France

6.3: Photograph: Cartlidge by permission of Bibliothek Benediktinerstift Admonten, Austria

6.5–6.12, 6.14–6.16: Trinity College Library, Cambridge

6.17, 6.20, 6.21, 6.22: Bibliothèque municipale d'Amiens

6.18, 6.24: Giraudon/Art Resource, NY

6.19: By permission of the Warden and Fellows of Keble College Library, Oxford

6.23: Civiche raccolte d'arte applicata ed incisioni, Castello Sforzesco, Milan

6.25: Pierpont Morgan Library, NY.

PREFACE

The pictorial art of the church has had such an influence on its theology and piety that it would not be inappropriate to insist that this art formed a Bible of its own, a sacred scripture which was handed down in parallel to the written Bible, the Lives of the Saints and the liturgies.

When tracing the development and use of the church's images of its heroes and their significant deeds one ought to pay close attention to the role that early Christian apocrypha have played in stimulating the imagination of those patrons and their artists who decorated churches, cemeteries, homes and the texts themselves. Virtually every cycle of Christian art exhibits its parallels with the Christian apocrypha, but studies of this phenomenon are unfamiliar to those outside professional art history.[1]

The relationship of Christian pictorial art to texts is a subject much under discussion. The old iconographical dictum that texts are the influence which led to specific cycles of images and discrete images is undergoing considerable change and Chapter 1 addresses these issues. The old consensus tended to look to texts first and to announce that a particular text influenced the atelier or painter in such a manner that the primacy of the text was maintained. The developing consensus is that oral traditions, texts (rhetorical arts) and the pictorial arts all interact so that *all* the arts demonstrate the church's 'thinking out loud' in both rhetorical and pictorial images.

This monograph attempts to make available to those interested on an academic level as well as to the general reader the power and influence upon the faith of the church carried by the art of Christian apocrypha. As there are thousands of such images, this book does not pretend to be exhaustive. It should, however, be able to raise the understanding of its readers of the significance of these apocrypha both in rhetorical and pictorial forms and to lead the reader into further exploration of the 'Art of the Apocrypha' as well as into an interest in the texts.

Chapters 2–6 describe and illustrate the rhetorical and pictorial representation of images and events that belong to the non-canonical stories about Jesus, his family and his earliest followers. Thus Chapter 2 focuses on Mary, the mother of Jesus, particularly her origins and early life, but also, briefly, her death. Chapters 3 and 4 are concerned with images of Christ and with episodes relating to his life, mission and destiny. Chapters 5 and 6 feature events parallel to the popular apocryphal Acts, which relate a large number of incidents involving the earliest apostles and followers of Jesus, both male (predominantly Peter, Paul, Andrew, John and Thomas) and female (the most noteworthy being Thecla).

An index of some 2,000 images displaying scenes and persons where there seem to be parallels with the apocryphal New Testament has been assembled over many years by Dr David R. Cartlidge, the Ralph W. Beeson Professor Emeritus of Religion at Maryville College, Maryville, Tennessee, USA. This is not an exhaustive index and is regularly updated and added to. Images found in that index form the basis of the descriptions and figures reproduced in the present book. The full database of that index is available on www.maryvillecollege.edu/cartlidge/homepage.htm

The contents of Chapters 1–6 have been written primarily by Professor Cartlidge, who wishes to acknowledge the help received from the chairperson of the Division of Humanities, Dr Susan Schneibel, and the staff of Lamar Memorial Library (with special thanks to Mr Roger Myers) at Maryville College.

Dr J. Keith Elliott, Professor of New Testament Textual Criticism in the Department of Theology and Religious Studies at the University of Leeds in England, has been collaborating with Professor Cartlidge for several years. They have been present together at symposiums on Christian apocrypha in Switzerland and the USA. Professor Elliott's translations of New Testament Apocrypha have been drawn upon throughout this book. His introductory notes to these texts precede the first chapter.

Both authors wish to thank Catherine Bousfield and Richard Stoneman of Routledge Ltd, for their help and advice in the preparation of this book.

Note

1   Two technical German monographs (J. Weis-Liebersdorf, *Christus- und Apostelbilder: Einfluß der Apokryphen auf die ältesten Kunsttypen*, Freiburg im Breisgau, Herder, 1902, and U. Fabricius, *Die Legende im Bild des ersten Jahrtausends der Kirche*, Kassel, Oncken, 1956) attempt to show the influence of the apocrypha on art. This is not the approach of the present book.

INTRODUCTION
The Christian apocrypha

Where parallels exist between a pictorial representation of a scene and a written form, it is tempting to assume that the artist has been inspired and influenced either directly from the literary source or indirectly from his having heard a story from a literary antecedent. This book does not wish to defend that position as a rule of thumb. Sometimes it may well be the case that the reverse is more likely. For example, illustrations of Jesus' appearance or of Paul's may precede the written descriptions of those images. It will be argued below that certain other images, the meeting of Peter and Paul in Rome, or Peter's striking the rock and its issuing of water, or the boiling in oil of St John preceded the written forms of these events.

However, where we are dealing with a sequence of illustrations and a written version of the same story, as is the case with the ubiquitous cycles of the life of Mary or of one of the Saints, it seems more likely that an artist has referred to an already existing written narrative for inspiration and guidance. One thesis in this book is that early written documents would themselves have been illustrated and that those could therefore have provided exemplars and precedents for painters, mosaicists and carvers of a later time.

We do not of course know what texts an artist had at his disposal or what books, illustrated or not, were available. In the West the widespread availability of Jacobus de Voragine's *Golden Legend*[1] makes it likely that this collection of lives of the Saints and early Christian events lies behind artistic representations of those episodes. However, most of the pictures with which we are concerned here come from a period much earlier than the composition of the *Golden Legend* in *c*. 1260. Literary parallels to artistic representations of works that date from the thousand years before that time can often be located nowadays in collections of what are commonly referred to as the New Testament Apocrypha.

In many ways this umbrella title 'The Apocryphal New Testament' is misleading and somewhat of an anachronism. The definite article implies that there is one agreed and exhaustive collection comparable to the canonical New Testament of twenty-seven books, or to the generally agreed contents of other Biblical collections, such as printed editions of the Septuagint or the Latin Vulgate. The extra-canonical Christian texts, many quite early, which may make up a published collection of 'New Testament Apocrypha' are numerous, extant in many different languages, often appearing in a variety of textual forms, lacking critical or definitive editions, and from a wide geographical and chronological range. In recent years the preferred description for these texts is 'Early Christian Apocrypha'.

Modern editors must make decisions about what to include and what to exclude in such a collection. Two of the most influential printed editions of Christian apocrypha in the twentieth century were the collections originally published by Edgar Hennecke[2] and by Montague Rhodes James.[3] These have been revised in recent times.[4] Other collections exist in French,[5] Spanish[6] and other languages including two very full collections in Italian, one edited by L. Moraldi,[7] the other by M. Erbetta.[8] Obviously some of the earliest and most influential texts appear in all these editions, but each has different contents.

Although several of these early non-canonical Christian texts were popular, were translated into different languages and seemed to have been best-sellers over several centuries these were not the books which were accorded canonical status. Quite the reverse. In many cases the church authorities expressed their disapprobation of the contents of these writings by including them in lists of books deemed unsuitable for reading. The Christian writings finally accepted by the church both East and West as its scriptures achieved canonical status in the fourth century and formed the 'New Testament'; these books had been extensively used as authoritative foundation documents for at least two centuries prior to that time.

Many of the so-called New Testament Apocrypha included on the lists of censored texts have disappeared without trace; some are known only by a title found in one of the registers of books declared inappropriate for the faithful to read; some are known only from limited extracts of their contents cited in writings by the Church Fathers. Nevertheless, others have survived – some even in multiple manuscript copies dating from over several centuries. It is rather surprising that so many of these rejected texts are extant. We shall note in Chapters 2–6 an irony, namely, that details found in those relegated books often appear in iconic, pictorial, form in churches, on Christian sarcophagi and on liturgical utensils – all clearly with the church's sanction and promotion.

The sheer chance of survival has meant that we sometimes possess only one recently recovered copy of a work. The Gospel of Thomas, composed probably in the second century, has survived in its entirety only in a Coptic manuscript dating from the fourth century and unearthed in 1945/6 among the codices discovered at Nag Hammadi. Similarly, the apocryphon known from antiquity as the Gospel of Peter was rediscovered, albeit only in part, by a French archaeological team working in Egypt in 1886/7.

Those and many other early Christian texts originating from the second century onwards provided the faithful with popular reading matter. Much of their contents is unsophisticated, sensational, superstitious and magical to modern tastes. It is in that sense of 'secondary,' 'spurious' and 'derivative' that the quasi-pejorative term 'apocryphal' is applied to these non-canonical texts. (With a couple of exceptions, the word 'apocryphal' in the literal sense of 'hidden' or 'concealed' does not properly apply to these texts, as most of them do not claim to have been written clandestinely.)

Despite the judgment of the ecclesiastical authorities about the status and contents of the rejected books in our 'Apocryphal New Testament,' most of the books are 'orthodox' when judged alongside the official canon. Many may seem theologically uncritical but few of these texts are deliberately unorthodox or against the mainstream party lines. Occasionally gnostic and other heresies are to be found within its pages, but full-blown gnosticism, such as is found in many of the texts found in Nag

Hammadi, is not characteristic of the New Testament apocrypha. (Obviously, when speaking of those texts which were written in the first few Christian centuries, it is to be understood that we are being anachronistic in using words like 'apocryphal,' 'canonical,' 'heretical' and 'orthodox.')

Throughout this book reference is made to several apocryphal texts. Extracts from these works are quoted to show parallels with (but not necessarily direct literary influence upon) the examples of artworks described or illustrated. The most common texts from which extracts are included or which are referred to in the chapters following are now given. These are subdivided below into their conventional, but by no means necessarily appropriate, categories of apocryphal gospels, acts, epistles and apocalypses.

Apocryphal gospels

The Protevangelium of James

Like all the apocryphal books and many of the New Testament writings the author of the *Protevangelium* is unknown. The book was probably written in the second half of the second century. Many manuscripts survive in Greek (its original language) as well as in many early translations. The *Protevangelium* was the inspiration behind other written apocrypha, most notably the *Gospel of Pseudo-Matthew* (see below) and the *Gospel of the Birth of Mary*.

The title by which this book is conventionally referred to is intended to show that its contents precede the events found in the canonical gospels. The story tells of the Virgin Mary's parents, Anna and Joachim, Anna's divinely encouraged pregnancy, the birth of Mary, her upbringing in the Temple, her betrothal to Joseph, the virginal conception of Jesus and his birth. Like many of these apocryphal gospels the motive for its composition seems to have been the padding out of stories found in the Gospels of Matthew and Luke. The emphasis now given here to Mary indicates the growing interest in her and itself created much of the later and increasing devotion to Jesus' mother.

The Infancy Gospel of Thomas

This apocryphon, also from the second century, tells of the childhood deeds of Jesus from the age of five to his visit to the Jerusalem Temple at the age of twelve. The stories fill a perceived gap in the biography of Jesus, and show him (often as an *enfant terrible*) having power over life and death and able to perform some improbable and precocious miracles. The cycle of childhood stories here was made use of in later rewritings of the early career of Jesus.

The Gospel of Pseudo Matthew

This work, probably composed in the eighth or ninth century drew extensively on the *Protevangelium of James* and on *Infancy Thomas* (although it altered and added to its sources). This was the main vehicle for popularizing the contents of those earlier Gospels in the West in Latin.

The Arabic Infancy Gospel

This Christian equivalent of the *Thousand and One Nights* also drew heavily on the *Protevangelium* and *Infancy Thomas*, but added many stories, especially those set on the Holy Family's sojourn in Egypt.

The Armenian Infancy Gospel

Like the Arabic cycle this too seems to have been based on a (now lost) Syriac archetype. That archetype may have been written in the fifth or sixth century although the Armenian version is several centuries later.

The Arundel Infancy Gospel (Arundel 404)

This is one of several medieval Latin infancy gospels. It is housed in the British Library. The earlier infancy gospels are behind this apocryphon, but its distinctive description of the birth of Jesus may parallel some iconic images of the birth and it is in that context, below, that an extract from this work may be found.

The Gospel of Thomas (not to be confused with the Infancy Gospel of Thomas referred to above)

This is a rare apocryphon in that it seems to refer to the ministry period – most apocryphal gospels are set at the beginning or the very end of Jesus' life. It is also unusual in that it contains very little narrative and is a collection of 114 sayings, nearly all attributed to Jesus. As a sayings document it may be compared with Q, one of the supposed sources used by Matthew and Luke. This is one of the few apocrypha which has close parallels with the canonical books – several of the logia of Jesus here are identical with, and others (but by no means all) close to, words of Jesus in the New Testament. For that reason it is one of the few apocrypha where theologians legitimately seek historical material that may have originated with Jesus. Thus some of the contents of *Thomas* go back to the first century although the form in which we have it now is a second-century composition.

Three fragments from this Gospel were discovered in Greek (its probable original language) at the end of the nineteenth century and the beginning of the twentieth among the Oxyrhynchus papyri, but it was not until the discovery of the Gnostic library at Nag Hammadi that the text in its entirety became known to the scholarly world. The full text survives only in Coptic.

The Gospel of Peter

This Gospel, known in modern times only from a large fragment found in 1886/7 and two tiny scraps discovered more recently, tells of the death and resurrection of Jesus. Despite some recent claims that this may in effect be a fifth and separate first-century gospel to relate Jesus' Passion, its independence of the canonical gospels is questionable. In fact it seems to have been a second-century rewriting, perhaps even a deliberately harmonizing rewriting, of the four canonical gospels. Apparent tinges of gnosticism or docetism in it probably account for the apocryphon's dismissal and its virtually complete disappearance.

The Gospel of Nicodemus

This is another Passion Gospel and, like many other apocryphal texts, fills in gaps in Jesus' story. Early legends about Pilate (which are also to be found in medieval apocrypha such as the *Mors Pilati* and the *Paradosis Pilati*) are to be found here. There was a growing curiosity about the biography of Pilate, especially his end, as well as about the theological ambiguity of his role in the sentencing of Jesus. So expansions of the exiguous references to him in the first-century accounts were created. Likewise the roles of other *dramatis personae* in the story of the death and burial of Jesus were elaborated in this apocryphon. Such stories are to be found in the first half of the *Gospel of Nicodemus* known as the Acts of Pilate. The second half, usually known as the *Descensus ad Inferos* tells, as its name suggests, of Jesus' descent to the underworld in the period between his death and the discovery of the empty tomb. Once again a tantalizing gap in Jesus' story is filled by an ingenious elaboration of a possible interpretation of 1 Peter 3:19 in order to answer a theological problem about the status of those who had died prior to the time of Jesus' ministry. The *Descensus* relates Jesus' entry into Hades and his releasing of the faithful dead. This scene, often known as the Harrowing of Hell, was an extremely popular influence on artists, on the mystery plays and on theology. Both parts of the *Gospel of Nicodemus* go back to the fifth–sixth centuries, but the two halves are likely to have been separate stories originally before they were combined in later manuscripts where the text of one runs into the other. The dual work, the *Gospel of Nicodemus*, became a widely known work particularly in the medieval West.

Vindicta Salvatoris

The well-known legend about Veronica and her kerchief that captured the image of Christ's face gave rise to many artistic representations. The literary parallel occurs in the medieval Latin text known as the *Vindicta Salvatoris*, although the character Veronica (or Berenice in Greek) is to be found earlier in the Acts of Pilate where she is identified as the woman healed by Jesus of haemorrhaging.

The Dormition of Mary

Although not normally classified under 'Apocryphal Gospels' the many stories about Mary's death (dormition or assumption) provide ample literary parallels to depictions of her parting. There are various stories about her death in several languages in the apocryphal tradition, but the one quoted in Chapter 2 comes from the Greek narrative *The Discourse of St John the Divine concerning the Falling Asleep of the Holy Mother of God*. Other extracts below include the versions attributed to Joseph of Arimathea and Pseudo-Melito. The history of the traditions and the interrelationship of the various accounts in the different languages are largely unknown. It is likely that the earliest written traditions about Mary's death are from the fourth century. These had a profound effect on Christian theology and practice in both East and West.

The Passion of Matthew

This is a late martyrdom quoted below because of its references to the visions of Jesus as a 'beautiful child.' It exists primarily in Greek and Latin.

Jewish–Christian Gospels

These are conventionally divided into three separate texts, the *Gospel according to the Hebrews*, the *Gospel of the Nazareans* and the *Gospel of the Ebionites*. These titles were known in antiquity but the books themselves are lost. Recent reconstructions of some of their contents have been taken from appropriate citations found in various patristic sources, primarily Jerome, Origen, Epiphanius and Clement of Alexandria who attribute certain quotations to gospels of a Jewish–Christian character.

The Gospel of the Egyptians

Another lost gospel, some of whose contents are also known only from a patristic source, is the *Gospel of the Egyptians*. This probably flourished in the second century. A reference to a quotation found in Clement of Alexandria from the *Gospel of the Egyptians* is given below in the context of androgynous pictures of Jesus.

The apocryphal *Acts*

The five major *Acts*, those of Andrew (incorporating possibly the *Acts of Andrew and Matthias*), of John, of Paul, of Peter, and of Thomas are likely to have been composed in the second century. Only one (the *Acts of Thomas*) survives in its entirety. The others have many gaps and they have had to be reconstructed from extant fragments and from later rewritings and catholicized or expurgated versions based on the second-century originals. These later rewritings ensured the survival of the concluding sections of the earlier *Acts* because those tell of their eponymous hero's death, typically by martyrdom. Whatever doubts the church may have had about the racy narratives in the bulk of these often prolix Christianized novels, the martyrdoms were deemed not only to be inspirational and educational in a church determined to honor the memory of its founders and famous apostles but also to be of relevance at times when self-sacrifice and abstinence were virtues worthy of emulation – hence the preservation of distinctively Christian examples to serve as role models. In addition to the text of the second-century apocryphal *Acts*, some of the later bowdlerized versions, such as the *Martyrdom of Peter* attributed to Linus, the *Passion of Peter and Paul* by Pseudo-Marcellus, the *Virtutes Iohannis* by Pseudo-Abdias and the *Acts of Andrew* by Gregory of Tours, provide stories for which we have iconic parallels.

Apocryphal epistles

By their very nature the contents of letters (such as the alleged correspondence between Seneca and Paul) did not lend themselves to artistic parallels. Pictorial art commonly matches narratives or descriptive passages. However, the Letter of Lentulus, which contains the famous description of Jesus' face, is one of the best known apocryphal letters. This is a thirteenth-century concoction, originally written in Latin. The relevant portion of this text is quoted in Chapter 4. Another famous letter (also quoted in Chapter 4) is the so-called Letter of Christ which occurs within the account of the Abgar legend. This comes from Eusebius' Church History in Greek (and in Rufinus' translation into Latin); a Syriac version of the Abgar legend is also extant (the 'Doctrina Addai'). The relationship between the Syriac and Greek is disputed, but the original traditions behind these two seem to have come from the second century.

Apocryphal apocalypses

There are several such apocrypha. The images and word-pictures in these written apocalypses are of a piece with a view of the world (and the other world) found in many paintings and other iconic manifestations of the medieval mentality and its preoccupations. However, citations from these texts do not occur in the pages following. Although there are, as one would expect, works of art illustrating the other world, the Last Judgment, the horrors of Hell and the like – all themes that are to be found in these apocryphal apocalypses – these do not seem to have unique parallels with the Christian apocrypha. Instead their inspiration, insofar as it can be paralleled with literary sources, may be traced to Jewish apocalyptic writings or the Book of Revelation. Milton and (especially) Dante did draw on these apocryphal writings for their poems, but a direct influence on art is more difficult to define.

The *Questions of Bartholomew*

Often classed as an apocalypse is the *Questions of Bartholomew*, the form of which is a dialogue between Bartholomew and the risen Christ. It deals *inter alia* with the descent of Jesus to Hades. (It is included below in the section on the Resurrection in Chapter 4). The main text is in Greek (its original language) and Latin. A Slavonic version also exists. The earliest form seems to have originated between the second and sixth centuries.

1

TEXT, ART AND THE
CHRISTIAN APOCRYPHA

Christian theology has elevated the rhetorical arts in written form to the predominant position in its traditions. In addition, most Christians have a canon of written texts which they declare to be exclusively the rule and practice in the church's life, although not all Christians agree on the contents of the canonical list of the Old Testament. New manuscript discoveries such as the Nag Hammadi codices have enlivened continuing discussions of the theological validity or wisdom of a 'closed canon.'[1]

None of the above is news. That most Christians possess a canon of written literature and confess this canon to be the required basis by which to judge all other forms of faith and practice raises at least two problem areas for this particular study. Our subject is (1) the importance of extra-canonical traditions in (2) their iconic forms.

The church, the chirograph and the other arts

The church turned to the chirograph, that is, the written text, from its foundational art forms, namely from oral tradition in narrative (stories) and poetry.[2] The consequences of this shift of medium have had lasting and defining effects upon the content of the Christian faith.[3] Not the least of these effects is that the written text reigns over all media in the church's judgment about the value of an expression of faith.

In respect to the medium of pictorial arts, one of the most influential passages in that written word, Exodus 20:4–6, may be and has been interpreted to forbid the iconic arts in the church.[4] The Second Commandment was echoed and paraphrased in statements from certain early church theologians.[5] Canon 36 of the Synod of Elvira (300–306 CE), which was a local and limited gathering,[6] employs the language of Exodus to declare that *picturas in ecclesia esse non debere, ne quod colitur et adorabitur in parietibus depingantur* ('There should be no pictures in the church building, lest what is worshipped and adored might be painted on the walls,' or, '. . . lest what is painted on the walls should be worshipped and adored'). Discussions of the so-called aniconic texts from the early church abound in the histories of art.[7] With early church pronouncements buttressed by the belief that the Judaism of late antiquity was aniconic and further strengthened by the apparently late appearance of recognizable Christian art objects (from the beginning of the third century, at the earliest), a consensus arose among many historians which stated that it was virtually a miracle that there was any Christian iconic art. Pope Gregory the Great is credited with the rescue of pictorial art for the Western Church. In his letters to the Bishop of Marseilles in 599 and 600 CE (*Epistolae*, IX, 209; XI, 10) he declared that church decorations are 'for the instruction of the ignorant, so that they might understand the stories and so learn what occurred.' Gregory's pronouncements were not mainly intended to rescue an art form, as Kessler points out; Gregory's intention was a clever missionary plan.[8] In the Eastern Church, the iconographic wars and their aftermath settled the clash between iconic and aniconic voices.

But the existence of a prolific art early in the church's history, set over against the perceived standpoint of the church's theologians against such art, creates a dilemma for historiography. The historical question, in the light of seemingly strong resistance to iconic representations in the church (and Judaism), becomes: How does one account for the development of a Christian art? André Grabar puts the dilemma in the form of a challenge:

> Whatever the degree of relationship between the two iconographies, Jewish and Christian, may have been, and the causes of the interdependence of their images, the historian of Christian iconography is faced with the question: Why did the two traditionally aniconic religions, which existed side by side within the Empire, equip themselves with a religious art at the same [i.e. the Severan] period?[9]

The dominant theory in answer to Grabar's question was that, at least until the 'baptism' of pictorial art after Constantine's triumph (*c.* 315), Christian art was a folk art which stood over against the wishes of the clergy and other church officials. Christian pictorial art developed 'from below,' from the laity. In particular, the art was desired by pagan converts who were used to images in worship, in the face of official doctrinal resistance.[10] Sister Charles Murray calls this the 'classical' theory of the development of Christian pictorial art.[11]

The 'classical' theory is itself under challenge. The early texts, under scrutiny, turn out to be less condemnatory of all images and more precisely aimed at the idolatrous use of images than the classical hypothesis maintains. In addition, there have been several developments in the history of art which have added weight to these challenges. There has been the discovery of profusely decorated places of worship in both Judaism and Christianity (at Dura Europos and other sites). The art of these early places of worship, as well as that in the catacombs, shows strong evidence that (1) it developed from prolifically illustrated sacred texts, such as copies of the Septuagint,[12] and (2) that the existing art (from the beginning of the third century) reveals signs that it had considerable antecedents. Third, a study of the texts of the Judaism of the Imperial Period shows that Judaism was not a consistently aniconic tradition which took a fundamentalist attitude toward the Decalogue, especially in regard to pictorial art.[13]

It still holds, however, that there is no extant art which can be identified as indisputably Christian before the end of the second century. This fact does not, however, completely rule out the possibility that such art never existed. It is well known in iconographical circles that the Christians borrowed their art forms from the existing art vocabularies available to them in the wider social matrix. There is virtually no Christian iconic symbol in the earliest extant material that does not have a pagan counterpart. Thus, the earliest Christian art is often difficult to distinguish as Christian. The hypothesis of the classical theory mentioned above has become even more difficult to hold with the discovery in the 1950s of the catacomb below the Via Latina in Rome. There, Christian and pagan art mingle in startling fashion, but, more importantly, some of the images at Via Latina, like those of the church and synagogue at Dura Europos, display signs that they had a considerable iconographic tradition behind them.[14]

The problems accompanying the relatively late appearance of recognizably Christian art can be at least partially solved if we pay attention to estimates of the growth of the numbers of Christians in the Empire. Rodney Stark has provided some very important sociometric data to this point. Stark demonstrates that until about the year 150 CE, Christians would have made up about 0.07 percent of the total population. Between 150 and 250 CE, Christians would have grown to 1.9 percent; from 250 to 350 CE they increased to 10.5 percent in 300 CE and 56.5 percent by 350 CE. Given the generally accepted estimated population of the Roman Empire, that is, about 60 million people, there would have been only about 7,500 Christians in the Empire in the year 100 CE, 40,000 in 150 CE, 1 million in 250 CE, and just over 6 million in 300 CE.[15]

The population growth of early Christianity was therefore exponential. A curve of our accumulation of pictorial artifacts from the early church would show a similar pattern. The number of such artifacts which we can safely say are Christian is sparse at the end of the second century and through the middle of the third century; the number of these artifacts increases dramatically during the period of the greatest growth in Christian population in the Empire, that is, during the late third and fourth centuries. It should be noted as well that the number of rhetorical artifacts which have come down to us from the early church is also consistent with those of iconic items. With the possible exception of Papyrus Bodmer V (*Protevangelium Jacobi*), we have only fragments of early Christian writings until the fourth century.[16] We assume that many of these fragments are from complete manuscripts of, say, the gospels or the epistles.

There is no doubt that certain elements in both Judaism and Christianity were suspicious of pagan practices and, of course, idolatry was a subject of ardent Christian suspicion. Ernst Kitzinger rejects the 'classical' hypothesis' belief that it was the Second Commandment which delayed the appearance of Christian art and believes that it was the church's abhorrence of paganism which accounts for the absence of Christian iconic art prior to *c.* 200 CE.[17] The attitude of both the Christian and Jewish traditions toward the development of pictorial art appears actually to be in a distinction they made between the function of art as decoration and for heuristic purposes as opposed to the pagan idolatrous function, that is, the worship of an art-object. The latter was anathema.

Just when Christians began to use and to create pictorial art is therefore not settled. Both issues fall into the 'Abominable Snowman' problem. That is, it is virtually impossible to prove that something does not exist; it is also easy to summon hypotheses to theorize that this something might have existed, whether it did or not. There are a number of images which fall on the cusp between the Christians' using images which they acquired from pagan culture and their creation of images as 'their own.' In his lecture at a symposium connected with the Metropolitan Museum of Art's exhibition, 'The Age of Spirituality,' immediately after he insists that Murray is in error in her insistence that Christian art appeared earlier than what she calls the classical theory would allow, Kitzinger gives a brilliant 'reading' of one of the sarcophagi [Figure 1.1] in the exhibition to show how this art object is Christian and how Christians would have seen it. Ironically, it is this very sarcophagus which, in the published catalog of the exhibition, Carder employs to show how some very early 'Christian' art may or may not be Christian.[18]

Paul Corby Finney[19] has added a fruitful element to the discussion of the 'beginning of Christian art.' Noting that the first collection of Christian iconic art is in the cemetery of S. Callistus (Callixtus) from which there are funereal decorations (frescoes) which were painted approximately at the end of the second century, he employs the Callistus paintings as a paradigm for the cultural and social development of Christian iconography. It is no accident, says Finney, that this development took place at about the same time as the early Christian apologists were writing. Both were a sign that a hitherto small, poor and loosely organized group, that is, the Christians, began to go public. The paintings in the catacomb, including their decorations (borders, birds, fish, and so on), demonstrate a group who were employing the basic funereal iconography of paganism and beginning to Christianize it. A chief element in this development was the fact that Christians had begun to arrive at a period in their growth when they were (1) organized enough to plan for such a project, and (2) had the economic means to purchase the land and to pay for the excavation and decoration of the cemetery.

Finney also points out that the development of such an iconographic enterprise as the digging and the decoration of S. Callistus does not preclude the employment of pagan personal or household art in Christian homes. Finney employs the well-known Wulff oil lamp (Wulff 1224)[20] as his main example. Several of the 'Shepherd Lamps' can be acceptably dated in the period of 175–225 CE. It is not only on lamps of the late second and early third centuries that the Good Shepherd appears. We know that Tertullian mentions the use of the image on Christian drinking glasses. Finney, building on studies which have identified an Annius as a major manufacturer of these lamps in the period, concludes:

> Thirty years later, on the example of the painted shepherd carrying the oversize sheep in the lunette decoration over the Dura baptismal font, the practice had spread from Rome to the Syrian *limes*. In Rome, the shepherds carrying their sheep began to appear around 260 in relief sculpture . . . commissioned by the new religionists. Last but not least, within the literary culture of the new religionists . . . there existed a long-standing exegetical tradition that associated the founder of the movement with shepherding metaphors. Under such circumstances as these, it is reasonable to suppose that at least an occasional Christian customer will have been prompted to purchase one of Annius' shepherd lamps on the basis of its discus [a roundel on the top of the lamp which contains an image or inscription] subject.[21]

In short, from evidence such as that presented by both Finney and Stark, we can reasonably assume that there was 'Christian art,' that is symbols available and acquired on artifacts from the larger social matrix which Christians interpreted as Christian, before we find iconic representations that can be positively identified as produced by a Christian aesthetic.

MVNIFICENTIA LEONIS XIII P. M.

Figure 1.1 Teaching scene and orant. Sarcophagus, late third or early fourth century. Museo Pio Cristiano, Vatican. Found in the Via Salaria, near the Mausoleum of Licinius Paetus. Photograph: Graydon F. Snyder.

The church clearly did overcome whatever reluctance it had toward pictorial art, although in the East it required passage through a bloody war before the issue was settled. One central criticism of pictorial art from an author of the early church, however, still rings powerfully within the church and is relevant to anyone who would employ Christian pictorial art to establish Christian theology. Eusebios, in the beginning of the fourth century, after a Christian iconic art had been functioning for at least a century and a half, sums up in a letter to the Empress the several arguments against the use of iconic art in the church:

> You wrote me concerning some supposed image of Christ, which image you wished me to send you. Now what kind of thing is this that you call the image of Christ? [Eusebios speaks of Christ's two forms] i.e. Is it the true and unalterable one which bears His essential characteristics, or the one which He took up for our sake when He assumed the form of a servant? . . . You seek his image as a servant, that of the flesh . . . But that is also, as we have been taught, mingled with the glory of His divinity so that the mortal part was swallowed up by Life. [Eusebios then speaks of the ascension and the transfiguration] when his face shone like the sun and His garments like light. Who would be able to represent by means of dead colors and inanimate deliniations (*skiagraphiai*) the glistening, flashing radiance of such dignity and glory, when even His superhuman disciples could not bear to behold him in this guise and fell on their faces, thus admitting that they could not withstand the sight? How can one paint an image of so wondrous and unattainable a form – if the [form] is at all applicable to the divine and spiritual essence – unless, like unbelieving pagans, one is to represent things that bear no possible resemblance to anything . . .? . . . But if you mean to ask of me the image, not of His form transformed into that of a God, but that of the mortal flesh before its transformation, can it be that you have forgotten the passage in which God lays down the law that no likeness should be made either of what is in heaven or what is in the earth beneath?
>
> Once . . . a woman brought me in her hands a picture of two men in the guise of philosophers and let fall the statement that they were Paul and the Savior – I do not know where she had had this from or learned such a thing. With the view that she nor others might be given offence, I took it away from her and kept it in my house, as I thought it improper that such things ever be exhibited to others, lest we appear, like idol worshipers, to carry our God around in an image. . . . It is said that Simon the sorcerer is worshipped by godless heretics painted in lifeless material. I have also seen myself the man who bears the name of madness [Mani] [painted] on an image and escorted by Manichees. To us such things are forbidden. For, in confessing the Lord God, Our Savior, we make ready to see Him as God, and we ourselves cleanse our hearts that we may see Him after we have been cleansed.[22]

Eusebios refers specifically to images of Christ and the worship of these images in the manner that he believes pagans worshiped their divine statuary and paintings. Eusebios is not, however, consistently against pictorial art. In his *Life of Constantine* he 'records complacently the Emperor's generosity in adorning many churches with pictures, and mentions without reprobation the statues of the Good Shepherd and of Daniel among the lions which [the emperor] erected in Constantinople to adorn public fountains.' In his *Church History*, he 'describes without a word of criticism the statue of Jesus which he saw at Caesarea Philippi and which was said to have been erected as a sign of gratitude by the woman who was healed at Capernaum of an issue of blood. In spite of all this . . . Eusebius is reckoned as an opponent of Christian art.'[23]

Beneath the common aniconic elements of Eusebios' letter to Constantia, i.e. his abhorrence of idolatry and his insistence that Exodus 20 is binding on the church, there is a theological condemnation of iconic art in the church, namely, that pictorial art, as a medium, is theologically inadequate, for 'Who would be able to represent by means of dead colors and inanimate delineations (*skiagraphiai*) the glistening, flashing radiance of such dignity and glory, when even His superhuman disciples could not bear to behold him in this guise and fell on their faces, thus admitting that they could not withstand the sight?' Eusebios, who at this point seems to be in concord with Clement of Alexandria,[24] is speaking specifically of Jesus' transfiguration, but his suspicion of the theological reliability of the medium transcends the particular subject matter of his plaint and lives on in discussions of the function of iconic art as a medium in the church and in historiography.

Eusebios does not indicate that his rhetorical, written description of 'glistening, flashing radiance of such dignity and glory' is problematic, even though one's reading it is a visual experience, and the sentence is 'dead letters' which the reader must turn into a 'living voice' (to cite Papias).[25] But his comments bring up several questions which are still alive in historiography and theology in regard to the pictorial arts.

Art history as a science is greatly indebted to Aby Warburg and Erwin Panofsky. Panofsky's influential work[26] saw pictorial images as cultural 'symbols' which were as revealing as other artifacts of the heart of a culture. His employment of texts – in his case judiciously – to help identify the subject and meaning of a given image, however, set many art historians off with the idea that the text actually established the meaning of the painting or sculpture. Panofsky himself was not happy with this trend in iconography.[27] Further, the search for texts to give meaning to pictures tended to undergird further the priority of the chirograph in historiography and theology.

In recent developments in iconography and art history, an outcry has arisen against what Leo Steinberg calls 'textism, [which] as I define it is an interdictory stance, hostile to any interpretation that seems to come out of nowhere because it comes out of pictures, as if pictures alone did not constitute a respectable provenance.'[28] Steinberg's comment is an immediate response to one of his hypotheses, a response that demanded that he have texts to back up what he interpreted a number of paintings to express.[29]

For the historian who is accustomed to work with texts, pictorial art is difficult to turn into historical and/or theological data. What, when we look at a picture, did the artist intend for us to see, and what did the artist's audience actually see? That pictures represent a respectable provenance is no less relevant in respect to church history than it is to art history. Thomas F. Mathews points out in his discussion of images of Jesus in the early church that pictorial art is a valid and powerful medium through which the church and its faithful expressed their faith. As such, pictorial expression is as meaningful and helpful to historiography and theology as are theological texts. As Mathews says,

To [the converts of the early church, Christ] was still utterly mysterious, unde-finable, changeable, polymorphous. In the disparate images they have left behind they record their struggle to get a grasp on him; the images were their way of thinking out loud on the problem of Christ. *Indeed, the images are the thinking process itself.*[30]

If that be true, that pictorial art images are as much an indication of the church's 'thinking out loud' as are the rhetorical images of the early church thinker, how can we justify the pictorial arts as of lesser importance in our church historiography and our theological constructions than texts?[31]

For the general historian to venture into the field of art history is also a problem of practice. To deal with both text and art is an interdisciplinary hurdle which is often formidable. Most theologians are, so to speak, buried in their texts; they are trained in the study of texts and committed to that study. Robin Jensen puts it succinctly:

Thus while many intellectual historians find visual art beautiful and interesting, even provocative, they may be unsure how to evaluate it as primary research data and intimidated by the scholarly apparatus of the practitioners of art history.[32]

At the same time, the reverse is true for art historians. They are often not as skilled as textual historians in the study of chirographs. Cassiday spells out the problem: 'Even assuming that early painters or their advisors did refer to texts for guidance, it was certainly not to the versions brought to us by Migne or Loeb.'[33]

Even if we assume that we can 'read' the 'message' in an iconic work of art, how does one translate the seen into the heard or read? Even more telling for this study is the question of what honor does the church give to an expression of faith which is not 'in the book?' The theological weight of pictorial art in the church is therefore a crucial question, given the power that has generally been handed to the chirograph in church theology. If, however, one takes seriously the current trends in our study of Christian literature, namely, that Christian literature, in both oral and written human communication, is always an art form, it seems likely that calls to regard the parity of all Christian art forms as expressions of human encounters with the divine ought to be taken seriously.[34]

Art and the Christian apocrypha

The church's pictorial art has been and remains an extremely powerful medium by which the tradition informed the faith and piety of the community. We of the modern era often forget that, until the invention of the printing press, most of the faithful learned about the Nativity of Christ, the Crucifixion, the life of the Virgin Mary, and the lives of Christian heroes, saints and apostles from liturgies, sermons and church and funerary decorations, and not from books. Mathews' evaluation of the 'imaging' of Jesus extends to all Christian art:

once they imaged Christ, he *became* what people pictured him to be. The trans-lation of the Gospels from Greek into Latin altered their content only marginally;

the translation of the Gospels from literature into visual images profoundly affected their content. Images are not neutral; they are not just stories put into pictures. Nor are they mere documents in the history of fashion. Images are dangerous. Images, no matter how discreetly chosen, come freighted with conscious or subliminal memories; no matter how limited their projected use, they burn indelible outlines into the mind. . . . Eventually, of course, they invite worship. One cannot write history without dealing with the history of images.[35]

There are no Christian narrative cycles in pictorial art that represent the stories exactly as they appear in the New Testament. That these cycles are interpretations of oral and textual narratives insures that as a fact; they are the transference of a story from one art medium to another. But even if an iconic picture allowed the viewer to see noetically what he or she read – an unlikely occurrence – when the reader considers the lives of the saints, the life of the Virgin, the Birth, Mission and Passion of Christ, and virtually every other cycle of narrative images from the church, what the people of the church believe is strongly colored by the pictures at least as vividly as by what they have read or heard from Matthew or Luke or the *Acta Sanctorum*. Each of these narratives in iconic form often contains elements which are paralleled in text form only in the Christian apocrypha. If we look behind these narratives in either text or pictorial form, we appear to see similar or parallel traditions which gave birth to both art forms.

The term apocrypha (secret, hidden) breathes on the texts of early Christian apocrypha[36] an air of the clandestine or of the forbidden. In contemporary publication, certain mass-market books containing early Christian apocrypha sell well to a kind of theological pruriency; there are hints that the Christian apocrypha are texts that the church concealed or suppressed to guard the faithful against theological corruption.[37] This conception is often heightened by the publications' employment of old translations in what appears to be quasi-biblical language. In the wider theological world, however, it is more accurate to say that the churches have focused attention on the canonical writings and that this concentration has resulted in the church's ignoring the Christian apocrypha rather than on its suppressing them. In addition, the church's by-passing of these materials has been historically and theologically buttressed by judgments which declared the texts to be late or pseudonymous or heretical or marginal; such declarations were by far the more prevalent after the Reformation. The title of a book published in the last third of the nineteenth century sums up the problem: 'Canonical *Histories* and Apocryphal *Legends* Relating to the New Testament.'[38]

In recent years, there has arisen a renewed interest in Christian apocrypha. A detailed discussion of the causes of this renewal are outside the focus of this volume, but certainly among them are the increasing ecumenicity in church and academy, the discovery of the Coptic library at Nag Hammadi (and especially the library's containing the *Coptic Gospel of Thomas*), and the growth of cross-disciplinary studies. However, in spite of the aura of the forbidden and, most debilitating, of the irrelevant which has surrounded them, certain of the early Christian apocrypha have, from their inception, continually influenced substantially the faith and the piety of the Christian church. This influence has mainly been fostered by the liturgical and the pictorial arts of the church. In modern Protestant churches, particularly in the United

Figure 1.2 The Nativity of Christ and the Magi observing a star. Sarcophagus fragment with two
scenes, late fourth century. Musée lapidaire d'art chrétien, Arles. Photograph: Graydon
F. Snyder.

States, the influence of Christian apocrypha carries on virtually unnoticed; nevertheless, even among these churches, the presence of Christian apocrypha has been at work
quietly but effectively. Many Christians, clergy and laity, can immediately recognize
a portrait of Paul of Tarsus, whether it be in stained glass, stone, or manuscript illumination. This recognition is in spite of the fact that there is no description of the
apostle to the Gentiles in the New Testament. Such a description, and one which
appears to have greatly influenced portraits of Paul from the very first images that
are extant, is in the apocryphal *Acts of Paul* 3 (see Chapter 5, below). Even if the
viewer of an image does not recognize the typical facial features of Paul – long face,
pointed, dark beard, receding hair-line – the apostle is usually presented carrying a
sword, a symbol of his martyrdom. It is common knowledge that Paul was beheaded,
by Nero or by Domitian, although the New Testament does not describe Paul's death

at all, much less the nature of his martyrdom. The scene does, however, occur in the *Martyrdom of Paul* and other early apocrypha related to the *Martyrdom*.[39]

It is customary that scenes of Christ's Nativity depict the ox and the ass either nearby in the place of Jesus' birth or, more typically, with their heads leaning over the crib in which the Christ Child lies [Figure 1.2]. We declare in poetry and song that

> Ox and Ass before him bow,
> And he is in the manger now.
> Christ was born for this!
> Christ was born for this![40]

These common figures in pictorial representations of Christ's birth are not mentioned in the New Testament; they occur in the apocryphal *Gospel of Pseudo-Matthew* 14 (from this point *Pseudo-Matthew*; c. 8th or 9th centuries).[41] This element of the Nativity became an almost universal feature in pictorial representations of Jesus' birth. Arguably the first extant sculpture of the Nativity is what remains of a sarcophagus; it is now in the pulpit at the Church of Saint Ambrose in Milan. [Figure 1.3]. It shows a child in a crib, flanked by an ox and an ass; to our eyes, the other figures which we expect to see in every Nativity scene are strikingly absent: no Joseph, no Mary, no shepherds. The sarcophagus fragment probably comes from the late third or early fourth century.[42] The presence of the ox and ass at the Nativity likely precedes by a lengthy time the writing of *Pseudo-Matthew*, and the existence of this detail in the story of the Nativity is first witnessed by the pictorial arts.

The ox and ass, and thus the witness of *Pseudo-Matthew*, have become common elements of the larger culture. In a cartoon in the *New Yorker* magazine, the scene is in a stable. A woman is in the lower left, facing half right, seated, veiled, not nimbed; a child, nude, not nimbed, is in her lap. A man stands center, facing frontally; he is bearded. The innkeeper stands right, facing the left background. Behind the father is an empty crib. The inscription reads: 'Sorry, folks, but your insurance doesn't cover more than one day in the manger.' An ox and ass lean over the crib.[43]

The continuing power of Christian apocrypha in iconic form is demonstrated not only by details in what would later be 'canonical' stories but by entire series of tales and lives that come from the same church traditions that underlie the written apocryphal texts. The tales of the lives of the apostles and of the early saints and heroes of the church appear in Christian art from at least the middle to the end of the third century. During the medieval period, these lives were popularized in chirographs, such as Jacobus de Voragine's *Golden Legend* (middle of the thirteenth century). But both the *Acts of the Saints* and the *Golden Legend* rely to a great extent upon very early *Apocryphal Acts of the Apostles*, several of them from the second century, such as the *Acts of John* and the *Acts of Paul*, and extra-canonical gospels.

There exists in the church what one could call a Whole Gospel. It is part of the faith in which the church believes and of the faith by which the church believes. It consists not only of the biblical (and the so-called Old Testament Apocrypha) texts but also of the nearly two millennia of commentaries, liturgies, sermons, church disciplines, the church's arts and, as the center of this study, the Christian apocrypha and the pictorial arts which parallel this apocrypha. We suggest and hope to show that

Figure 1.3 Nativity. Sarcophagus lid fragment, third century, Rome. Now in the Church of S. Ambrose, Milan. Photograph: Deutsches Archäologisches Institut, Rom, InstNegNr. 41.2665 (detail).

the iconic versions of the Christian apocrypha have played a strong role in the make-up of this Whole Gospel. The influence of these materials upon the church warrants close observation by those who would reconstruct the history of Christian beginnings and of subsequent church development. We argue that the endurance of Christian apocrypha and its related contributions to the accumulated faith of the church is stronger than most Christians imagine and that its influence in the pictorial arts is consistently underestimated.

2

MARY

There are few Christians, especially those in the Western Church, who know of the existence of an early Christian text called the *Protevangelium Jacobi* (*Proto-Gospel of James*). Yet this so-called 'infancy gospel,'[1] along with its sister texts, *The Gospel of the Nativity of Mary* and the *Gospel of Pseudo-Matthew* has had an influence on the faith and piety of the church which rivals that of the canonical gospels. There is little doubt that the pictorial versions of these gospels have put their stamp on the faith and piety of the church at least as much as have their textual forms.[2] This influence specifically has manifested itself in the church's understanding of Mary, the mother of Jesus (we would be more precise if we called these works the 'Marian gospels'), and of the Nativity of Jesus.

The importance of Mariam of Nazareth in history can hardly be overstated: '[she] has been more of an inspiration to more people than any other woman who ever lived.'[3] With the exception of her son, the number and variety of pictorial images of the Virgin exceeds by a large factor those of any other figure in the Christian tradition. The sheer number of these images demonstrates the emotional and theological importance in the Christian tradition that Mary holds. She has served as the model of what it means to be feminine in the church, a model which has been both celebrated and bitterly attacked. The Virgin has been a prototype of Christian fidelity and of purity. She has provided a model of feminine faith to a church strongly inclined toward patriarchy. In modern Protestantism, in spite of its suspicions of certain honors given to Mary, there has been a renewal of interest in her, especially as women have begun to assert their roles in the church; what it means to be a female Christian is a vibrant issue in all Christian churches.

For all her fame, the material about Mary the mother of Jesus in the New Testament is, again in Pelikan's words, 'tantalizingly brief.'[4] It has been the role of the Marian gospels to supply the major portion of what the church believes Mary to have been. These gospels tell of her parents, her childhood, her service in the Jerusalem temple, and of her marriage to Joseph, as well as their supplying alternative Nativity stories which have also had great influence upon the church's faith and practice.[5] Mary's physical characteristics – other than that she was young when married to Joseph and was a virgin with child – also are supplied by later stories. There is a legend in a Menologion (Mount Athos, Monastery of Esphigmenou, Menologion, Cod. 14) in which the Magi commission a portrait of the Virgin and the Child. The legend is illuminated (folio 407ro) [Figure 2.1].

The many narratives in the apocryphal gospels about the Virgin Mary, in both

Figure 2.1
The making of the portrait of the Virgin and
the Christ-child. Manuscript illumination,
eleventh century. Monastery of Esphigmenou,
Mount Athos, Menologion, Cod. 14, fol. 407ro.
Photograph: Ekdotike Athenon.

rhetorical and iconic images, are not simply late additions to the glimpses we gain of her in the New Testament. It cannot have been long after the narratives about Jesus began to form in oral and then written tradition in the church that the church began to extend the history of redemption back into the story of the mother of the Redeemer. The stories which came to make up the *Protevangelium* and its companion gospels seem to have been a part of the life of the church during the first generations. The early appearance of the *Protevangelium* attests to this, as do witnesses of other early church authors.[6]

The *Sitz im Leben* of these gospels is often described as the need in the church to 'fill in the gaps' which the brief infancy narratives in Matthew and Luke have left open. Put that way, one must assume that the canonical stories were, in a sense, the starting point of these gospels, especially of the earliest, the *Protevangelium*. This has been the prevailing consensus, at least until recently. There are, however, some growing adjustments to this hypothesis. Elliott and Hock move toward a description of the author of the *Protevangelium* as having several sources – which may have included the sources from which Matthew and Luke received their material.[7]

A theological impetus in the early church was to tie together the story of redemption in the history of Israel with that of the early church; the infancy narratives in Matthew and Luke, also witness to this theological drive. This is a main theme in the *Protevangelium* and in *Pseudo-Matthew* as well. A connecting of the old and new covenants stands out in virtually every scene of the Marian gospels. In addition, and not in a small measure, the story of the Virgin in her gospels has a didactic purpose, namely, to spell out the exemplary Christian life, in purity, service and fidelity. Mary is exalted to a cosmic, royal status in these writings, yet, at the same time, she is the model of what it means to be faithful and pure, especially, but not exclusively, for women in the church. The purity of Mary certainly is a dominant, maybe the predominant, theme in the *Protevangelium*.[8] The suggestions that the work had didactic and/or apologetic purposes are not mutually exclusive.[9]

In their iconic form, these gospels express all the themes of the textual forms, but with the added power of visual images. The story is that of how *Ave fit ex Eva*, and this was both a transmutation theologically and in praxis. As a result, there is virtually no image of the Virgin in the church, in text or in picture, which the Life of the Virgin cycle in the church's pictorial art has not affected. No portrait in fresco, mosaic, or sculpture can really be said to have avoided the influence of the early church's visualization of Mary in its scenes which are paralleled only in the Christian apocrypha, particularly in the Marian gospels.

Two classical examples of this iconographic cycle, one from the West and the other from the East, set the example of what we can call the 'mature' cycle. The Western version, among the many churches which have these cycles, is represented by the justly treasured Cappella degli Scrovegni (Arena Chapel) in Padua. At the beginning of the fourteenth century (*c.* 1304–5), the Count degli Scrovegni built this chapel as a devotional gift to the Virgin. He chose an outstanding interior decorator, namely, Giotto. The choir of the chapel contains an extensive Life of the Virgin, beginning with the story of Joachim and Anna, Mary's parents, when Joachim was expelled from the temple, his offering refused because he and Anna were childless. The cycle contains some twelve scenes, lined along the right and left top rows of the nave, extending out from the arch.[10] These scenes include the story of Joachim and Anna meeting at

Figure 2.2 Giotto: Joachim and Anna meet at the Golden Gate. Fresco, *c.* 1305. Cappella degli Scrovegni, Padua. Photograph: Art Resource, NY.

the gate [Figure 2.2], the birth of the Virgin [Figure 2.3] and a controversial image which may be either the 'Handing Over of the Virgin (Marriage Procession)' or a 'Procession of Temple Virgins' (at the time that Mary enters service in the temple)[11] [Figure 2.4].

In the Eastern Church, the Kariye Djami (Camii), also known as the church of the monastery of the Chora, in Istanbul, contains an exemplary cycle of the Life of the Virgin.[12] There are some eighteen scenes.[13] This church's decoration, also of the fourteenth century, is in mosaic, and it stands as one of the great masterpieces of the so-called Paleologan Renaissance.[14]

The images at the Kariye Djami are excellent examples of the Byzantine (Eastern) cycle of the Life of the Virgin. They include the famous story which describes the choice of a suitor for the Virgin (after she has come of age). The suitors bring staves to the choosing, and Joseph's staff bursts into flowers [Figure 2.5]. This image is very

Figure 2.3 Giotto: The Birth of the Virgin. Fresco, *c.* 1305. Cappella degli Scrovegni, Padua.
Photograph: Art Resource, NY.

popular; Giotto's series in Padua also contains this scene of Joseph's being chosen. In stained glass windows, the scene of the flowering rod is in Lincoln Cathedral, the north transept, rose window, panel D2. The Kariye Djami images also display events in the Life of the Virgin which are main events in the life of any family, but, since they were in the family of the Theotokos, became events for a feast day. Such a picture is that of the infant Mary's first steps [Figure 2.6].

In these cycles, a central image is that of the Annunciation to the Virgin. The Annunciation serves as the climax to the Life of the Virgin, the beginning of the Life of Christ, and as a bridge between the two cycles. As this scene technically, in iconographic discussions, begins the cycle of the Infancy of Christ, we will discuss it in the next chapter.

The Cappella degli Scrovegni and the Kariye Djami are the recipients of a long history of two versions of the Life of the Virgin in pictorial art. These histories parallel

Figure 2.4 Giotto: The Procession of Virgins to the Temple or The Wedding Procession of the
Virgin and Joseph. Fresco, *c.* 1305. Cappella degli Scrovegni, Padua. Photograph: Art
Resource, NY.

two rhetorical versions. In the East, the *Protevangelium* is the rhetorical work closest
to the iconic cycle; in the West, the textual parallels are *The Gospel of the Nativity
of Mary* and *Pseudo-Matthew*. One cannot, however, simply assume that because a given
scene from the story of Mary is in a Western or Eastern Church that the artist knew
only the stories from his region's preferred infancy gospel. There were exchanges of
technique, style and subject matter between East and West, particularly as
Constantinople was such an important aesthetic center for the church up through the
early middle ages.

Lafontaine-Dosogne's work on the cycle of the Life of the Virgin is fundamental
and close to exhaustive.[15] What follows is a chart of the two cycles, dependent upon
Lafontaine-Dosogne's work. Each of the listed subjects is depicted in some medium
of pictorial art created before the fifteenth century.[16]

Figure 2.5
The miracle of the flowering rod. Fresco, *c.* 1320. Kariye Djami, Istanbul. Photograph: Art Resource, NY.

Figure 2.6 The Virgin's first steps. Fresco, *c.* 1320. Kariye Djami, Istanbul. Photograph: Art Resource, NY.

The cycle in the West	The cycle in the East
The marriage of Joachim and Anna (*Pseudo-Matthew* 1)	
Joachim's generosity	
Anna and Joachim marry	
Anna and Joachim give alms	
Kinship of Anna	
Joachim, offering refused (*Pseudo-Matthew* 2)	**Joachim, offering refused** (*Protevangelium* 1–2)
Anna and Joachim return home	The return of Anna and Joachim to their home (Syriac)
	Joachim consults the Book of the Twelve Tribes (He actually speaks to the tribes in the Syriac, Armenian and Georgian)
	He then returns home (Syriac) and then Joachim leaves Anna
Annunciation to Anna (*Pseudo-Matthew* 2)	**The Annunciation to Anna** (*Protevangelium* 2)
An angel announces to Anna her conception	Euthine reproaches Anna about her sterility (the headband)
The servant (not named) reproaches Anna	Anna laments in the garden
	The annunciation to Anna
Annunciation to Joachim (*Pseudo-Matthew* 3)	**The Annunciation to Joachim** (*Protevangelium* 4)
Joachim returns to the desert	Joachim returns to the desert
Joachim and his shepherds	Joachim and his shepherds and flocks
Joachim makes a sacrifice in the wilderness	Joachim prays in the desert
Annunciation to Joachim	The annunciation to Joachim (that Anna has conceived in her womb – apart from Joachim. Other texts disagree)
Joachim's song	
Joachim leaves the mountain	Joachim returns

The cycle in the West *(cont.)*	The cycle in the East *(cont.)*
Anna and Joachim meet at the Golden Gate (*Pseudo-Matthew* 3)	**The meeting of Anna and Joachim at the gate** (*Protevangelium* 4)
Anna and the messengers	Anna and the messengers (in Pr-Jac they are messengers and not angels)
The meeting at the Golden Gate	The meeting of the couple
The immaculate conception	The immaculate conception of Anna
Anna and Joachim at home	Anna and Joachim at their house
	The offering is accepted
The birth of the Virgin (*Pseudo-Matthew* 4; *Gospel of the Nativity of Mary* 5)	**The birth of the Virgin** (*Protevangelium* 5)
	The birth and the bath
	Offering
Anna nurses the infant Virgin	Anna nurses the Virgin
	Gathering of representatives of the twelve tribes (reunion of the phylarques)
	Anna's acts of charity
	Anna invokes David
The babyhood of the Virgin (*Pseudo-Matthew* 4)	**The babyhood of the Virgin** (*Protevangelium* 6)
First presentation of the Virgin at the Temple (modeled on Luke)	
The first steps	The first steps
Anna with the infant Virgin	The closeting of the Virgin in her room
Anna teaches the Virgin to read.	The caresses
[Anna, the Virgin and the Infant Jesus (Anna-Trinity) (14th C)]	Anna caresses the infant
	Anna and Joachim caress the infant
The Holy Family	The blessing of the priests at Joachim's banquet
	Preparations for the banquet (on the Virgin's first birthday)

The cycle in the West *(cont.)*	The cycle in the East *(cont.)*
	Presentation of the child and the blessing
	The Virgin goes back to her room
	Anna sings a hymn of joy
	Anna holds the infant Virgin
	Anna nurses the Virgin
The presentation of the Virgin to the temple (*Pseudo-Matthew* 4; *Gospel of the Nativity of Mary* 6)	**The presentation of the Virgin to the temple** (*Protevangelium* 7, 8)
The Virgin goes to the temple	Discussion of Anna and Joachim about the Virgin
The Virgin climbs the steps to the temple	A cortège accompanies the Virgin
The Virgin is greeted by the priest	Presentation and housing of the Virgin at the sanctuary
The Virgin prays before the altar	
Paroghita (daughter of Anna – Syriac only)	
The life of the Virgin at the temple (*Pseudo-Matthew* 6; *Gospel of the Nativity of Mary* 7)	**The life of the Virgin at the temple** (*Protevangelium* 7,8)
The Virgin fed by an angel	The Virgin fed by an angel
The Virgin embroiders at the temple	Visions of Zacharias
The Virgin and her companions	The Virgin educated in the temple
The Virgin is educated at the temple	Anna and Joachim visit the temple
The largesse and miracles of the Virgin	
The 'marriage' (handing over) of the Virgin to Joseph (*Pseudo-Matthew* 7)	**The marriage (handing over) of the Virgin to Joseph** (*Protevangelium* 8, 9)
The Virgin's refusal to marry	Meeting of the priests
Convocation of the priests	A dream-oracle comes to Zacharias
The suitors carry their rods	Gathering of the widows
Prayer of the high priest and prophecy	Zacharias prays over the rods
The choosing of Joseph	The appearance of the flowering rod

The cycle in the West *(cont.)*	The cycle in the East *(cont.)*
The Virgin is informed of the choice	The Virgin is given to Joseph in 'Marriage.'
The handing over of the Virgin to Joseph	
The scenes after the handing over (*Pseudo-Matthew* 8; *Gospel of the Nativity of Mary* 8)	**The Virgin and Joseph set up housekeeping** (*Protevangelium* 9)
The Virgin bids farewell to the temple and its occupants	Farewell of the Virgin at the temple
Joseph leads the Virgin away	Joseph takes the Virgin to his house
The marriage procession	The housing of the Virgin at Joseph's house
Joseph leaves on a trip	Joseph takes a trip and warns the Virgin
The Virgin returns to the house of Anna and Joachim	Joseph reproaches the Virgin (*Protevangelium* 13)
The Purple, or the distribution of riches (*Pseudo-Matthew* 8)	**The distribution of alms** (*Protevangelium* 10)
The Virgin is named 'Queen of the Virgins'	

The main outline of both the Eastern and Western series is essentially the same. The Western cycle begins, however, with the marriage of Joachim and Anna and a demonstration of Joachim's piety and its accompanying generosity, while the Eastern version commences with the expulsion of Joachim from the temple. Scenes of the marriage of Joachim and Anna are rare, according to Lafontaine-Dosogne.[17] The Western cycle follows almost religiously the text of *Pseudo-Matthew*, while the Eastern version has parallels in several versions of the *Protevangelium*, such as the Syriac, Coptic and Armenian versions. A Western image of Joachim's distributing alms to the poor is in the *Wernherlied von der Magd*, fol. 7vo.

The illustrated manuscript of the *Wernherlied von der Magd* in Berlin (Staatsbibliothek, germ. 8, 109, *c.* 1225 CE) is the sole representative of the full Western cycle as we know it.[18] There does not appear to be one monument which contains the whole of the Eastern cycle; it must be assembled from various sources. Further, this assemblage is difficult in that it depends to a great extent upon inference from post-iconoclastic Byzantine art. However, in Cappadocia and in some of the preserved churches in the Balkans and Russia, there is ample evidence that the complete cycle of the Life of the Virgin existed in the early Byzantine period.[19]

The Eastern version is in its likely most complete form in the two twelfth-century manuscripts of *The Homilies of the Monk James*, one in the Vatican Library (Vatican cod. gr. 1162), the other in Paris (Bibliothèque nationale, cod. gr. 1208). These two codices are virtually identical, although they do not contain precisely the same illustrations, and they do not include all the images in the cycle of the Life of the Virgin. They are undoubtedly from the same scriptorium (probably Constantinopolitan), and together they strongly indicate the existence of a very early, fully illuminated manuscript of the *Protevangelium*.[20] Of considerable interest for the relationship of text to pictorial image is the frontispiece of the Paris manuscript (fol. 1vo) which shows John Chrysostom looking at a book entitled *biblos geneseos* (cf. the title of *Protevangelium*, namely, *genesis Marias*).[21]

There are two cycles in the Church of San Marco, Venice, which are of importance in our view of the cycles of the Life of the Virgin and of the Infancy of Christ (Chapter 4, below). The first is the mosaic cycle in the south and north transepts of the church. The south transept portion of the cycle begins with the scene in which Joachim's offering is refused and ends with the presentation of the Virgin for temple service. This group of mosaics is 'only preserved as a complete transformation of the late seventeenth century.'[22] The images of the north transept start with the gathering of the suitors for the Virgin's hand in marriage and end with the scene of the twelve-year-old Jesus among the doctors in the temple (an image which usually belongs to the cycle of the mission of Christ). This group of mosaics has also been reworked but retains much of its medieval character.[23] The complete cycle contains the following images:

South Transept:

1   Joachim's offering rejected.
2   Anna and Joachim return home from the temple.
3   A curious scene in which the inscription indicates that there were scenes of Joachim's searching the records of the twelve tribes; the annunciation to Anna; Joachim's return to the wilderness. Instead, the Baroque designer has Anna and Joachim reading at home, on the left.[24]
4   The annunciation to Anna.
5   Joachim returns to the wilderness.
6   Joachim's lament.
7   The annunciation to Joachim.
8   The meeting at the Golden Gate.
9   The birth of the Virgin.
10   Anna lactans.
11   Anna giving thanks to God.
12   The blessing of the priests.
13   The presentation of the Virgin to the temple; the Virgin is fed by an angel.

North Transept:

1   The suitors are gathered.
2   The handing over of the Virgin to Joseph.
3   The annunciation to the Virgin at the spring.
4   The Virgin receives the purple.
5   The visitation.
6   Joseph remonstrates with Mary.
7   Joseph's first dream.
8   The journey to Bethlehem.
9   Joseph's third dream.
10   The return from Egypt to Nazareth.
11   Christ in the temple with the doctors.[25]

Demus proposes that the model for the mosaic cycle was an illuminated manuscript.[26]

Figure 2.7 Procession of virgins escorting Mary to the Temple or Parable of the Ten Virgins. Fresco, *c.* 250. House church at Dura Europos. Photograph: Yale University Art Gallery.

The second cycle is in sculpture on the ciborium columns at the high altar in San Marco. The cycle differs from the mosaic decorations in that it contains the contre-temps between Anna and her maidservant and Joachim's offering in the desert. These columns will re-appear in later discussions; they are very important in Christian art history as well as for the particular subject-matter of this book. San Marco stands as a monument to the crossroads of the Byzantine and Western art traditions, and the church and its decorations are also, in many ways, a bridge between what one may call the art of the early church and that of the medieval church. The columns, espe-cially column A (the left-rear column), contain scenes in which 'l'inspiration des scènes sculptées . . . est certainement préiconoclaste et orientalisante.'[27] The images of this Life of the Virgin on column A include (1) Joachim's offering refused; (2) Joachim consults the book of the twelve tribes; (3) the Annunciation to Joachim; (4) The reproach of Anna by the maidservant (including the mysterious presentation of a head-band to Anna);[28] (5) the messenger comes to Anna; (6) the angel comes to Joachim; (7) Joachim among the shepherds; (8) the meeting of Anna and Joachim; (9) the birth of the Virgin; (10) the offering is accepted at the temple; (11) Anna nursing the infant Mary; (12) servants kill a calf (for a feast); (13) the first steps of the Virgin [Text 2.A]; (14) the Virgin is presented to the priests; (15) Anna's hymn of joy; (16) the presentation of the Virgin to the temple for service; (17) Mary is fed by an angel while she is serving in the temple; (18) the Handing Over, or, Marriage of Joseph and Mary.

2.A

The months passed, and the child grew. When she was two years old Joachim said, 'Let us take her up to the temple of the Lord, so that we may fulfil the promise which we made, lest the Lord send some evil to us and our gift be unacceptable.' And Anna replied, 'Let us wait until the third year, that the child may then no more long for her father and mother.' And Joachim said, 'Let us wait.' And when the child was three years old Joachim said, 'Call the undefiled daughters of the Hebrews, and let each one take a torch, and let these be burning, in order that the child may not turn back and her heart be tempted away from the temple of the Lord.' And they did so until they had gone up to the temple of the Lord. And the priest took her and kissed her and blessed her, saying, 'The Lord has magnified your name among all generations; because of you the Lord at the end of the days will reveal his redemption to the sons of Israel.' And he placed her on the third step of the altar, and the Lord God put grace upon her and she danced with her feet, and the whole house of Israel loved her.

The Protevangelium of James 7.1–3

There are images in some of the earliest extant Christian pictorial scenes which parallel the rhetorical images in the Marian gospels. In the case of some of these scenes, this parallelism is questionable. One of the decorations in the house church at Dura Europos shows a procession of women who are approaching a large architectural structure which has open doors.[29] [Figure 2.7]. As the scene (on the east wall) shows only the feet and the bottom of the garments of five women approaching an architectural structure, there are competing identifications of this image. On the west wall there are three women identifiable, each carrying a lit candle. Whether the Eastern and Western images represent a unified and balanced theme is in question. Dinkler suggests that the women carrying candles represent the five wise virgins (Matthew 25).[30] Another identification of the image is that the scene represents the women coming to Christ's tomb.[31] Schiller believes that the women are a procession of temple Virgins as described in Protevangelium 7; Pseudo-Matthew 10; Nativity of Mary 7, 8.[32] If the latter be correct, it is the earliest known image parallel with the apocryphal Marian gospels and their account of the life of the Virgin. The key to the scene's identification is the architectural structure; is it the temple or the open tomb? A similar confusion exists in a scene in the catacomb of the Via Latina, cubiculum C. This image has been identified as 'The Raising of Lazarus' (Ferrua) and 'Joshua Leading the Children of Israel into the Promised Land' (Tronzo). As is the case in the Dura Europos image, the key is an architectural structure which can be either the tomb or the temple.[33] The identification of the scene at Dura as parallel with the Protevangelium is clearly not certain. However, in the necropolis at the Bagawat Oasis, in Egypt, the so-called 'Exodus Chapel' (Chapel 30), there is an image, possibly as early as the fifth century, of the temple virgins' procession [Figure 2.8]; the scene is labeled as such (that is, parthenoi).[34] This scene has also been doubly identified as the Virgins in the Marian gospels and those in the parable of the Wise and Foolish Virgins.[35]

On a sarcophagus in Le Puy, at the Musée Grozatier, there is a scene which Lafontaine-Dosogne identifies as 'the marriage' or 'handing over of the Virgin' to Joseph. In the image, a man holding a scroll joins the hands of a man and woman in the *junctio dextrarum*. The scene is followed by one of the 'Song of Joseph.'[36] The close proximity of the two scenes allows Lafontaine-Dosogne to identify the former scene as the Marriage of the Virgin. Lafontaine-Dosogne also calls attention to the possibility that a scene on a sarcophagus in Ravenna (the so-called Pignatta sarcophagus) is of the marriage of the Virgin. A male figure and a woman, not veiled, join their hands in the *junctio dextrarum*, in this case, '[t]he absence of a central figure who joins the man and woman is notable.' The scene is in a small section of the Pignatta sarcophagus and is next to one of the Annunciation to the Virgin. 'Ces deux illustrations n'ont pas de caractère apocryphe, elles sont inspirées des évangiles canoniques, en relation avec la Nativité du Christ,' is Lafontaine-Dosogne's comment, a comment which illustrates the problems of the relationship between text and image.[37] It is the custom of art historians to assume that a text must underlie an image. Those who come at the problem from the side of textual studies are more likely to suggest that traditions, oral or written, underlie both the apocryphal texts which we have received and the canonical texts. In this case, the narratives – not necessarily 'canonical' – which underlie the apocryphal gospels' scenes of the wedding of the Virgin may have indeed inspired the image on the sarcophagus, but the iconographical 'fixing' of the scene as we find it in later church illustrations has not yet occurred.

Figure 2.8
Procession of virgins and S. Thecla in the flames. Fresco, fifth through seventh centuries. Chapel 30 (Exodus chapel), Christian necropolis at the Kharga Oasis, El Bagawat, Egypt. Photograph: after a photograph by Dr Ahmed Fakhry.

Figure 2.9 The Virgin preaching in the Temple. Drawing of a carving in a stone slab, fifth century. Basilica of Sainte-Madeleine, Saint Maximin la Sainte Baume, St Maximin, Provence, France. Drawing: Cartlidge.

A more clearly identifiable early image of the Life of the Virgin cycle is in a crypt in the Church of St Maximin in Provence [Figure 2.9]. It is a stone slab upon which there is engraved the figure of a woman, veiled and *orans*.[38] There is an inscription which reads 'MARIA VIRGO MINESTER DE TEMPULO GEROSALE.' Here, also, we have a scene of the Life of the Virgin which represents a time in which the iconography classically associated with that particular scene has not yet been established.[39]

Several ivory carvings of the fifth and sixth centuries display scenes which are clearly parallel with the *Protevangelium* and in which the classical iconographical form for these scenes appears. The earliest is an ivory in the Hermitage, St Petersburg, on which there are scenes depicting Anna [Figure 2.10]. These two plaques are portions of a diptych which has been broken up so that portions of it are in several museums.[40]

On this ivory are the Annunciation to Anna and Euthine's reproaches to Anna. In the first scene, the Annunciation to Anna, which takes place in a garden, there are birds in the trees. This detail recalls Anna's lamentation which the angel has interrupted: 'Even the birds are fruitful before you' (*Protevangelium* 3:2) [Text 2.B]. The second scene contains one of the more mysterious elements in the Life of the Virgin cycle: the headband which is given to Anna by her servant. The other portions of this plaque also show evidence of parallelism with *Protevangelium* in their depiction of other scenes from the Life of the Virgin.

Figure 2.10 Above: The Annunciation to Anna in the garden, with elements (the birds in the trees) of Anna's lament. Below: The affront to Anna by the presentation of the headband. Ivory, fifth or sixth century. The State Hermitage Museum, St Petersburg, Russia, Omega 300. Photograph: State Hermitage Museum, St Petersburg.

2.B

And Anna sighed towards heaven and saw a nest of sparrows in the laurel tree and she sang a dirge to herself:

'Woe is me, who gave me life
What womb brought me forth?
For I was born a curse before them all and before the children of
　　Israel,
And I was reproached, and they mocked me and thrust me out of
　　the temple of the Lord.
Woe is me, to what am I likened?
I am not likened to the birds of the heaven;
for even the birds of the heaven are fruitful before you, O Lord.
Woe is me, to what am I likened?
I am not likened to the beasts of the earth;
for even the beasts of the earth are fruitful before you, O Lord.
Woe is me, to what am I likened?
I am not likened to these waters;
for even these waters are fruitful before you, O Lord.
Woe is me, to what am I likened?
I am not likened to this earth;
for even this earth brings forth its fruit in its season and praises
　　you, O Lord.'

And behold an angel of the Lord appeared to her and said, 'Anna, Anna, the Lord has heard your prayer. You shall conceive and bear, and your offspring shall be spoken of in the whole world.' And Anna said, 'As the Lord my God lives, if I bear a child, whether male or female, I will bring it as a gift to the Lord my God, and it shall serve him all the days of its life.'

And behold there came two angels, who said to her, 'Behold, Joachim your husband is coming with his flocks for an angel of the Lord had come down to him and said to him, "Joachim, Joachim, the Lord God has heard your prayer. Go down from here; behold, your wife Anna shall conceive."'

The Protevangelium of James 3.1–4.2

Another early ivory with scenes paralleled in the *Protevangelium* is the Lupicin Diptych [Figures 3.9; 3.10]. On the left-hand column of the right leaf of the diptych is the Annunciation to the Virgin, who is doing wool-work (see Chapter 4, below), and the confrontation between Anna and her servant, Judith, in which the maid is brandishing the headband. As Thierry points out, this scene has often been wrongly identified as one of the visitation of Elizabeth and the Virgin.[41] The Lupicin ivory has images on the right-hand column of the 'water trial' of the Virgin, *Protevangelium* 16 (see Chapter 3, below), and of the journey to Bethlehem, with Joseph supporting Mary and conversing with her (*Protevangelium* 17). The headband in the annunciation to Anna scene is found also on the ciborium column A in San Marco, Venice, and on the cycle in the Anna Chapel of the Church of Kizil Cukur (ninth century) in Cappadocia.

The headband appears in a few of the earliest renditions of the 'reproach' scene, and then, as Nicole Thierry has pointed out, it disappears and is forgotten in the Byzantine world.[42] The headband is a symbol, especially in the oriental areas of the Greco-Roman world, of royalty. Its presence in a scene in which a servant is berating her mistress is anomalous. Indeed, the idea of a servant's reproaching her mistress because of her sterility is strange in itself. It is sufficiently out of place that, according to Thierry, the various versions of *Protevangelium* begin to change it. Only the Syriac and Greek retain the scene in its basic form. It appears that the iconography follows the same pattern. The reproaches are tempered with the headband as a sign of royalty, and then both the scene of the reproach and the headband become less and less common. It does not do for the mother of the *regina caeli* to be dressed down by a servant.

The scene of the headband is a paradigm for the images of the Virgin's life-cycle as they develop in the early church. The drift is toward exaltation of the principal characters. The parents of an exalted Virgin are naturally exalted as well. The Virgin is always dressed elegantly, if often demurely, in the iconic arts. If the purposes of the rhetorical forms of the *Protevangelium* are apologetic (to rebut charges of Mary's humble lineage) or encomiastic,[43] both of these purposes are settled in favor of the Virgin by the iconic form of the narrative.

It would be difficult to find any image of the Virgin which has not been affected by the iconic version of the *Protevangelium* and its sister documents. Mary's images in the cycle, portraits of the Theotokos which stand by themselves, and images parallel with canonical sources bear the imprint of the early versions of the cycle of the life of the Virgin. The iconic version of these gospels puts a visual and therefore very decisive stamp upon the way in which the church saw the Virgin in its theology. The elevation of the Virgin surely is part of the cycle's purpose. But this is far from the text's or the image cycle's only purpose. The cycle and the images which have been derived from this cycle, in a way consistent with other early Christian art, tie the events of redemption from the time of prophecy to that of the life of the Redeemer.

The story of God's saving acts is a story of a royal salvation. Mary is the offspring of important people in Israel. Beyond that, she is the model of a pious child, one who will be the benchmark for the ideal of purity in Christian behavior. A servant in the temple, she endures the mocking of her companions. It is she who is chosen to weave the veil of the temple, the very veil which, at the death of her son, will be torn to open the grace of God to all people. That she is the 'most blessed among women' is depicted in the reception she has from the priests and the blessing she receives when her father holds a feast for the priests. She is the epitome of the chaste woman, even of the conventual woman, forced to marry only by a miracle. Yet, she becomes the model of motherhood. The daughter of those who give alms almost to excess, she is the image of the charitable, learned child and grown woman.

At the same time, surrounded by the miraculous, the iconic images depict a touching and very attractive humanity. Destined to be Theotokos, even the first steps [see Figure 2.6] of Mary are significant. The images of the first steps become part of the feast icons of the Eastern Church. She is the truly loved child. Unexpected, a miraculous joy to her parents, their caressing of her becomes a favorite image, as does her suckling at Anna's breast. Depictions of her departure from her parents to become a servant of the temple are, in the hands of great artists, symbols of the pathos between parent and child when there comes the inevitable separation from a child as she grows up. Albrecht Dürer demonstrates this pathos beautifully. [Figure 2.11] In a woodcut from his 'Life of the Virgin,' the child, with hair unbound, climbs the high staircase to the temple where the priests await her. Her parents stand below, almost obscured by the crowd. Vendors and other townsfolk do not notice the momentous event; indeed, the greed on the faces of the temple's money-changers obscures everything other than their business. There is a Brueghel-like quality to the truly world-changing event which passes unnoticed by virtually everyone.

The Life of the Virgin cycle also celebrates the new position in which the church of the second through the sixth centuries finds itself. It is, as an inscription on S. Maria Maggiore says, 'the people of God.' The former heirs to the kingdom reject her father's offering. He is turned from the temple in disgrace; in some images he is force-fully turned away. It is only when the girl-child wins the priesthood back to a true path that Joachim's offering is accepted and Zacharias brings about the marriage to Joseph the carpenter. The history of salvation is set once again on its right path.

Iconography traditionally ends the cycle of the Life of the Virgin with the events immediately preceding the Annunciation to the Virgin. But the story of the Virgin in images paralleled in Christian apocrypha continues. Mary is the resigned and mournful mother, almost always in stricken, yet faithful, stance at the Crucifixion. Then she is the most faithful of followers in the worshiping of her dead and risen son, both *mater fidelis* and *mater dolorosa*.

In the iconographic tradition, the Virgin begins to be present in scenes where the New Testament does not place her, but, because of the iconography, her presence is theologically accepted. The most notable of these scenes is the presence of the Virgin at the Ascension of Christ, almost always standing *orans*. The Nag Hammadi document, *The Dialogue of the Savior*, includes a question which Mary (either Magdalene or the Virgin, although, in a gnostic document the figure is likely Magdalene) puts to Jesus at the occasion of the Ascension. Whatever the text, by the sixth century, much of the iconography of the Ascension places the Virgin there. She is usually standing in the lower center of the scene, her hands in *orans* position, and she is flanked by the apostles. Christ ascends in a mandorla, supported by four angels. The pilgrim ampullae at Monza and Bobbio have several of these scenes as does a pilgrim's reliquary from the sixth century in the Vatican, Treasury of the Sancta Sanctorum.

Clavis Apocryphorum[44] lists some sixty-four different texts of the Life of the Virgin after the Passion of Christ. They differ considerably, and the many attempts to establish

Figure 2.11 Albrecht Dürer: The Presentation of the Virgin for Temple Service. Woodcut, *c.* 1503–4. Boston Museum of Fine Arts, Boston, MA, Maria Antoinette Evans Fund, 30.1158. Photograph: Boston Museum of Fine Arts, Boston.

Figure 2.12 The Dormition of the Virgin (Koimesis). Manuscript illumination, *c.* 980. The British Library, Collection of the Duke of Devonshire, Benedictional of S. Aethelwold, ms. Add. 49598, fol. 102vo. Photograph: British Library.

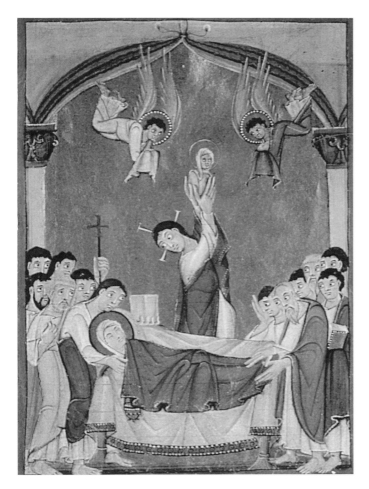

Figure 2.13 The Dormition of the Virgin (Koimesis). Manuscript illumination, *c.* 1000. Herzog
August Bibliothek, Wolfenbüttel, Germany, Cod. Guelf. 84.5, fol. 7vo. Photograph:
Herzog August Bibliothek, Wolfenbüttel.

a lineage of these texts do not agree. They all, however, concentrate on her fidelity to
her son, her piety, and her death and assumption (Dormition; Koimesis; Transitus). It
is the Dormition which has generated the majority of scenes. The announcement of her
impending death is given to her by either her son or by an angel.

Early scenes of the *transitus Mariae* in the West are 'three scenes remaining from
a fresco cycle'[45] in the Church of S. Maria Egiziaca, Rome. They likely date from the
period of 872–82.[46] Eastern iconic versions of the *transitus* (the Dormition and
the Assumption) from before the ninth or tenth centuries do not survive. A fresco
in the Church of Agac Alti (*c.* 850–950), Cappadocia, pictures the Virgin on her bed,
with John the Evangelist holding a palm and Jesus at her side.[47] The earliest extant
image demonstrates the early period in which the legends of Mary were known in
the British Isles, namely, a carving on the Wirksworth Slab (late eighth or ninth

century). The Slab is of 'rectangular red sandstone . . . which probably once formed part of a stone shrine or sarcophagus.'[48] The scene, which is left center in the upper register of the Slab has also been identified as 'the Virgin being borne to her burial.'[49]

Another group of early Marian scenes parallel with Christian apocrypha in the British Isles is in the tenth-century *Benedictional of S. Aethelwold* (c. 973). The *Benedictional* contains beautifully wrought scenes of the Annunciation to the Virgin, the Nativity (with an ox and ass), the Adoration of the Magi and the Dormition (fol. 102vo)[50] [Figure 2.12]. The Dormition of the Virgin in the *Benedictional* is also the occasion of her crowning.

At her death, according to the *Transitus Mariae* and other such documents, the Virgin continues to be the model of the faithful person. The typical iconography is of the Virgin, encouched, surrounded by the disciples, with her son behind the couch, handing her soul to angels [Figure 2.13]. The soul is in the form of an innocent and pure child: *sicut erat in principio et nunc et semper* [Text 2.C].

2.C

And as the Lord thus spoke, Mary arose from the ground and laid herself on her bed, and giving thanks to God she gave up the ghost. But the apostles saw her soul, and it was of such whiteness that no tongue of mortal men can worthily express it, for it excelled all whiteness of snow and of all metal and silver that shines with great brightness of light.

Then the Saviour spoke saying, 'Arise, Peter, and take the body of Mary and bear it to the right-hand side of the city toward the east, and you will find there a new sepulchre in which you shall place it, and wait till I come to you.'

And when the Lord had spoken, he delivered the soul of the holy Mary to Michael, who was set over paradise and is the prince of the people of the Jews; and Gabriel went with them. And immediately the Saviour was received into heaven with the angels.

Now the three virgins who were there on guard took the body of the blessed Mary to wash it after the custom of burials. And when they had stripped it of its apparel, that holy body shone with such brightness that it could indeed be touched as a rite, but the appearance could not be looked upon for the exceeding flashing of light; and a great splendour appeared in it and nothing could be sensed when the body was washed, but it was most pure and not stained with any manner of defilement. And the body of the blessed Mary was like the flowers of the lily, and a great sweetness of fragrance issue from it: nothing like that sweetness could be found elsewhere.

Pseudo-Melito, The Assumption of the Virgin 8–10

3

IMAGES OF THE CHRIST

The polymorphic Jesus

One Christian apocryphon contains a detailed rhetorical description of Jesus:

> . . . a man in stature middling tall, and comely, having a reverend countenance, which those who look upon may love and fear; having hair of the hue of an unripe hazel-nut and smooth almost down to his ears, but from the ears in curling locks somewhat darker and more shining, flowing over his shoulders; having a parting at the middle of the head according to the fashion of the Nazareans; a brow smooth and very calm, with a face without wrinkle or any blemish, which a moderate red colour makes beautiful; with the nose and mouth no fault at all can be found; having a full beard of the colour of his hair, not long, but a little forked at the chin; having an expression simple and mature, the eyes grey, flashing, and clear; in rebuke terrible, in admonition kind and lovable, cheerful yet keeping gravity; sometimes he has wept, but never laughed; in stature of body tall and straight, with hands and arms fair to look upon; in talk grave, reserved and modest, fairer than the children of men.[1]

This description is in a letter purported to be from Lentulus, a Roman official during the period of Tiberius Caesar. The Latin text is from the thirteenth century. Its description is of a Jesus who is more European than Middle Eastern, and it reads, as M. R. James says, as if the author were looking at a medieval portrait of Jesus when he wrote.[2] The so-called letter was a popular piece; there are Syriac, Persian and Armenian versions, all of which are medieval in origin.[3]

Pictorial images of Jesus which are parallels to the description in the Lentulus letter are essentially the standard in the church – particularly in the European and North American churches. With some ethnic variants, there is a consistency in these portraits of Jesus, a consistency which is in painting and in Christians' visions of Jesus. It is safe to say that, within the confines of one's own community of faith, everyone can describe what Jesus looked like, in spite of the fact that there is no physical description of him in the New Testament.

There is an image of Jesus considerably older than the rhetorical description in the Lentulus letter which also bears the distinction of its being a model for the Jesus pictures which followed it. It is one of the two most famous images 'not made by hands' (*acheiropoietes*) in Christian legend. Known as the Mandylion, it is an iconic image of the Christ, and it is associated with Christian apocrypha. The apocryphon is, in turn, about an historical figure, Abgar who was the king of Edessa (*c.* 4 BCE– 3 CE and 13 CE–50 CE). According to Eusebios (*Historia Ecclesiastica* I.13) a very ill Abgar heard of Jesus' healing powers and wrote a letter to Jesus, asking him to come and heal him. Jesus responded that he was unable to come to Edessa; he must fulfill his destiny and go to his Passion. After Jesus' Ascension, Thomas sends Thaddeus to Abgar and heals him. At Thaddeus' arrival, the king, according to Eusebios, who says he is translating from what may be an early Syriac version of what we call now *Doctrina Addai* ('The Doctrine of Addai') 3–4, sees a vision on the face of Thaddeus. Thus was born a further legend. There are several versions of the healing of Abgar. Among these legends (in the *Doctrina Addai*) is that Hannan, the messenger whom Abgar sent to Jesus, was a painter and brought to Abgar (with the letter) a portrait of Jesus painted on a 'kerchief' (*mandulion*). Another version of the legend has Jesus wiping his face with the cloth (or letter) and the imprint miraculously reveals the 'true image' of Jesus.[4] Abgar was healed, and he and his kingdom embraced Christianity.

According to its legends, the Mandylion was hidden in the walls of Edessa during a war and rediscovered in 544. Then in 944 the relic was taken to Constantinople at which time an 'official' tradition of the Mandylion was written at the behest of the Emperor Constantine Porphyrogennetos.[5] The Mandylion was supposedly transported to France during the crusades and was lost in the French Revolution. Copies of the image, however, were extremely popular in the Middle Ages.

The earliest extant image of the Mandylion's miraculous portrait is on an icon, [Figure 3.1] likely originally part of a triptych, at the Monastery of S. Catherine, Mount Sinai.[6] It shows Abgar, on the upper right panel, seated on a throne, holding the Mandylion. In the upper left panel is Thaddeus, beardless, also seated. Both of them have their heads turned slightly toward the upper center of the icon. Weitzmann argues that the missing central panel of the triptych was devoted to a copy of the Mandylion.[7] The image which Abgar holds and, as Weitzmann reconstructs it, the central, large image, are tenth-century copies and bear the signs of that time's style of portraits of Jesus.

A legend similar to that of Abgar and the Mandylion is that of the veil of Veronica [Figure 3.2]. The legend relates that this image was created by a woman's (Veronica) taking pity upon Christ's suffering on the *via dolorosa*; she wiped his face with a cloth, and a miraculous imprint of Jesus' face appeared. The story is in late apocrypha, *Mors Pilati* and *Vindicta Salvatoris*. The only texts of this apocryphal story are medieval [Text 3.A]. The woman (Berenice/Veronica) who Origen claimed had a statue of Christ (Origen, *Contra Celsum* VI.34; cf. Eusebios, *Historia Ecclesiastica* VII.18) was thought to be, in early periods, the woman who had an issue of blood (see *Acts of Pilate* 7.1). Through legends Berenice was identified with Veronica of the veil. There were popular images of S. Veronica holding her veil beginning with the fourteenth century.[8]

In the earliest stages of the portrayals of Jesus, the rhetorical arts show diversity. Each of the four canonical gospels is a theological portrait of Jesus. Behind the four different prose portraits of Jesus in the canonical gospels there reside earlier rhetorical images of Christ. Underlying the Jesus of Matthew and Luke is the Jesus of 'The Synoptic Sayings Source' ('Q') and the miracle working Jesus of the aretalogical catenae which Achtemeier has convincingly demonstrated.[9] The Gospel According to John builds upon the Jesus of the so-called 'Semeia Source' or 'signs source'; whether there

Figure 3.1 Thaddeus, King Abgar and four Saints. Abgar holds the Mandylion. Icon, tenth
century. Monastery of S. Catherine, Mount Sinai. Photograph:
Michigan–Princeton–Alexandria Expedition to Mount Sinai.

were other sources which John uses, such as a collection of discourses, is an open
debate. Each of the twenty or more known gospels that did not make it into the New
Testament display to us various rhetorical portraits of Jesus, e.g. Jesus in the *Coptic
Gospel of Thomas*, in the *Gospel of Truth*, in the *Gospel of Philip* and in the *Gospel of
Peter*. In addition, the rhetorical versions of the gospels are grounded in a vital oral
tradition.[10] In view of the many different views of Jesus presented by the early church,

3.A

Then they made a search with great diligence to seek the portrait of the Lord; and they found a woman named Veronica who had the portrait of the Lord. Then the emperor Tiberius said to Velosian, 'How have you kept it?' And he answered, 'I have it in clean cloth of gold, rolled up in a shawl.' And the emperor Tiberius said, 'Bring it to me, and spread it before my face, that I may fall to the ground and bending my knees, may adore it on the ground.' Then Velosian spread out his shawl with the cloth of gold on which the portrait of the Lord had been imprinted; and the emperor Tiberius saw it. And he immediately adored the image of the Lord with a pure heart, and his flesh was cleansed and became as the flesh of a little child. And all the blind, the lepers, the lame, the dumb, the deaf, and those possessed by various diseases, who were there present, were healed, and cured, and cleansed. And the emperor Tiberius bowed his head and bent his knees, and pondered the words, 'Blessed is the womb which bore you, and the breasts which you sucked' and he groaned to the Lord, saying with tears, 'God of heaven and earth, do not permit me to sin, but confirm my soul and my body, and place me in your kingdom, because in your name do I always trust: free me from all evils, as you freed the three children from the furnace of blazing fire.'

Vindicta Salvatoris 32–4

Figure 3.2 Veronica holds the sudarium on which is the Image of Christ. Manuscript illumination, fifteenth century. Ambrosian Library, L58 sup., fol. 67ro.
Photograph: Cartlidge.

the apocryphal *Acts of Thomas* 153 aptly describes the situation: 'Glory to thee, many-guised (*polymorphos*) Jesus . . .' [Text 3.B].

The iconic arts also present to us theologically diverse and often competing depictions of Jesus. The early church has left for us a wide array of iconic Jesus figures. One art historian has dubbed this phenomenon 'Christ Chameleon.'[11] It is common knowledge that the New Testament in its presentations of who Jesus was or is does not give us a rhetorical description of what Jesus looked like. But some of the early Christian apocrypha do. As several of the many different pictorial images of Christ are paralleled in the rhetorical arts only in Christian apocrypha, it is fitting that the apocryphal *Acts of Peter* 20 should put it succinctly: '[Jesus] is huge and very little, beautiful and ugly, child and old man . . . He is all things.'

Augustine, who was not known as a happy companion of Christian figurative arts – Peter Brown calls him a 'spoilsport'[12] (in regard to Christian art) – believes it natural that 'even the countenance of our Lord Himself in the flesh is variously fancied by the diversity of countless imaginations, which yet was one, whatever it was.'[13] The one Jesus who appears in many forms to the faithful, appears to be a reluctant boon to Augustine. To this, there is a fascinating exchange in Origen's *Contra Celsum*:

3.B

'For when he had chosen Peter and Andrew, who were brothers, he came to me, and to my brother James, saying, "I have need of you, come unto me." And my brother said, "John, this child on the shore who called to us, what does he want?". And I said, "What child?" He replied, "The one who is beckoning to us." And I answered, "Because of our long watch that we kept at sea you are not seeing straight, brother James: but do you not see the man who stands there, fair and comely and of a cheerful countenance?" But he said to me, "Him I do not see, brother; but let us go and we shall see what it means." And so when we had landed the ship, we saw him helping us to beach the ship.

'And when we left the place, wishing to follow him again, he again appeared to me, bald-headed but with a thick and flowing beard; but to James he appeared as a youth whose beard was just starting. We were perplexed, both of us, as to the meaning of what we had seen. But when we followed him, we both became gradually more perplexed as we thought on the matter. Yet to me there appeared a still more wonderful sight; for I tried to see him as he was, and I never at any time saw his eyes closing but only open. And sometimes he appeared to me as a small man and unattractive, and then again as one reaching to heaven. Also there was in him another marvel; when I sat at table he would take me upon his breast and I held him; and sometimes his breast felt to me to be smooth and tender, and sometimes hard, like stone, so that I was perplexed in myself and said, "What does this mean?"

'At another time he took me and James and Peter to the mountain, where he used to pray, and we beheld such a light on him that it is not possible for a man who uses mortal speech to describe what it was like. Again in a similar way he led us three up to the mountain saying, "Come with me." And we went again and saw him at a distance praying. Now I, because he loved me, went to him quietly as though he should not see, and stood looking upon his back. And I saw that he was not dressed in garments, but was seen by us as naked and not at all like a man; his feet were whiter than snow, so that the ground there was lit up by his feet, and his head reached to heaven so that I was afraid and cried out, and he turned and appeared as a man of small stature, and took hold of my beard and pulled it and said to me, "John, be not unbelieving, but believing, and not inquisitive." And I said to him, "What have I done, Lord?" And I tell you brethren, I suffered such pain for thirty days at the place where he took hold of my beard, that I said unto him, "Lord, if your playful tug has given me so much pain, what if you had given me a beating?" And he said to me, "Let it be your concern from henceforth not to tempt him who is not to be tempted."

'But Peter and James were angry because I spoke with the Lord and beckoned me to come to them and leave the Lord alone. And I went, and they both said to me, "Who was speaking to the Lord when he was on top of the mountain, for we heard both of them speaking?" And I, when I considered his great grace and his unity which has many faces, and his wisdom which without ceasing looked upon us, said, "This you shall learn if you ask him."

'Again when all of us disciples were once sleeping in a house at Gennesaret, after wrapping myself up I watched what he did, and first I heard him say, "John, go to sleep." And thereupon I feigned to be asleep; and I saw another like him whom I also heard saying to my Lord, "Jesus, those whom you have chosen still do not believe in you." And my Lord said to him, "You are right, for they are men."

'Another glory I will tell you, brethren. Sometimes when I meant to touch him, I met a material and solid body; and at other times again when I felt him, the substance was immaterial and bodiless and as if it were not existing at all. Now, if at any time he were invited by one of the Pharisees and went where he was invited, we went with him. And there was set before each one of us a loaf of bread by our host, and he also received a loaf. And he would bless his own and divide it amongst us; and from that little piece each of us was filled, and our own loaves were saved intact, so that those who had invited him were amazed. And often when I was walking with him I wished to see whether the print of his foot appeared upon the earth – for I saw him raising himself from the earth – but I never saw it. Now, these things, dear brethren, I speak to you to encourage you in your faith towards him, for we must at the present keep silent about his mighty and wonderful works, inasmuch as they are mysteries and doubtless cannot be uttered or heard.'

The Acts of John 88–93

In VI.75 Celsus says, 'If a divine spirit was in a body, it must certainly have differed from other bodies in size or beauty or strength or voice or striking appearance or powers of persuasion. For it is impossible that a body which had something more divine than the rest should be no different from any other. Yet Jesus' body was no different from any other, but, as they say, was little and ugly and undistinguished.'

Origen replies:

> Admittedly it is written that the body of Jesus was ugly, but not, as he asserted, that it was also undistinguished; nor is there any clear indication that he was little. The passage is written in Isaiah . . . [53:1–3] . . . Celsus paid heed to these words, since he thought they would be useful to him with a view to attacking Jesus; but he did not pay any attention to the words of the forty-fourth Psalm where it is said: 'Gird thy sword upon thy thigh, mighty one, with thy beauty and fairness; and exert thyself and ride on and rule.' [in VI.76, Origen attacks Celsus for his picking the prophecy that suits his own argument. In rebuttal, Origen describes the transfiguration.] [VI.77] *how did {Celsus} fail to notice that his body differed in accordance with the capacity of those who saw it, and on this account appeared in such form as was beneficial for the needs of each individual's vision?*[14]

Behind Celsus' attack upon the Christians' use of images lie Greco-Roman expectations in respect to the appearance of gods and heroes. With the exception of a few divine characters, e.g. Socrates, a divine man (*theios aner*) was expected to be beautiful; they were usually portrayed as such. Origen's reply may contain more than a *soupçon* of docetism, even if we grant that his model is the Transfiguration. But the point we would emphasize is that Origen is arguing within the context of theological 'vision.'

In both rhetorical and pictorial art, an image of Jesus in the church was a theological choice, a choice which was at the heart of the Christians' existence. As Mathews points out in a passage which we have already quoted,[15] the various images of Jesus in the early church were the church's thinking out loud theologically. The many different Christs who appear in the numerous gospels of the church and those whom we can see in sculpture, fresco, mosaic and other media are not happenstance nor are they simply the early church's thoughtless grasping at images which were available in the culture in which the early church came to be. It is unwarranted to believe that the early Christians, who undoubtedly employed Greco-Roman images of savior gods to picture Jesus, were mindless imitators of Greco-Roman practices or that they were unaware of what they were doing. One art historian recently declared in a popular article, 'It is clear that the early Christians were unconcerned by Christ's actual appearance.'[16] This is not the case. The many-guised Jesus should be taken seriously as evidence of the early Christians' struggles to come to understand the object and content of their faith, a struggle which has continued throughout the history of the church.

The beautiful youth (and Good Shepherd)

The most popular choice of the pre-Constantinian Christians for their first depictions of the person of Jesus in the early church's art is Jesus as a comely youth. The first image which arguably falls under that heading, and which was the most popular figurative Jesus image in the very beginnings of Christian iconic art, is the *criophoros* (literally, the ram-carrier), the Good Shepherd. The figure is usually of a young man, beautiful and, most often, a beardless youth; he is dressed for outdoor work, that is, with a short tunic and boots or high-laced sandals; he stands carrying a sheep across his shoulders. This image is featured in the baptistery of the house church in Dura Europos, one of the earliest datable pieces of Christian pictorial art. It is well known that the image of the ram-carrier was originally pagan and was at least a thousand years old before it was used by the Christians. Hermes, Apollo and Dionysos were all represented by the ram-carrier.

The metaphor of the shepherd who cares for his flock is prolific throughout the early church's literature (and not only in John 10 and Luke 15:3–7). The image did not carry over to the church only in the traditions it received from ancient Israel (as in Psalm 23); the shepherd as leader of the flock permeates the Greek and Roman cultures of the Mediterranean basin from before the times of the *Odyssey*. It is not therefore the rarity of the image which gives rise to considerable and often contentious discussions about early Christians' use of the iconic *bonus pastor*; the case is just the opposite. The image is employed so often and is so permeated with a pagan scent that it seems the Christian use of these images had to be justified in some way by art historians and theologians.[17]

The most common device in art history's canonization of the Good Shepherd has been to suggest that it is an 'abbreviated representation,' and the image therefore points to scriptural passages, namely, Luke 15:3–7 and John 10. Dinkler, in reference to the Good Shepherd in the baptistery of Dura Europos says that '[the] broader presentation of a sheep carrier with his flock introduces a bucolic theme, which, in this context, is to be understood as a symbolic reference to John 10:11.'[18] Given that the gospels came into being in stages and that long histories of oral and written tradition underlie our present versions of these writings, it is likely more accurate to say that the image of the Good Shepherd at Dura would exist for the early Christian viewer in the context of the various traditions that also contributed to John 10.[19]

The Christian apocrypha join virtually the whole corpus of early Christian literature in their employment of references to Jesus as Shepherd. The *Acts of Thomas* 39 uses the phrase 'Good Shepherd' (*agathos poimen*). That the *Shepherd of Hermas* uses the image is self-evident in the title given that work; it is an especially relevant image in the fourth vision. The list of passages throughout Christian literature is vast, and in the rhetorical images it is not only Jesus who is the shepherd. God and the apostles are also shepherds of the flock. In the latter reference, the phrase in the *Acts of Paul and Thecla* 21 is poignant and touching: Thecla, having been condemned to be burned, 'as a lamb in the wilderness looks around for the shepherd, so Thecla kept searching for Paul. And having looked into the crowd she saw the Lord sitting in the likeness of Paul and said, "As if I were unable to endure, Paul has come to look after me." '[20]

This passage may give us a clue as to what an early Christian would have seen (in the sense of one's 'seeing internally' or 'noetically'[21]) when he or she went shopping for a common household implement such as an oil lamp. After a look through a workman's displays, the purchaser would have likely come across a lamp which had upon it the figure of a Good Shepherd.[22] The Good Shepherd was, depending upon the context of the purchaser's life at that time, for the buyer, the church, a favorite apostle, the pastor of the church, Jesus or God – or all of these at once.

To borrow a symbol, and the Christians, as we know, appropriated, in addition to the Good Shepherd, every pictorial image they had from the artistic vocabulary available to them in the Greco-Roman world, is to bring over to one's camp the meaning of the symbol as well as the image itself: 'the sign taken over, because it is a sign, comes with a meaning.'[23] If the symbol is taken over from one's competitors, the meaning that comes with it must be adapted or tamed. Tertullian, for example, mentions with some disapproval the Christian use of drinking goblets which had images of the Good Shepherd engraved on the bottom.[24] The context, however, is Tertullian's dislike of the *Shepherd of Hermas*; he believed that the *Shepherd* allowed fornicators, if they repented, to return to the communion: 'In other words, this is not an example of Tertullian's rigorism in a matter of art but the treating of a particular symbol with contempt because it was used by Christians for whom he felt contempt.'[25]

This incident involving Tertullian also illustrates the way in which an image or any other symbol carries with it an aura of meaning. The Good Shepherd of the *Shepherd of Hermas* brought with it, in the case of some Christians, drinking and other carousing as part of a package of meaning, at least in Tertullian's eyes. The borrowing community attempts to recolor the aura; it is always only partially successful.

We have iconographic evidence of the church's reworking both the pagan symbol and the meaning that comes with it in the evolution of the Good Shepherd image itself. Compare, for example, the statue of the Good Shepherd among the Cleveland marbles[26] [Figure 3.3] or that in the Catacomb of Domitilla[27] with the highly Christianized shepherd in the mausoleum of Galla Placidia in Ravenna.[28] The Good Shepherd in Cleveland and that in the Domitilla cemetery would be hard to distinguish from pagan images, if they had not been found in Christian contexts. The fresco in the Domitilla catacomb is Christ as Orpheus – the shepherd carries a pan-pipe.[29] The Good Shepherd in the mausoleum of Galla Placidia, on the other hand, sits on a rock in a manner much more pacific than is the stance of the first two, and he carries a cross-headed staff. He is nimbed, wears a long, loose-fitting tunic, and chucks a lamb under the chin. He is the Christian Good Shepherd from head to toe.

The popularity of the Good Shepherd began to wane in the latter fourth century, and it virtually disappears in the fifth century. Jensen suggests that the church's emphasis upon its establishment of 'specific manifestations of Jesus' divinity' contributed to the image's loss of popularity.[30] The image did not disappear entirely. One re-occurrence of the image, in modern times, has a quirky history. A recent cleaning and restoration of the images in the Mission San Xavier del Bac, Tucson, Arizona, included what had been believed to be a *c.* 1797 painting of the Good Shepherd [Figure 3.4]. The restorers now believe that the image is actually the Virgin as a Good Shepherdess (*bona pastora* ?) and entitle the image 'La Divina Pastora.' The picture shows a shepherd (or shepherdess) figure seated, wearing a broad brimmed, Spanish hat, a scarf is under the hat and is tied under the figure's chin; he/she holds a crook in the left hand. The right hand reaches down to pet a lamb at his/her feet. Other sheep surround the shepherd, who is dressed in a red tunic with blue cloak, with a gold belt around the waist.[31]

As the Good Shepherd began to wane in popularity (at the beginning of the Constantinian period), the image of Jesus as a beautiful youth emerges as what is really the first 'portrait' of Jesus himself. The classical form of this image is of a young man, beardless, usually with long-locked, loose hair. These images most often appear

Figure 3.3 The Good Shepherd. Marble statuette, 50 × 27.7 × 15.9 cm, *c.* 270–80. Asia Minor, probably Phrygia (Central Turkey). Copyright: The Cleveland Museum of Art, 2000, John L. Severance Fund, 1965.241.

Figure 3.4 'La Divina Pastora.' Fresco, *c.* 1797. Mission San Xavier, Tucson, AZ. Photograph: Helga Teiwas.

on monuments which also contain images of the apostles. In every case, the Jesus-figure differs dramatically from those of the apostles. The latter are almost always dressed in the philosopher's style of tunic, that is, with the tunic slung open at one shoulder. Their hair-style is typical of other portraiture in the Greco-Roman world, that is, relatively short-cropped and, if they are bearded, the beard is well-trimmed and groomed.[32]

This figure is strikingly different from the Jesus-depictions that began to take its place in the fourth century, namely, Jesus as a bearded, mature man. There has been considerable discussion by art historians of the relationship of these two images of the Christ and of the circumstances by which the bearded, mature Jesus became the more popular (but not exclusive) image. The volume of literature is huge in content and diverse in its conclusions. It has been widely publicized in works on iconography how these Jesus-as-youth images are virtually the same as certain images of Dionysos, Apollo and other popular pagan savior-figures in the Greco-Roman world. Art history books which do not emphasize this are rare. The commonly accepted version of the emergence of 'Christ Pantocrator' to replace the 'Christ the Youth' depictions is that the emergence of the Christian imperial Holy Roman Empire resulted in Jesus' being figured along the lines of portraits of the emperor. Thomas Mathews has raised penetrating questions in which, in the words of Peter Brown, he has 'rattled the cage' of this consensus.[33]

It is not, however, as common to find these beardless, long-locked images of Jesus and of his other manifestations (as an old man, and even as a woman) discussed in parallel with Christian apocrypha.[34] The rhetorical descriptions of Jesus as a youth occur predominantly in the apocryphal acts of the apostles; even a partial list of rhetorical parallels to the iconic images is long.

> *Acts of Peter* 5: At the baptism of Theon 'a young man, radiant in splendour, appeared and said to them "Peace be with you"' (Elliott, *The Apocryphal New Testament*, p. 402).
>
> *Acts of Peter* 21: This is an important passage for one's discussion of the 'many-guised Jesus.' Jesus appears in a vision to a number of Christians gathered in a household in which Peter has just read the story of the transfiguration. The vision of Jesus presents him to the many who saw it in many different guises – Quae dixerunt: Quoniam seniorem vidimus, speciem habentem qualem tibi enarrare non possumus; *aliae* autem: iuvenem adulescentem; *alii* autem dixerunt: Puerum vidimus tangentem oculos nostros subtiliter; sic nobis aperti sunt oculi. ('We saw an old man whose appearance we cannot describe. Some (fem.) said, "We saw an adolescent youth"; others (masc.) said, "We saw a boy tenderly touching our eyes; thus our eyes were opened."' (Elliott, p. 415).[35]
>
> *Acts of Peter and Andrew* 2: Jesus appears 'in the form of a little child' (Elliott, p. 299).
>
> *Acts of Peter and Andrew* 16: 'The saviour appeared in the form of a boy of twelve years.' (Elliott, p. 300).
>
> *Acts of John* 73: At the tomb of Drusiana 'we saw a beautiful youth smiling.' (Elliott, p. 331).
>
> *Acts of John* 76: 'I saw a beautiful youth covering her with this cloak.' (Elliott, p. 332).
>
> *Martyrdom of Matthew* 1: 'Behold, in the form of a child harp-player in a pleasure garden Jesus appeared to Matthew' (Lipsius and Bonnet, *AAA*, II.1, 217).[36] The overtones of the youthful Jesus as reflecting the Christ-Orpheus connection appear to be indicated in this passage.
>
> *Martyrdom of Matthew* 13: 'and behold, a beautiful youth came down from heaven' (Lipsius and Bonnet, *AAA*, II.1, 232).
>
> *Martyrdom of Matthew* 24: 'we all saw Matthew, as if getting out of bed and going into heaven, led by the hand by a beautiful youth" (Lipsius and Bonnet, *AAA*, II.1, 250). 'And we saw the youth . . . crown Matthew . . .' (*AAA*, II.1, 251) [Texts 3.C, D, E, F].

There are also other extra-canonical materials in which the description occurs:

> *Passion of Perpetua and Felicitas* 12: 'And we saw sitting in that place . . . a man . . . he had white hair and the face of a youth.'
>
> In Cyprian, *Vita et passio S. Cypriani per Pontium* 12: 'He appeared to me as a very large youth (iuvenis ultra modum enormis).'

3.C

And when they had been sealed, there appeared to them a young man holding a blazing lamp, so that the other lamps were darkened by the emanation of its light. And he went out and disappeared from their sight. And the apostle said to the Lord, 'Your light is too great for us, Lord, and we cannot bear it. For it is too much for our sight.'

The Acts of Thomas 27

3.D

On the 20th of Tobi we came to her and found her amazed. She explained that that night, after she had finished the 'little office *(synaxis)*', she slumbered and saw a beautiful youth about thirty years of age, and Peter and John standing at his right hand, with garments in their hands. She perceived that it was Jesus, and he told her that the garments were her shroud; and he vanished.

Theodosius, *The Discourse on the Assumption* 2

3.E

The holy Matthew remained alone on the Mount praying, in the apostolic robe, barefoot, and Jesus appeared to him in the form of one of the children that were singing in Paradise.

The Passion of Matthew 1

3.F

It was about the sixth hour, and Plato looked out to sea seven stadia away, and saw Matthew standing on the sea between two men in bright apparel, and the beautiful child before them. And they said, 'Amen, Alleluia.' And the sea was like a crystal stone, and before the child a cross came up out of the deep, and at the lower end of it the coffin of Matthew; and in a moment it was set on the land where they were.

The Passion of Matthew 26

Both Weis-Liebersdorf and Fabricius have discussed these connections at length, with diverse conclusions as to their history of religions origin and their place in the church.[37] That the early church's imaging of Jesus as a youth mirrors the depictions by pagans of their gods is not in question, but how and why the early church picked up these representations to portray Jesus have been widely discussed.[38] The identification of the portrayal of Christ as a youth with pagan imagery apparently began with Raoul-Rochette.[39] Weis-Liebersdorf rejects the general interpretation, which is to see the early church's adoption of these images as the result of 'Volksreligion' among the pagan converts to Christianity.[40] These Christians associated the new god, Jesus, with the characteristics of the pagan gods they had known, e.g. Jesus' healings connected him with Asklepios; his miracle at Cana was Jesus doing what Dionysos had done, and so forth. Weis-Liebersdorf, on the other hand, points out that some of the apocryphal acts (especially the *Acts of John*) are gnostic. Hence, he is inclined to believe that the Christ as youth originated in '*Die Gnosis*.'[41]

Weis-Liebersdorf's assigning the origins of the early church's adoption of the Good Shepherd and Christ as youth to gnostic influences reflects the history of religion's assessment of gnosticism at the beginning of the twentieth century. The discoveries in the mid-twentieth century of the Coptic Library at Nag Hammadi have well-established that 'gnosticism' was a much more subtle phenomenon than was believed in Weis-Liebersdorf's time (i.e. *c.* 1900). The theology which we call gnostic ranged from elements of a common Hellenistic religious piety, which expressed a strong world-rejection and in whose vocabulary much of the early church shared, to the full-blown systems of gnostic theology that we find in Valentinus and other early Christians. Virtually the whole early church in some way participated in the 'gnostic' impulse of late antiquity.

We must be careful as well to recognize that to equate 'gnostic' with 'heretical' is an anachronism. To make such a connection in the paleo-Christian scene is to apply a post-Nicene category to pre-Nicene church history. This is as much an anachronism as to use 'canonical' and 'apocryphal' as distinctions which would have been recognized by those Christians of the first three centuries.

The portrayal of Jesus as a youth is so overwhelmingly the image of choice in the early church that it is difficult to believe that the vast majority of church leaders, lay or clergy, who oversaw the art in the catacombs, early basilicas and other Christian *loci* were all in some surreptitious way 'influenced' by gnostic theologies which they ought to have seen were 'heretical.' Christianity was a young religion, full of youth and vigor and possessing what it considered to be a vital key to the reality of life in the cosmos. It is not surprising that the early Christians would choose to depict their savior-god in the aesthetic vocabularies available to them, vocabularies already rife with images of a savior of youthful vigor. It was not only the Hebraic tradition (Psalm 23) which carried this image. So did virtually every Greco-Roman religion. Behind both the Christian Good Shepherd and Jesus the youth lay tens of centuries of savior gods as the *criophorus* and as a comely young man.

The actions of Jesus as they are portrayed in early Christian art reflect the atmosphere in which the church was born. When we look at what Jesus does in the pictorial images in the early church, this borrowing from the aesthetic vocabulary of the Greco-Roman world, including the existing Jewish aesthetic which had already borrowed from that world, becomes an illustration of a natural impulse. In narrative representations, Jesus the youth is almost always depicted as healer and wonder-worker. He turns water into wine, he multiplies the loaves and the fishes, he raises Lazarus. In these scenes he is often holding a wand, a *virga*. Thus, Jesus is also a *magos*. When he is portrayed in the Passion in the earliest images, it is by a kind of visual abbreviation, namely, he is before Pilate. The crucifixion itself is usually expressed symbolically in the Chi-Rho, or various Old Testament scenes of martyrdom, such as Abraham's Sacrifice of Isaac.

Thomas Mathews employs a metaphor of competition to place these early Christian images in context. The early church was in competition with other savior Gods, Serapis, Apollo, Dionysos, and others. These gods were often portrayed as the vigorous, beautiful youth, brimming over with life. It is from these portrayals that the figure of Jesus as the beautiful savior-god was drawn, and that figure supplanted those of the pagan's gods:

> The Christ who emerges (in early Christian art) is far more vigorous and more versatile than we had been led to believe. His rightful place is among the gods of the ancient world. It is with them that he engaged in deadly combat, and it is from them that he wrested his most potent attributes.[42]

The Christ who appears in these young and vigorous forms in the early church performs the functions that one would expect in the divine representative of the growing new religion in its world: he takes his place among the

> rhythms of Mediterranean life [which] continued to draw, for secular as well as for religious purposes, on a long-established Mediterranean imagery to express common human needs and hopes – triumph, pleasure, and the yearning to 'put off the cares of this life'.[43]

Eusebios is not surprised to have seen a statue of Jesus which reflects this competition. The statue belonged to a woman who had

> an issue of blood, and, as we learn from the sacred Gospels, found at the hands of our Savior relief from her affliction . . . there stood on a tall stone at the gates of her house [at Caesarea Philippi] a bronze figure a relief of a woman, kneeling and stretching out her hands . . . opposite to this there was another of the same material, a standing man, clothed beautifully and extending his hand to the woman; at his feet there grew a strange plant, which climbed up to the border of the double cloak of brass, and was an antidote to all kinds of disease. This statue, they said, bore the likeness of Jesus . . . we saw it with our own eyes. And there is nothing astonishing that those heathen, who long ago had good deeds done to them by our Savior, should have made these objects, since we saw also images of His apostles, of Paul and Peter, and indeed of Christ himself, preserved in colored pictures. And this is what we should expect [because it was a pagan habit to have images of their gods].[44]

Jesus also assumes the role of the master of a ship, of the helmsman in early pictorial art and in apocryphal rhetoric. The popularity of the ship as a Christian symbol of salvation and refuge in a stormy world in the very earliest of Christian art makes it almost a natural progression that Jesus would be portrayed as the ship's master.[45] He is described in this role in the *Acts of Andrew and Matthias* 5ff., in which the youthful Jesus appears as a ship's captain, accompanied by his crew (two angels transformed to look human) and skilfully sails Andrew to Myrmidonia to rescue Matthias[46] [Text 3.G]. There is a bronze lamp, known as the lamp of Valerius Severus, in the Museo Archeologico, Florence. It is likely of the fourth or fifth centuries. It depicts a man of the Peter-type (see Chapter 5) in the bow, and a beardless man at the helm. Both Gough and Weis-Liebersdorf identify the helmsman as Christ.[47] A fourth-century sarcophagus fragment in the Museo Pio Cristiano, Inv. 233 [Figure 3.5], has a ship with a long-locked, beardless Jesus (named) at the helm. There are three oarsmen, John, Luke and Mark (named). The bow and the bow-stroke are broken off; presumably the missing oarsman was Matthew.[48] This image is interesting in the order of the evangelists depicted. A third image, an ivory of the fourth century in the Museo Sacra at the Vatican, also has Jesus named as the helmsman of a ship named 'piety.'[49]

3.G

Rising early in the morning, Andrew and his disciples went to the sea, and when he descended to the shore he saw a small boat and seated in the boat three men. The Lord by his own power had prepared the boat. He himself was in the boat like a human captain, and he had brought on board two angels whom he transformed to look like humans, and they were sitting in the boat with him.

When Andrew saw the boat and the three men in it, he was overjoyed. He went to them and said, 'Brothers, where are you going with this little boat?'

'We are going to the city of Myrmidonia', answered the Lord.

Andrew looked at Jesus but did not recognize him, because Jesus was hiding his divinity and appeared to Andrew as a human captain. 'I too am going to the city of the Myrmidons,' Andrew answered, 'so take us to this city, brothers.'. . .

After boarding he sat down by the sail of the boat, and Jesus said to one of the angels, 'Get up and go below to the hold of the boat, bring up three loaves, and place them before all the brothers, so that the men may eat in case they are hungry from having come to us after a long trip.' He got up, went below to the hold of the boat, and brought up three loaves, just as the Lord had commanded him, and set out the bread for them.

Then Jesus said to Andrew, 'Brother, stand up with those in your party and take bread for nourishment, so that you might be strong enough to endure the turbulence of the sea.'

'My children,' Andrew told his disciples, 'we have experienced great generosity from this person, so stand up and take bread for nourishment, so that you might be strong enough to endure the turbulence of the sea.'

His disciples could not respond to him with as much as a word; they were already seasick. Then Jesus insisted that Andrew and his disciples take bread for nourishment.

'Brother,' said Andrew, unaware he was Jesus, 'may the Lord grant you heavenly bread from his kingdom. Just leave them alone, brother, for you see that the servants are queasy from the sea.'

'Perhaps the brothers have no experience of the sea,' Jesus told Andrew. 'Ask them if they want to return to land and wait for you until you finish your task and return to them again.'

Then Andrew asked his disciples, 'My children, do you want to return to land and wait for me there until I finish the task for which I was sent?'

'If we separate from you,' they answered Andrew, 'we may become strangers to the good things that you provided us. We shall be with you now wherever you go.'

Jesus said to Andrew, 'If you are indeed a disciple of the one called Jesus, tell your disciples the miracles your teacher did so that their souls may rejoice and that they may forget the terror of the sea, for we are about to push the boat off shore. Jesus at once said to one of the angels, 'Cast off the boat', and he cast the boat off from land. Jesus went and sat at the rudder and piloted the craft.

The Acts of Andrew and Matthias 5, 7–8

Figure 3.5 Christ as helmsman; the Evangelists as oarsmen. Sarcophagus fragment. Museo Pio Cristiano, Vatican. Photograph: Robin M. Jensen.

In one of the oldest and most published images of Jesus, he frequently takes on the form which paganism employed for Helios, the sun god. This image, likely from the middle of the third century, is in Mausoleum M (Julii) in the pre-Constantine mausoleum at St Peter's in Rome. Christ is in a chariot, drawn by horses. He is beardless and nimbed with a sunburst.[50] This image has a Jewish parallel. In Hamat Tiberias, on a mosaic floor, David is depicted as Helios in the center of a Zodiac form. The outer ring of the zodiac has beasts. Above is a rectangle with Menorahs and the tabernacle; below are inscriptions and lions.[51] The Christian identification of Christ as Helios is not paralleled in the text of a recognized Christian apocryphon. However, it is in a poem which is reconstructed from a quotation of a section in a quasi-apocryphal text and another in the Epistle to the Ephesians:

Awake, sleeper,
Rise from the dead,
And Christ will shine upon you;

(Ephesians 5:14)

The Sun of the Resurrection,
He who was born before the dawn,
Whose beams give life.
(Clement of Alexandria, *Protrepticus* IX.84)[52]

Christ androgynous[53]

Arguably the most long-lived and intense taboo in the history of Christian discussion has been that of the sexuality of Jesus. Although this topic has appeared recently and frequently in respect to texts,[54] in the case of pictorial images in the early church, the taboo appears to be much more intense.[55] The subject of Jesus' sexuality involves two inter-related topics. The first falls under the category of incarnational theology; did the incarnation include the physiological and psychological elements of a sex-drive? In regard to this, one of the critics of Steinberg's book gives what Steinberg calls an X-rating: 'For advanced students only, one is tempted to say . . . And only for rather specialized tastes perhaps is the question of [Christ's] erection [at the Crucifixion].'[56]

The second issue involved in discussion of Jesus' sexuality in an iconographic context arises because of certain images in the early church's pictorial art which appear to present Jesus with androgynous or feminine features. It is a much debated topic, because it is timely and, to some, heretical. It is also an inescapable topic, because the images exist, and because there are rhetorical parallels in early Christian apocrypha.

The most famous and undoubtedly most notorious of the images in the early church which displays feminine characteristics (namely, gynomastia and other secondary sexual characteristics) is a statuette in the Museo Nazionale delle Terme in Rome [Figure 3.6]. First identified as a 'seated poetess,' it has now been compared with the images of Jesus on the sarcophagi and identified as Jesus. The statuette has long been recognized as having feminine implications, and this recognition has brought

Figure 3.6 Christ as a young boy. Statuette, fourth century. Museo Nazionale delle Terme, Rome, Italy. Photograph: Art Resource, NY.

forth some fancy and intricate academic footwork. Some of this dodging and weaving seriously dulls Occam's Razor as well as its application of one of the most-used ploys in the academic studies of iconographic and rhetorical materials for the dismissal of the importance of a text or of an iconic artifact, namely, that it looks gnostic:

> The artist must have taken as his model a statue of Serapis, which he transformed into a statue of Christ by putting in one hand a roll to represent the Gospel, and by elevating the other to imitate the gesture of a teacher . . . I believe Wilpert is right in saying that this likely was a Gnostic production and in remarking that the dealer was not far wrong when he described it as 'a Hellenistic poetess.'[57]

The image in the National Museum in Rome is not the only early Christian art work which displays androgynous characteristics. Several sarcophagi exhibit Jesus-images with more than hints of gynomastia:

> In Ravenna, the Church of S. Francesco, there is a fourth- or fifth-century sarcoph-agus with five niches having rounded arches and strigilated columns. In the center niche is Jesus, beardless, short-haired, soft-faced, with gynomastic upper torso, enthroned, extending his right hand to Paul (Peter, says Grabar).[58]

> In the Musée Reatu, Arles, is a columnar sarcophagus of about 380 CE. Christ stands, bearded, long-locked, orans, upon a small heap of demons. His feet are flanked by two lambs. He is dressed in a tunic and shows a hint of gynomastia. In his left hand is an unrolled scroll which stretches into the niche to the right. There Peter, a cock or eagle at his feet receives the other end of the scroll. He is accompanied by a beardless apostle. On the left, another bearded apostle (Paul) stands facing the triumphant Christ, a scroll in his left hand. He is accompanied by a beardless apostle who carries a scroll in his left hand.[59]

> Also in Ravenna, in the Museo Archeologico is a sarcophagus in which Christ, long-haired, bearded, slightly gynomastic, nimbed with a Chi Rho in the nimbus, stands facing frontally, his right hand raised; in his left hand is a scroll which he hands to Peter, on the right, who holds the scroll on a towel. On the left is Paul. A female is on the far right; a male, dressed as a soldier, on the left.[60]

Mathews also calls his readers' attention to the form of Christ in the dome mosaic of the Arian Baptistery in Ravenna. In this scene of Christ's baptism, the figure of Christ is very different from other baptism scenes. Jesus is beardless, long-locked, and his body is shaped very softly.[61]

The image in the Arian Baptistery is similar in its presentation of Jesus as is that in a famous mosaic in the apse of the Church of Hosios David in Thessalonica [Figure 3.7]. The church's date of construction is a matter of considerable debate, but it is surely one of the precious few pre-iconoclastic structures left in the East. As is the case with many such artifacts, the church comes with a full cargo of legends. Among them is the story of the rediscovery of the apse mosaic. According to the story an elderly Egyptian monk, Senouphios, was pulled by a divine revelation to rediscover the mosaic – it had been hidden during a persecution – and he died in ecstasy at its

Figure 3.7 Christ in Majesty, surrounded by the Vision of Ezekiel. Apse mosaic, fifth or sixth century. Church of Hosios David, Thessalonica. Photograph: Research Team for New Testament and Archaeology, Harvard University.

sight.[62] The problem with these accounts is that the church was not erected until at least the mid-fifth century. Although there is doubt about the dating of the church's construction, the building certainly pre-dates the iconoclastic period. As such, its mosaic may be the only surviving example of what was the look of the earliest apse mosaics in pre-iconoclastic Constantinople.[63]

The mosaic at Hosios David is iconographically related to images of the vision of Ezekiel, with Christ, beardless and soft-figured, sitting enthroned upon a rainbow; he holds a scroll in his hand. He is in a mandorla which is surrounded by beasts. Mathews recalls a legend about the creation of the mosaic, in which the daughter of a pagan emperor Maximian/Galerius (287–305) was a closet Christian. She pretended illness and asked for a small house near healing waters, so she could recover. Her father gave her permission to do so. While her father was away persecuting Christians, she re-built the house (which already had water for baptism) into a chapel:

> When this had been done, she ordered that a painter [mosaicist] be fetched imme-diately so as to paint the pure Mother of God in the eastern apse. So this image was painted and the work was nearly finished when, the following day, the painter came along intending to complete the picture and saw not the same painting, but a different one, indeed one that was altogether dissimilar, namely that of our Lord Jesus Christ in the form of a man, riding and stepping on a luminous cloud and on the wings of the wind.[64]

Mathews sees the visual characteristics of the figure of Christ in the apse mosaic as a pictorial parallel with that legend: 'The apse is a bare ten feet across. Yet within the narrow confines of this space the mosaicist has created a hallucinatory vision that might easily have suggested miracles to the believing eye.'[65] That is the figure of Christ exhibits feminine characteristics. Mathews' judgment about this painting and other images which we have mentioned and which appear to give Jesus an androgy-nous cast has brought forth some rather irate criticism.[66] Some of the responses to the concept that some of the early Christians produced an androgynous Jesus reveal more about the critic than about the issue. As one reviewer put it:

> The most provocative part of Mathews's analysis of the mosaic in Thessalonica concerns his visual reading of the physiognomy of the figure of Christ as femi-nine. This is simply untrue. This Christ figure is not effeminate or androgynous. It would be more accurate to characterize it [as] – *neither overtly masculine nor overtly feminine*.[67]

The viewer will have to make judgment about the Hosios David mosaic. That there were images in the early church in which the figure of Christ exhibited features which were decidedly those of pagan divinities (including his long-locked hair) is hardly disputable. One may dismiss this material as 'gnostic' or as belonging to some other Christian group which orthodoxy subsequently placed on the deviant fringes of the church. However, it is not disputable that Jesus as being both male and female was part of the early church's theological discussion. Epiphanius reports a Christian sect, the 'Quintillians' who report that one of their leaders, Priscilla, saw a vision of Jesus as a woman[68].

There are a number of apocrypha in the Nag Hammadi codices in which Christ presents himself in an androgynous form.

> *Apocryphon of John* (II.2) (p. 105):[69] 'I am the one who is [with you] always. I [am the Father], I am the Mother, I am the Son.'

> (II.4) (p. 517): 'It is she who is prior to them all, the Mother–Father, the first man, the holy Spirit, the thrice-male, the thrice powerful, the thrice-named androgynous one.'

> *Trimorphic Protennoia* (XIII,1) (42, 45) (p. 517): 'I am called "She who is syzegetic."'

> 42 (p. 517): 'I am a single one (fem.) since I am undefiled. I am the Mother of the Voice.'

> 42 (p. 517): 'Now I have come the second time in the likeness of a female and have spoken with them.'

> 45 (p. 519): 'I am androgynous. [I am Mother (and) I am] Father since I copulate with myself.'

Another text from the Nag Hammadi codices sends mixed signals about androgyny. In the *Coptic Gospel of Thomas* there are logia which celebrate the 'coming together of opposites' (*coencidentia oppositorum*), that is, 'the two becoming one.'[70] The same text assumes that to enter the Kingdom Mary must be made [by Christ] as male (logion 114). As the coming together of opposites is a commonly occurring theme in the history of religions,[71] it is not surprising that it expresses itself in early Christianity both in text and in pictorial image.

To what extent the early church carried on such discussions about the gender of Jesus (and of the Christians themselves) we do not know. Such discussion began early, as Galatians 3:28 witnesses. If one is to create an iconic representation of the Christian and his/her Lord as 'neither male nor female,' how else is this to be accomplished except through images of androgyny? The vast majority of extant early Christian images do not carry on the androgynous characteristics which appear in the few images which do. Nevertheless, the polymorphic character of the Christ abounded in the church's images. The rhetorical equivalent of these images is preserved for us primarily in early Christian apocrypha.

The Ancient of Days

It should be said that one must take into account that the descriptions we find in the apocryphal Acts are epiphanic appearances to the apostles and other of the faithful; they are all post-Easter. One could argue that these visions differ from the post-resurrection appearances in the canonical materials, which attempt to show that the risen Christ in the period before the ascension is identical with the crucified Christ. That is, these appearances claim that Jesus' resurrection was a bodily resurrection. There is a strong emphasis within the canonical materials' desire to maintain the humanity of Christ, the reality of the Incarnation; as is well known, this was one of

Figure 3.8 Portrait of S. John the Evangelist (center medallion); Christ in three forms, left to right: Pantocrator, Ancient of Days and Immanuel. Manuscript illumination. Bibliothèque nationale, Paris, ms. gr. 74, fol. 167ro. Photograph: Bibliothèque nationale.

the most difficult theological tasks of the early church. Thus, the canonical materials and some of the apocryphal materials follow what is generally known as the Pauline-type gospel creed (see 1 Corinthians 15:1–4; and see Paul's emphasis on the reality of the cross in Philippians 2:5–11). There are, however, ambiguities even within the canonical materials. Particularly in John 20, there is ambiguity about the 'bodyliness' of the resurrection. Mary at first thinks that Jesus is a gardener, and in his appearance to the disciples Jesus walks through a closed door and then his solid flesh and its wounds are touched by Thomas. In Luke 24:13–22 the men walking on the road to Emmaus do not recognize Jesus until he identifies himself to them. Their 'eyes are opened' only after Jesus instructs them about the Law and the Prophets and celebrates a eucharist with them. As a rule of thumb, in the post-resurrection appearances, particularly in the second-century writings, Jesus could be described as having been seen by a believer in any form.

Figure 3.9 Diptych of S. Lupicin. Center: Christ as Ancient of Days, flanked by Paul and Peter. Left: healing of the blind man; healing of the lame man who carries his bed. Right: woman with an issue of blood; healing. Below: Christ and the Samaritan woman; the raising of Lazarus. Ivory book cover, sixth century. Bibliothèque nationale, Paris, Cabinet des médailles. Photograph: Bibliothèque nationale.

The discussions of the persona of Jesus eventually settled down, so to speak, into basically three forms: Christ as youth; Christ as a mature man, usually bearded; Christ as an old man. As the *Acts of Peter* 20 says, 'He is both young and an old man.' Weitzmann, in a discussion of the Byzantine traditions refers to a manuscript illumination in a Paris Gospel Book, in which the three classic forms of 'Christ Pantocrator,' 'Christ Immanuel' and 'Christ, the Ancient of Days' all appear and are labeled as such[72] [Figure 3.8].

This combination of Jesus in different forms appears early in the pictorial arts. A classic example is the Lupicin Diptych [Figure 3.9; 3.10], sixth-century ivory book covers. On the left plaque [Figure 3.9], Christ as the Ancient of Days appears in the center frame, while Jesus, performing miracles in the scenes of bordering frames, is

Figure 3.10 Diptych of S. Lupicin. Center: Virgin and child. Left: The Annunciation to the Virgin in her home; Anna is affronted by her servant (the headband). Right: Joseph and the Virgin; the journey to Bethlehem, with Joseph conversing with the Virgin. Ivory book cover, sixth century. Bibliothèque nationale, Paris, Cabinet des médailles. Photograph: Bibliothèque nationale.

a beardless youth.[73] There appears to have been a tendency, even after the establishment of the bearded, middle-aged Jesus as the predominant figure of Christ in the church, to show the miracle-working and the epiphanic Jesus as a youth. An intriguing early sixth-century set of mosaics in the Church of S. Apollinare Nuovo, Ravenna, has a set of some twenty-six mosaic scenes from the life of Christ. The scenes are mounted on the walls of the nave, thirteen on a side. In all the scenes of events which precede the Passion of Christ, Jesus is beardless. In those during and after the Passion, he is bearded. Whether or not this characteristic of the mosaics is significant depends on the judgment of some art historians who see the bearded and beardless Jesus figures as done by different artists.[74] As it stands, however, the series speaks as an historical allegory in which the miracle-working and teaching Christ is a beardless youth and the Christ of the Passion becomes Christ Pantocrator.

The discussions of the nature of the Christ appear in the rhetorical and pictorial portraits which portray his actual figure, and they appear in a form parallel with rhetorical descriptions in the Christian apocrypha. These representations speak to us of a church in the process of sorting out theologically just who is this Jesus of Nazareth. The 'many-guised' Jesus (*Acts of Thomas* 153) had to be considered in more specific form, both in rhetoric and in iconic representations. The pictorial forms which prevailed in various communities speak as loudly of the theological discussions within the communities as do the theological texts themselves.

4

THE LIFE AND
MISSION OF JESUS

Canonical Histories and Apocryphal Legends Relating to the New Testament is the title given to a facsimile edition of a delightfully illustrated fourteenth- or fifteenth-century manuscript in the Ambrosian Library (ms. L58 sup.).[1] In text and pictures the manuscript narrates the church's story of Jesus, beginning with the Infancy of Christ, through his childhood, his mission and the resurrection (Anastasis; Descensus ad Inferos), and Ascension. The images are basically drawings rather than miniature paintings, but they are evocative drawings. The work's text and pictures, blissfully unaware of the bibliolatry of certain contemporary churches, blend canonical and apocryphal materials into a continuous narrative. Among those gospels employed are Matthew, Mark, Luke, John, *Pseudo-Matthew*, the *Infancy Gospel of Thomas* (not to be confused with the *Coptic Gospel of Thomas* in the Nag Hammadi codices) and the *Gospel of Nicodemus (Acta Pilati)*. The title of the facsimile, *Canonical Histories and Apocryphal Legends*, represents the modern sensibilities of the book's sponsors. The manuscript itself is representative of a portion of the *de facto* diatessaron that the church created and which we name the 'Whole Gospel.'

The Ambrosian manuscript is not alone in this combination of materials. Another such manuscript is in Paris, Bibliothèque nationale, cod. lat. 2688. It contains some fifty-two illustrations of the texts which include the canonical gospels, *Pseudo-Matthew*, and the story of Abgar, King of Edessa, including the apocryphal story of the ill King Abgar's writing to Jesus the healer to help him.[2] In the Laurentian Library in Florence, an apocryphal Arabic gospel of the thirteenth century (*c.* 1299), contains a large number of illustrations. Weitzmann describes the Arabic manuscript as 'neither a simple Infancy Gospel nor a Passion Gospel, but [it] combines elements of both with a few interspersed events from the life of Christ, and Baumstark correctly calls it "Ein apokryphes Herrenleben."'[3] There are some fifty-four pen drawings 'which are intercalated in the text [and] are rather rough in style.'[4]

A third artifact, one of the most treasured of Christian objects of art, is a cross-reliquary in the Sancta Sanctorum of the Vatican, Inv. 1881 [Figure 4.1]. The cross was fashioned of gold decorated with enamel, and it is contained in a box made of gold and silver. The origin of the cross is either Syria or Palestine. Called a 'Reliquary of the True Cross,' on the side of the cross is enscribed 'Pascalis episcopus fieri iussit.' If this means Pope Paschal, a ninth century date is correct. Virtually every scene on the cross has some element which is paralleled in early Christian apocrypha. (1) At the crux is the Nativity with an ox and ass (*Pseudo-Matthew* 14) leaning over the crib; two midwives (*Pseudo-Matthew* 13) bathe the child, and a light in the heavens shines down on the scene. (2) At the top of the upright is the Annunciation to the Virgin. The Virgin holds a book (*Pseudo-Matthew* 6). (3) The Visitation is above the Nativity. (4) On the left arm of the cross is the Journey to Bethlehem. The Virgin is seated on the ass. Joseph, gray headed, follows on the left; one of Joseph's sons leads (*Protevangelium* 17). (5) The right arm of the cross has the Adoration of the Magi. The Christ-child is sitting up by himself on Mary's lap; he is not a neo-nate (*Pseudo-Matthew* 16). (6) Below the Nativity is the presentation of Christ to the temple. Simeon hastens (see below, p. 96) to adore the child. (7) On the bottom of the upright the scene is of the Baptism of Christ, with a small, beardless, gold-nimbed Christ center, nude, a dove descending; John the Baptist, not nimbed, is on the left. An angel (see below, p. 118) or prophet is to the right, holding an open scroll.

There is also a cross-shaped box for the reliquary which contains scenes that are paralleled with Christian apocrypha: (1) the Annunciation to the Virgin, with Mary's having been interrupted while she is working on the wool for the temple veil (*Pseudo-Matthew* 8; *Protevangelium* 10); (2) the bathing of the child with two midwives in attendance; (3) the Nativity with an ox and ass leaning over the crib; (4) the Adoration of the Magi, with the child sitting up on his own in Mary's lap; (5) the presentation of Jesus to the temple with Simeon 'hastening' to greet the child. We will discuss these elements below.[5]

The canonical gospels are not seamless. From the perspective of those whose boundaries do not go beyond the canon, they not only fail to cover the story of Mary; there is an intriguing silence in the canonical sources about what happened between the Flight to Egypt and Jesus' appearance in the Temple to confront the 'Doctors' (as medieval manuscripts put it); what, then, was the nature of Jesus' childhood? There are also other 'missing events' in the canonical stories. If Herod were really successful in his determination to kill all the little children in his realm and if Jesus escaped only by divine intervention, how did Jesus' new-born cousin, John the Baptist, escape Herod's murderous rage? In the first century, to travel from Bethlehem to Egypt was a difficult and peril-laden journey through a forbidding wilderness. Did anything untoward happen on the Flight to Egypt? The Holy Family's return to Nazareth would have raised similar questions.

At the conclusion of Jesus' mission there are also seams that call out to be smoothed over. Who were the two thieves crucified with the Lord? Who were the soldiers who stabbed Jesus and gave him the vinegar to drink while he was on the cross? One of the thieves crucified with Jesus was told that he would be with Jesus in paradise; what was his experience there? What was taking place during the three days Jesus was in the tomb? To fill out such stories in respect to divine persons is a quest which perhaps inevitably would arise simply from the special interest that the early Christians would have had in these characters. In addition, and possibly more influential on the formation of apocryphal narrative was the custom in the Greco-Roman world for the lives (*bioi*) of divine heroes to include the precocious deeds of these divine men (and sometimes women) when they were children.[6]

The convention of the *bios* is likely a powerful influence upon the lives of all the characters in the early Christian church's story-telling. One has only to look at the many examples from the pagan world to understand the power of this particular genre. The *bioi* of Alexander the Great, Plato, Caesar Augustus and Apollonios of Tyana are but a few of the famous for whom there were well-known encomiums. The genre was

Figure 4.1 Cross-reliquary. Enamel. Crux: The Nativity of Christ/Bathing of the Infant. Left arm: Journey to Bethlehem. Right arm: Adoration of the Magi. Upper: Annunciation to the Virgin; Visitation. Lower: The Presentation to the Virgin; Baptism of Christ. Sancta Sanctorum, Vatican, inv. 1881. Photograph: Vatican.

so prolific that Lucian of Samosata could stand it on its head to present an anti-encomium for the denigration of Alexander of Abunoteichos.[7]

The typical encomium *bios* began with stories of a miraculous birth, continued with emphasis upon the precocious deeds of the young hero, listed the protagonist's miraculous deeds (aretalogy and teratology), and usually climaxed with an honorable and often courageous death and the metamorphosis of the subject to a place among the immortals. This genre is persuasive to the point that one of the most well-known collections of Greek mythology, i.e. Ovid's *Metamorphoses*, is actually a long *bios* which glorifies (and climaxes) with the divination of the Julian household. It owes its pattern not only to ancient Greek sources but also to ancient Near Eastern stories of the founding of the Holy City (e.g. *Enuma Elish*; the 'David/Zion' story in the Old Testament).[8] Thus the pattern prevails in the rhetorical and iconic versions of the Whole Gospel. It begins in parts and is gradually assembled in the history of the church to become the church's continuous foundational story.

We have good reason to suspect that the apocryphal gospels which recite their extra-canonical tales about Jesus and those who surrounded him were formulated early in the church. We have already pointed out that the Marian tales in, for example, the *Protevangelium* were certainly known well enough by the mid-second century to be written down. They were certainly popular by the end of the fourth and the beginning of the fifth century. The Whole Gospel in its iconic version is a melting pot of the canonical stories, legends from the church fathers, the teaching and preaching of the church throughout its history, and the pictorial images which have decorated walls, coffins, windows, manuscripts and virtually any other surface which will hold an image or which can be sculpted into a likeness.

The degree to which the tales that became the Christian apocrypha have contributed to the iconography of Jesus and the Jesus-event can hardly be over emphasized. The iconic version of the Whole Gospel has in Christian art history what is perhaps its most persuasive and effective medium. The power of these images on the faith of the church and as an expression of this faith is not only due to the inherent power of pictures themselves. We must remember in our assessment of the influence of images upon faith that, until the invention of the printing press, only a small number of Christians would have read either the narratives in the texts, glosses upon these narratives, or theological discussions which stemmed from the stories. The artists, the patrons, and the audiences of Christian art were 'not intellectuals with minds well-stocked with abstruse learning.'[9] They learned about Jesus from stories told them from the pulpit, from these stories acted out in the liturgy of the church, and stories which were illuminated from the light which was reflected from paintings on the walls and which glowed upon them from stained glass.

The infancy of Jesus

The image-cycle of the Infancy of Christ traditionally begins with the Annunciation to the Virgin and ends with the return of the Holy Family from Egypt to Nazareth.[10] This cycle is informed not only by the Gospels According to Luke and to Matthew, but also by the numerous so-called infancy gospels and Marian gospels: *The Protevangelium*; *The Gospel of the Birth of Mary*; *Pseudo-Matthew*; *The Infancy Gospel of Thomas*; *The Arundel Gospel*. In addition, just as *Pseudo-Matthew* is in many respects a western version of the *Protevangelium*, there also existed Arabic, Syriac, Georgian and Coptic (Sahidic) versions of the *Protevangelium*, as well as several other recensions of the same cycle of legends.[11] The number of images in this cycle is huge, and virtually every image shows parallels with the story in its rhetorical form in Christian apocrypha. The formation of this pictorial cycle was dependent upon several factors, but, as Weitzmann points out, there were basically two factors involved: the popularity of the texts which were first illustrated and the story-telling promise of the images derived from the story.[12]

The Annunciation

There are three versions of the Annunciation to the Virgin in the narratives. In one version, Mary is at a spring to fetch water when the angel Gabriel approaches her (*Protevangelium* 11:1; *Pseudo-Matthew* 9) [Text 4.A]. Mary carries a pitcher in these images. The iconography of this image appears early. On the lid of a mid-fourth century sarcophagus in the National Museum in Syracuse (the so-called 'Adelphia Sarcophagus') on the far left is a carving in which the Virgin is at a spring, in the form of a gushing waterfall. She holds a pitcher and turns her head back to see the angel approaching. This sarcophagus lid also contains a scene of Jesus' Nativity (with the Ox and the Ass), the presentation of the Virgin to the temple, and, possibly, the scene of Mary's being mocked by the other temple virgins.[13]

Two ivories, one of the fifth-century in Milan, Cathedral Treasury,[14] and the other of the tenth century, in the Louvre[15] (Cat. Molinier 1896, n.11) are further examples of this version of the Annunciation. The fifth-century image is on a diptych, likely a book cover.

4.A

And she took the pitcher and went out to draw water, and behold, a voice said, 'Hail, highly favoured one, the Lord is with you, you are blessed among women.' And she looked around to the right and to the left to see where this voice came from. And, trembling, she went to her house and put down the pitcher and took the purple and sat down on her seat and drew out the thread. And behold, an angel of the Lord stood before her and said, 'Do not fear, Mary; for you have found grace before the Lord of all things and shall conceive by his Word.' When she heard this she considered it and said, 'Shall I conceive by the Lord, the living God, and bear as every woman bears?' And the angel of the Lord said, 'Not so, Mary; for the power of the Lord shall overshadow you; wherefore that holy one who is born of you shall be called the Son of the Most High. And you shall call his name Jesus; for he shall save his people from their sins.' And Mary said, 'Behold, [I am] the handmaid of the Lord before him: be it to me according to your word.'

The Protevangelium of James 11

Figure 4.2 The Annunciation to the Virgin at a well. Mosaic, fourteenth century. Kariye Djami, Istanbul. Photograph: Art Resource, NY.

The piece in the Louvre is an ivory casket. A later example is among the Kariye Djami frescoes [Figure 4.2]. The Virgin approaches the three-tiered well from the right, a pitcher in her right hand. She turns back, startled, as the angel, winged and nimbed, approaches her from the upper right. The scene is framed by architecture.[16]

The second two versions of the Annunciation place Mary in her house. By far the most prolific of the early Annunciation scenes has the angel appearing to the Virgin while Mary is working on the wool-work that she has been given as a task in the temple (*Protevangelium* 10:1–2; *Pseudo-Matthew* 8). Basically, the scene has Mary seated on a chair, although she has sometimes risen from it as the angel startles her. The iconography begins to appear in extant work at the end of the fourth or beginning of the fifth century. A textile burial cloth from Egypt in the Victoria and Albert Museum (number 1103–1900), a sarcophagus in Ravenna (the 'Pignatorum' sarcophagus in the Quadrarco di Braccioforte), and a fifth-century wood sculpture, also from Egypt (in the Louvre), are early examples. The famed sixth-century Chair of Maximinia, in the cathedral treasury, Milan, contains a beautiful example of the early classical style applied to the Annunciation in which Mary is doing the wool-work. Another especially beautiful example is an eleventh-century icon from the Monastery of S. Catherine, Mount Sinai [Figure 4.3]. One unusual example is a miniature at Mount Athos (Iveron, Gospel Book, cod. 5, fol. 222ro) in which the Virgin is accompanied on her right by a servant girl, spinning wool, who also looks up startled as the angel approaches from the left.

The Annunciation in which Mary was interrupted at her wool-work, it is safe to say, was the dominant image of the event in the pre-Carolingian period, and it persists in the Eastern Church to this day. In the West, Mary's occupation at the Annunciation began to shift from her working on the temple veil to an emphasis on her learning. In the Carolingian period, Mary holds a book, or is seated by a book-stand upon which is a Bible; she is reading the Psalms. (*Pseudo-Matthew* 6: 'No one could be found better instructed than [Mary] in the law of God and singing the songs of David.') This is an Annunciation scene which persists in the West [Figure 4.4]. In the *Benedictional of S. Aethelwold* (fol. 5vo) [Figure 4.5] the Annunciation is in the house; Mary holds what appears to be a spindle of wool in her left hand, and she has her right hand on an open book which rests on a lectern. The *Benedictional* is apparently directly influenced by the style of iconography which is represented by an ivory situla (bucket) in the Metropolitan Museum, New York (The Cranenburg Situla, *c.* 1000 CE) and by the ivory casket in the Louvre which we mentioned above (Cat. Molinier 1896, n.11).

The two versions of the Annunciation, the one outside the house, at the well, the other in the house, began to merge in some theologies into the concept that there were two stages to Annunciation to the Virgin. In the first, at the spring, the angel brings her the message that she will bear a child; the second involves the actual conception of the child. In some multiple-scene works, both stages of the Annunciation occur.

A ninth- or tenth-century ivory casket in the Louvre, mentioned above, probably of the Metz school, shows both the annunciation at the spring and the one in the house. There is a sixth-century ivory pyxis, in the Hermitage, which has both scenes.[17] The continuation of this tradition is shown in a sixteenth-century icon at the Church of St Basil-on-the-Hill, Pskov. On this icon, the two Annunciations are in series.[18]

The church has readily filled in narrative details which are not spelled out in its stories. Human curiosity being what it is, one of the prime questions which naturally came to the fore would be a much more detailed answer to Mary's question in Luke 1:34, 'How is this impregnation to take place?' Gabriel's reply 'The Holy Spirit shall come upon you, and the power of the Most High shall overshadow you' still leaves the question open in regard to detail. A delicate subject that, but it is one which the church was able to answer graphically and literally. If it was by the Holy Spirit that Mary would become pregnant, and, as the Spirit is closely associated with the Logos, then it was through the Virgin's ear that the impregnating word entered (*Protevangelium* 11). At S. Maria Maggiore the Annunciation is depicted formally. The Virgin sits enthroned, flanked by attendants and the angel of the Annunciation is at her right. Above her is another angel and a dove descending toward her head. Another

Figure 4.3 Annunciation to the Virgin. Icon, *c.* 1100. Monastery of S. Catherine, Mount Sinai.
Photograph: Michigan–Princeton–Alexandria Expedition to Mount Sinai.

Figure 4.4 Annunciation to the Virgin. Sculpture, *c.* 1925–8. Princeton University Chapel.
Photograph: Cartlidge.

such image is an illumination in the Pierpont Morgan Library.[19] So we see the Virgin
in these pictures with the dove descending toward her head and often toward her ear.

In the most hypostasized version of these images there is a tube extending from
the mouth of God and entering Mary's ear; half-way down this 'tube of the Word'
is the fetus of the Messiah. Such an image is on the tympanum in the North Portal
of the Marienkapelle am Markt at Würzburg, Germany [Figure 4.6]. This phenomenon has earned the appellation 'telephone babies.'[20] A manuscript illumination in
the Austrian National Library (Biblia pauperum, Ink. 2.D.32, fol. 1vo) [Figure 4.7]
pictures the Virgin, seated on the right, nimbed, veiled, a book in her lap. She is
faced by a winged, nimbed angel, who kneels before the Virgin. In the upper center
is a head in a mandorla; from the figure a dove descends on rays of light toward the
Virgin's head. Behind the dove is a fetus coming down the rays of light toward the
Virgin's ear. On the left is Eve, confronting the snake, while Adam is up the tree,
picking its fruit. On the right is Gideon with the angel. Above and below are busts
of paupers.

However, the logos also enters human consciousness through the eyes, especially
in a culture which features a religion of the book. At the monastery of Klosterneuburg,
Austria, is a twelfth-century enamel attributed to Nicholas of Verdun, in which the
Virgin has risen from her chair. She is facing a winged angel – who carries a banner
inscribed Ave Maria – and her hands are raised in start. The angel's right hand is
pointed at Mary, his first and index fingers forked. From their tips the light of the
Logos enters the Virgin's eyes.[21]

After the announcement from Heaven, Mary finishes the spinning of the purple wool
and takes it to the priests of the temple; they bless her (*Protevangelium* 12), and then
Mary visits Elizabeth, as the story goes in the canonical materials. But Joseph was disconcerted to find his virgin bride pregnant (as he is in the Gospel According to

Figure 4.5 Annunciation to the Virgin. Manuscript illumination, *c.* 980. The British Library, Benedictional of S. Aethelwold, ms. Add. 49598, fol. 5vo. Photograph: British Library.

Figure 4.6 Annunciation to the Virgin. Sculpture, fifteenth or sixteenth century. Marienkapelle am Markt, Würzburg, Germany. Photograph: after a photograph supplied by William Stroud (detail).

Matthew). His remonstrations to Mary are spelled out, along with his attempt to keep quiet their seemingly embarrassing family situation (*Protevangelium* 13:2; *Pseudo-Matthew* 10), until he was assured by an angel in a dream that all was well in God's plan (as in Matthew 1:23). The Kariye Djami mosaics combine two scenes in one space: (1) Joseph says farewell to Mary in the inscription: 'I leave you in my house while I go away to build.' (2) Joseph, on his return, reproaches the Virgin when he finds her pregnant. The inscription reads, 'Mary, what have you done?' Unfortunately, the scene is badly mutilated [Figure 4.8]. The scene of Joseph's remonstrating Mary also occurs twice in San Marco, Venice. One image is on the front left column of the ciborium; the other is in the mosaic cycle of the Life of the Virgin and the Infancy of Christ.[22]

Figure 4.7 Annunciation to the Virgin. Manuscript illumination, fifteenth century. Austrian
National Library, Vienna, Austria, Ink. 2.D.32, fol. 1vo. Photograph: Austrian
National Library (detail).

According to *Pseudo-Matthew* 10–11, Joseph asks forgiveness of the Virgin. This
she grants. The illuminations in the *Wernherlied von der Magd* illustrate this scene.[23]
It also occurs on the Anna portal of Notre Dame de Paris.

Joseph is reconciled to Mary, but the priests find out about what they considered
a gross scandal, even though Joseph attempts to keep Mary's pregnancy a secret
(*Protevangelium* 15). When the couple protest their innocence, they are forced to
undergo a trial of innocence, a water-test (*Protevangelium* 16; *Pseudo-Matthew* 12; see
Numbers 5:11–31). Joseph and Mary, of course, pass the trial. The scene occurs on
several early ivories. One, in the Louvre, Strognoff Collection, of the sixth or seventh
century, is a plaque with several scenes of the Virgin's life. The water trial is on the

Figure 4.8 Joseph's farewell to the Virgin and Joseph's remonstrating with the Virgin (partially destroyed). Mosaic, fourteenth century. Kariye Djami, Istanbul. Photograph: Art Resource, NY.

Figure 4.9 The Water Trial of the Virgin. Ivory plaque, sixth century. Chair of Maximinianus,
Museo Arcivescovile, Ravenna. Photograph: Art Resource, NY.

lower zone of the plaque.[24] The plaque also contains the Annunciation to the Virgin,
with the wool-work, and the Journey to Bethlehem.

One of the most famous early church artifacts, the Chair of Maximinianus in Milan's
Museo Arcivescovile, also has an image of the water trial [Figure 4.9]. The scene
appears to be a conflation of elements of the Annunciation and the trial. The Virgin,
right center, holds the bowl in her right hand. In her left hand she appears to carry
a skein of wool. She faces frontally with her head slightly turned and bowed toward
Joseph, who stands on the left, bearded with staff in his left hand. An Angel is above
the Virgin, a staff in his left hand, with his right hand raised in gesture of greeting.[25]

The water trial also is a frequent scene in frescoes in the rock churches of Cappadocia.[26] The scene occurs, for example, at Tokali Kilise, chapel 7, Göreme, at the
Church of St Eustace, chapel 11, and at Kiliclar Kilise, chapel 29.

Figure 4.10 A child warns Joseph to heed the Virgin's words on the journey to Bethlehem.
   Manuscript illumination, fifteenth century. Ambrosian Library, L58 sup., fol. 1vo.
   Photograph: Cartlidge.

The journey to Bethlehem

The images of the journey to Bethlehem, for the enrollment, very often show three
people on the trip. Mary rides on the ass, but the beast is usually led by one of
Joseph's sons – from another marriage (*Protevangelium* 17:2–3; *Pseudo-Matthew* 13) –
and/or the procession includes an angel. In some scenes, Joseph and Mary are shown
conversing, as they do in the Marian Gospels [see Figure 3.10]. Joseph is disconcerted
because Mary is alternatively 'sulking and laughing.' As is the case with many women
who are about to give birth, she has trepidations about her bringing a child into the
world. In Mary's case, she has a vision of the sorrow and of the joy that the son she
is to bear will bring to them. In the case of the birth of the Messiah, Mary's pregnancy mood-swings and pre-natal fears have theological importance. To emphasize
this point, a child is depicted in the Ambrosian ms. L 58 sup. [Figure 4.10], standing
in the middle of the road, his finger pointing at Joseph, and warning him of the
importance of her words, while Mary, on the left, holds the reins of the delightfully
depicted ass.[27]

The Nativity

The number of scenes of the Nativity is voluminous, as one would expect. In the early
art, there are both whole scenes and elements in other scenes which are paralleled in
Christian apocrypha, virtually without exception. Among these elements is the omni-
presence of the Ox and the Ass, which we have already mentioned (Chapter 1). The

Lucan gospel (Luke 2) gives the reader the impression that Jesus' birth took place in the stable in Bethlehem. Further, Luke mentions no one else who might have been present at the birth. It is not said in Luke whether the 'manger' is in a shed, a barn or in a cave. Matthew is silent in regard to a description of Jesus' birthplace, although, when the Magi arrive, they find the Holy Family in a house (*oikia*).

The *Protevangelium*, however, reports that Mary went into labor before she and Joseph completed their trip to Bethlehem. Joseph frantically finds a cave in the wilderness. It is there that the Nativity takes place (*Arabic Infancy Gospel* 2; Justin Martyr, *Dial.* 78; *Epistle of Barnabas* 11; *Protevangelium* 18; *Pseudo-Matthew* 13–14). In general one can say that the East favors the cave, the West the stable. These gospels make it clear that it is a very dark cave in which there is no light; it is a forbidding place. Joseph seeks help and finds a midwife (*Arundel Gospel; Protevangelium* 17; *Pseudo-Matthew* 13–14). At the birth, the dark and abandoned cave is suffused with light [Text 4.B] (*Protevangelium* 19:2; *Pseudo-Matthew* 13; *Arundel* 73). The iconic versions of the tale often depict rays of light descending from an arc in heaven into the cave and upon the Christ-child in his crib. This epiphany-light is not to be confused with the star of the Magi, especially in the earlier materials. In later works, in which the Adoration of the Magi becomes part of the Nativity scene itself, the star of the Magi and the miraculous light described in the Marian gospels become one.

4.B

As the time drew near, the power of God showed itself openly. The maiden stood looking into heaven; she became like a vine. For now the end of the events of salvation was at hand. When the light had come forth, Mary worshipped him whom she saw she had given birth to. The child himself, like the sun, shone brightly, beautiful and most delightful to see, because he alone appeared as peace, bringing peace everywhere. In that hour when he was born the voice of many invisible beings proclaimed in unison, 'Amen.' And that light, which was born, was multiplied and it obscured the light of the sun itself by its shining rays. The cave was filled with the bright light and with a most sweet smell. The light was born just as the dew descends from heaven to the earth. For its perfume is fragrant beyond all the smell of ointments.

The Arundel Infancy Gospel 73

Pseudo-Matthew is aware of the stories which appear in the canonical materials, namely, the Lucan story in which Jesus is born in a stable and of the tradition in which the child is born in a cave. In what appears to be a harmonizing effort, *Pseudo-Matthew* has the Holy Family move from the cave to a stable (ch. 13–14). Some later paintings preserve both the cave and the stable, as does a painting by Lorenzo Monaco in the Uffizi, Florence, or they maintain the mountainous terrain of the earlier cave setting while the Nativity takes place in a remote stable (see a painting by Campin on the Nativity in the Musée des Beaux-Arts, Dijon).[28]

The midwife (or midwives) in the stories play a significant role in both the rhetorical and iconic versions of the Nativity. In what is perhaps the most famous scene in the *Protevangelium*, one of the midwives (Salome) doubts that any woman could give birth to a child and still remain a virgin. She performs a gynecological examination of Mary, and, for her audacious disbelief, she suffers a withered hand. On a fifth-century ivory pyxis from Syria, now in the Monastery Church of Werden Abbey, Werden bei Essen, Joseph sits at the left, with a long staff, his chin in his left palm.[29] The Virgin is center, leaning against a rock (cave setting), with her left hand under her chin (in contemplation). Jesus lies in a masonry crib, with an angel orans between and behind the Virgin and Child, an ox and ass are at the far right leaning over the crib [see Figures 1.2; 1.3]. Salome, the midwife, stretches forth her injured hand to the Virgin for help, confessing her sin, and, in her new-found belief, she is healed (*Protevangelium* 20; *Pseudo-Matthew* 13). A sixth-century ivory plaque, in the John Rylands Library, Manchester, shows a very similar nativity scene – in the bottom zone [Figure 4.11]. Salome's plea for help occurs on at least two more such pyxes,[30] and upon the ciborium columns at San Marco, Venice. On the bottom the latter is part of a series of sculptures on the Life of the Virgin and are likely medieval copies of an ancient original.[31] A later version of this incident, in which Salome receives an epiphanic vision of the Christ-child, is on Ambrosian ms. L58 sup., fol. 3ro [Figure 4.12].

Salome's act as described in the *Protevangelium* is interesting in respect to the question of the post-partum virginity of Mary. It is possible that this particular Marian gospel was among those about whom Clement of Alexandria remarked 'a few say that when Mary gave birth she was found to be a virgin' (*Stromateis* 7.6).

In the Marian gospels (*Pseudo-Matthew* 13; *Protevangelium* 20) Salome believes and, according to a variant in *Protevangelium* is 'justified.'[32] In *Pseudo-Matthew* 13, Salome worships the child and 'many believed through her preaching.' A further development in the iconography indicates that Salome becomes a preacher and earned the appellation 'saint' – many Byzantine images inscribe her as *hagia Salome*. The manuscript drawings in Ambrosian L58 show an image of Salome preaching – to a crowd of women (fol. 4ro) [Figure 4.13].

The midwives bathe the infant; this scene occurs in a majority of Nativity scenes up to the Middle Ages. Usually, the bathing scene is in the lower center of the image, the 'bathtub' is in the shape of a baptismal font, and one midwife is washing the cross-nimbed infant, while the other is pouring water. There is no extant text in which the bath is described, although the image may be connected to two narratives in the *Arabic Infancy Gospel* in which Jesus' bathwater heals when poured over a sick human (*Arabic* 17, 18) [Text 4.C]. However, one should note that nativity scenes of great heroes and of divinities in the Greco-Roman world often showed the bathing of the child (Alexander the Great; Dionysos); the bathing of the new-born infant was a particularly important social event in the Greco-Roman world. It is natural that such a scene should work its way into the Nativity stories.

The further story of the midwives is a paradigmatic one in respect to the transmissional growth of narratives; they tend to become more complex. In *Pseudo-Matthew*

Figure 4.11 Salome extends her withered arm for help (lower register). Ivory plaque, sixth century. John Rylands University Library, Manchester, Ivories 6. Photograph: Reproduced by courtesy of the Director and Librarian, the John Rylands University of Manchester.

Figure 4.12 Salome extends her withered arm for help. Manuscript illumination, fifteenth century. Ambrosian Library, L58 sup., fol. 3ro. Photograph: Cartlidge.

4.C

On the day after, a woman took scented water to wash the Lord Jesus; and after she had washed him, she took the water with which she had done it, and poured some of it upon a girl who was living there and whose body was white with leprosy, and washed her with it. And as soon as this was done, the girl was cleansed from her leprosy. And the townspeople said, 'There is no doubt that Joseph and Mary and this child are gods, not men.' And when they were ready to leave them, the girl who had suffered from the leprosy came up to them, and asked them to take her with them.

The Arabic Infancy Gospel 17

Figure 4.13 Salome preaches to women. Manuscript illumination, fifteenth century. Ambrosian Library, L58 sup., fol. 4ro. Photograph: Cartlidge.

4.D

When the time of his circumcision arrived, that is on the eighth day, in accordance with the Law, they circumcised the child in the cave. An old Jewess whose son was a perfumer took the prepuce and placed it in a flask of precious ointment. She went to her son and said to him, 'Do not sell this flask even if you are given 300 dinars'. This flask is the one that Mary the sinner bought; she poured its ointment on Jesus' head and feet and then wiped them with her hair.

After ten days they took the child to Jerusalem; 40 days after his birth they presented him in the Temple in the sight of God and made the offering for him prescribed in the Law of Moses, that 'Every first-born male shall be consecrated to God'.

The Arabic Infancy Gospel 5

the number of midwives has become two; the second midwife picks up the name Zelomi, which appears to be a corruption of the name Salome. They are both named in some images. In other images one of the midwives is named Emeia (as at Castelseprio), which is likely a corruption of the Greek, *he maia*, or 'the midwife.'[33]

According to custom, on the eighth day, Jesus was circumcised. This took place either in the cave (*Arabic* 5) or in the temple in Bethlehem (*sic*), after they had moved from cave to stable (*Pseudo-Matthew* 15) [Text 4.D]. Ten days later, according to the *Arabic Infancy Gospel* – it places the circumcision and the presentation to the temple before the flight to Egypt – the Holy Family goes to Jerusalem to present Jesus to the temple. The iconic versions of the circumcision are of basically two types. In one, the circumcision is performed by Joseph. One example is that on the twelfth-century enamel at Klosterneuberg, Austria. There is, says Weitzmann,[34] no extant iconic depiction of the circumcision in the early church, but there are some Middle Byzantine images. An example of the second type of circumcision iconography for example is in an eleventh-century Lectionary in Vatican, cod. gr. 1156, fol. 283ro. In the image, the Virgin sits with the Child in her lap and Joseph stands behind her and in front of a house while a young Israelite performs the rite of circumcision.[35]

The Magi

As in the canonical accounts, in the Marian gospels the Magi traveled from the East to worship the new-born Christ. On the way to the cave (*Protevangelium* 21:3; *Arabic* 7) or to the stable, they unfortunately informed Herod of the purpose of their trip. When they made their journey is a problem. In many cultures, the Adoration of the Magi is celebrated directly after the Nativity, that is on January 6; it is part of the celebration of Christmastide (and in the East, the two feasts become one). However, there were stories in the early church that these magicians (soon to be transformed into kings; the church looked askance at magicians – thus the Phrygian caps of the Magi [see Figure 1.2] became crowns) did not arrive until two years after the Nativity (*Pseudo-Matthew* 16). In the majority of ancient pictorial descriptions of the Adoration the child is sitting up, sometimes on his own, and reaching out to take the gifts from the Magi. He is no longer a neo-nate; this depiction of Jesus is customary in images up to the Renaissance, and they are considered by many therefore to exhibit a parallelism with *Pseudo-Matthew*.[36] Perhaps the most well known of such images is the Adoration of the Magi on the Triumphal Arch at the Church of S. Maria Maggiore, Rome.

There is an element of the polymorphic Jesus in the cycles of the Nativity, in which one image depicts Jesus at the Nativity and the Circumcision as a neo-nate and the next image shows him sitting up as if he were a two-year-old. Those who are familiar with certain of the apocryphal acts of the apostles, e.g. *Acts of Peter*, *Acts of John*, know of the polymorphic Jesus in his appearances to the faithful. This element is emphasized in respect to the infant Christ by a series of manuscript illuminations at Mount Athos, Monastery of Esphigmenou, Menologion, cod. 14. This eleventh-century codex has a richly illustrated series on the Nativity. The series begins with a picture of S. Matthew (fol. 388vo), the Handing Over of the Virgin to Joseph (above) and Joseph's First Dream (below), fol. 389ro, a portrait of the prophet David (fol. 391ro), and Cyrenius, governor of Syria (fol. 389vo). The next folio (391ro) shows Mary and Joseph

Figure 4.14
Edmundo Arburola:
'Noel! Noel!'
Contemporary art,
Nicaragua. Photograph:
by permission of the
Nicaraguan Cultural
Alliance and Quixote
Center/Quest for Peace.

walking on the road to Bethlehem (above) and Mary's vision on the road (a vision painted in dark and menacing colors). Folio 391vo is a typical Byzantine Nativity with the ox and ass, the scene is in a cave, and the bathing of the infant is at the bottom of the image. There are separate images of the Annunciation to the Shepherds (fol. 393vo; 394ro; 394vo) and of angels singing ('all night') near the cave (fol. 394ro), as in *Pseudo-Matthew* 13. The Magi's journey in the track of the star (fol. 394vo) is followed by several miniatures about Persia and paganism (395ro–401vo).

The series picks up the Magi visiting oracles, meeting with King Cyrus and starting on their journey. The next images show the priest and scribes of Judea meeting with Herod, the Magi before Herod, the Magi meeting with the Jews, the Magi leaving Jerusalem, and the Magi before the cave of the Nativity (in which the Virgin and the infant are pictured, with Jesus swaddled and in a masonry crib; fol. 402ro through 405vo). We then see the Magi conversing with Mary; the child Jesus is still in swaddling cloths (fol. 406vo). The next image is of Mary and Jesus in the cave, but now Jesus sits up; he is a boy of two or three years (above). Below is an artist handing to the Magi a sheet upon which is the portrait of the zone above (fol. 407ro). The Magi embrace the child (fol. 407vo); they worship the child, who is now, suddenly, sitting up as a young boy of two or three (fol. 408ro). The next scene is of the Magi, sitting together with their entourage, discussing the alteration of the Christ-child's appearance. The images illustrate the text of the Menologion,[37] which is the legend in which one of the Magi saw Christ as a baby, the second as a thirty-year-old man, and the third as an old man (fol. 408vo). The story in the Menologion of the shape-shifting Jesus is very similar to one in an Armenian infancy gospel in which each of the Magi sees a different vision of Jesus at the Adoration. Gaspar saw a child, 'Son of God incarnate, seated on a throne of glory.' Balthasar saw him as the commander of the Lord's hosts. Melkon saw Jesus as a man dying in torment.[38]

In modern times, the elements surrounding the Nativity of Christ have tended to blend into one scene. Especially in the West, the birth of Jesus, the annunciation to the shepherds and their adoration of the child have become part of one feast, Christmas. Nevertheless, elements which the Christian apocrypha have contributed to the iconography of images remain. In the contemporary Nicaraguan artist Edmundo Arburola's 'Noel! Noel!' [Figure 4.14], the heavenly host who 'sing all night' are replaced by a marimba band of angels. The Magi are peasants bringing gifts of tropical fruit. The joyful babe is bathed in a light from heaven – merged with the star of the Magi. The ox and the ass are present and showing their traditional attention.

The Presentation

In certain images of the Presentation of the child Jesus to the temple (Luke 2:22–38), such as the one on the Triumphal Arch at S. Maria Maggiore, the priest is stepping quickly forward to greet Mary and Joseph, who hold the child. There are also three angels hovering over the scene. Fabricius[39] suggests that the attitude of the priest is a reflection of the text in *Pseudo-Matthew* 15: Hic (Simeon) cum vidisset infantem, exclamavit voce magna dicens Visitavit deus plebem suam, et implevit dominus promissionem suam. Et *festinans* adoravit eum ('[Simeon], when he saw the child, shouted with a loud voice, saying, "God has come to his people . . ." And he hastened

THE LIFE AND MISSION OF JESUS

to adore him'). The presence of the angels, according to Fabricius, is paralleled in the *Arabic Infancy Gospel* 6. The same iconography – less the angels – of the figure of the priest is on the marvelous, eighth-century enameled cross-reliquary in the Biblioteca Vaticana, Treasure of Sancta Sanctorum, Inv. nr. 1881[40] [see Figure 4.1]. The image of the priest suggests even more motion on two Sicilian mosaics. One is in the Cappella Palatina, above the East and West Arches of Crossing;[41] the other is in the Church of S. Mary's of the Admiral (The Martorana).[42]

The Massacre of the Innocents

Herod, as we know from both the canonical and the apocryphal accounts, moved to protect his throne from a new 'King of the Jews.' During the Massacre of the Innocents, Elizabeth, the mother of John the Baptist, fled to the mountains (*Protevangelium* 22:3) and made a miraculous escape from Herod's soldiers. This scene appears on a terracotta ampulla from Bobbio (fifth or sixth century),[43] at Castelseprio (a seventh-century fresco),[44] at Görëme, in Cappadocia,[45] and an icon at Mount Sinai (twelfth century),[46] among others. The Kariye Djami's mosaic of the flight of Elizabeth shows Elizabeth, holding the infant John the Baptist in her arms, hiding in a cave from a soldier who pursues them with a drawn sword.[47] Thus, John escaped the dark side of the Nativity, an escape which answers that vexing question we posed earlier: if John and Jesus were born only a few months apart, how did John escape the massacre?[48] Another legend, preserved in pictures, is of John's living in the desert as a child, led by an angel and instructed by God. According to a Life of John the Baptist, by Serapion, Elizabeth dies of old age in the desert, the Virgin and Jesus fly on a cloud to rescue him and to perform the necessary burial rites for Elizabeth. They then leave John in the care of angels: 'Instead of a desert full of wild beasts, he will walk in a desert full of angels and prophets.'[49] We have found no early images of John the Baptist's life in the desert as a child, but there is a thirteenth-century painting in Parma, which is part of the cathedral baptistery's cycle of the life of John the Baptist.[50] In addition, there is a painting in the Vatican, inv. nr. 185, fourteenth century, on this theme.[51]

In the *Protevangelium* 23, Herod is aware that the child John the Baptist is not among the dead infants. So he grills Zacharias about the whereabouts of the priest's son. Zacharias responds with a condemnation of Herod, and he is slain. The flight of Elizabeth and the murder of Zacharias appear on frescoes in the under Church of Deir Abu Hennis, at Antinoë, Egypt, in the sixth or seventh century.[52] A ninth-century miniature in the Bibliothèque nationale, cod. gr. 510, fol. 137ro,[53] has both events as did a lost cycle of frescoes in the 'Red Church' of Perustica, Bulgaria (seventh century).[54]

The murder of Zacharias and the selection of Simeon to take his place marks the end of the *Protevangelium*. But the cycle of the Infancy of Christ continues in *Pseudo-Matthew* and the *Infancy Gospel of Thomas*. It is *Pseudo-Matthew* who relates the story of the Flight to Egypt and the return to Nazareth. The *Infancy Thomas* picks up the story of the Holy Family's life in Nazareth up to the account of Jesus' confounding the learned men in the temple, at age twelve. A portion of *Pseudo-Matthew* (Part 2) basically follows the *Infancy Thomas*, and it 'seems to have developed from the Greek tradition [of the *Infancy Thomas*].'[55] If one can consider, for example, the *Coptic Gospel of Thomas* from Nag Hammadi, to which the *Infancy Thomas* appears to have no relationship, as an almost pure form of wisdom gospel – it contains no narrative, only sayings of Jesus – the *Infancy Thomas* is pure aretalogy. It consists of one miraculous deed of the child Jesus after another, with, at least to the modern mind, little redeeming theological importance. It did, however, have importance in the church, for it has contributed a number of images about Jesus in both rhetorical and iconic form.

The Flight to Egypt and the return to Nazareth

The only extant early church images of the Flight to Egypt of which we are aware are on the Triumphal Arch at S. Maria Maggiore – the image of the arrival at Sotina [Figure 4.15] – and on a fifth-century sarcophagus fragment in Istanbul (Arkeoloji Müzeleri).[56] The fragment's image shows only the latter half of the ass and Mary carrying Jesus. So we must turn to later images to view what earlier representations might have been.

An eleventh-century Gospel Lectionary at Mount Athos (Dionysiou, cod. 587, fol. 133vo)[57] shows one typical Byzantine form: Mary is on the ass, riding side-saddle and holding the child in her lap. The procession is led by Joseph's son; Joseph brings up the rear. There are actually three basic iconographies in Byzantine art: (1) Joseph's son leads the ass and Joseph follows – found in Cappadocian frescoes and elsewhere; (2) Joseph leads and the son follows; this is in the Vatican menologion (Menologion of Basil II, p. 274); (3) Joseph carries the child on his shoulders – in the Florentine Gospels.[58] In addition, there is often an angel present, and, in a few cases, the Holy Family is accompanied by one or more servants. All of these elements are described in *Pseudo-Matthew* 18f.

In the Swiss village of Zillis, the Romanesque Church of S. Martin has 'unquestionably the earliest extant wooden ceiling with Romanesque paintings.'[59] The ceiling paintings are the only decoration of the eleventh-century church, and 'clearly owe a debt to book-illustration.' In company with striking and wonderfully spare paintings

Figure 4.15 The Flight to Egypt/Arrival in Sotina. Mosaic, *c.* 432. Triumphal Arch of the Church of S. Maria Maggiore, Rome. Photograph: Art Resource, NY.

Figure 4.16 The Flight to Egypt/The Miracle of the Date Palm Tree. Wooden ceiling panel, *c.* 1120. Church of S. Martin, Zillis, Switzerland. Photograph: Peter Heman.

of the Annunciation and of the Nativity (with the Ox and the Ass) and other images from the Life of the Virgin and the Infancy of Christ, Zillis' ceiling paintings include an explicit visual reference to the miracle of the date palm tree (*Pseudo-Matthew* 20) [Figure 4.16]. The drawing of this scene in Ambrosian ms. L58 sup. fol. 10ro has an iconographical scheme somewhat different than that in the Zillis illustration [Figure 4.17].

In one of the most charming stories in the cycle of Christ's Infancy, the Holy Family rests on their dash to safety in a foreign land (*Pseudo-Matthew* 20). The rest allows artists to depict the Holy Family in repose. Zillis has one of the earliest (*c.* 1120) depictions [Figure 4.18], if this scene is intended to show the Holy Family's rest. More modern artists sometimes play with the traditional iconography, in which the Holy Family is simply shown seated, with Mary holding the child Jesus. Caravaggio, in his typical 'I will do this differently' style, has the angel in the form of a Greek muse, playing the violin. Joseph holds the music for the angel-muse, while the music accompanies the sleep of the exhausted mother and child (cover illustration: paperback version). The charm is not only in the narrative device of a time of peace during a very dangerous journey; it is also the occasion from which we have the legend of

Figure 4.17 The Flight to Egypt/The Miracle of the Date Palm Tree. Manuscript illumination, fifteenth century. Ambrosian Library, L58 sup., fol. 10ro. Photograph: Cartlidge.

the date palm tree's bending down at the Infant's command so that Mary may have refreshment from its fruit (*Pseudo-Matthew* 20). The Zillis image seems to be a reflection of the earliest iconography. Often, as in Dürer's 'Flight to Egypt,' (Bartsch, B. 89) the Virgin sits on the ass, her back to the viewer, the child is supported in her arms (only his head is visible). The ox and ass are together, as in a Nativity scene. Joseph leads the procession, in a forest, as they are about to cross a bridge over a stream. There is a date palm, which is clearly a reference to the miracle of the palm tree [Text 4.E].

In northern European countries, England, for example, date palms are a rarity, so the tree becomes a cherry tree and provides us with one of the most delightful bits of verse in English song:

> So Joseph flew in anger
> In anger flew he,
> Let the father of the baby
> Pick cherries for Thee . . .
> The Cherry tree bent low down
> Bent low down to the ground.
> And Mary picked the cherries
> While Joseph stood around.[60]

Figure 4.18 The Rest on the Flight to Egypt. Wooden ceiling panel, *c.* 1120. Church of
S. Martin, Zillis, Switzerland. Photograph: Peter Heman.

The date-palm tree narrative also reflects the use of the palm branch as a symbol
of martyrdom, a symbol which is common in Christian iconic art. The palm's occurrence in an image, especially when it is held by a figure in that scene, symbolizes to
the viewer that that person has fulfilled the statement in *Pseudo-Matthew* 21: 'You
have attained the palm of victory.'

On the journey to Egypt, in the spirit of *Pseudo-Matthew* and the *Infancy Thomas*,
there are many occasions upon which the child Jesus exhibits his powers. When the
group reaches a cave in which they wish to rest, they discover it is full of dragons.
Jesus subdues them and orders them to hurt no one (*Pseudo-Matthew* 18). The text is
accompanied in Ambrosian L58 sup. 8ro with a picture. In the image, the child Jesus
stands on the right, facing the cave full of wild beasts. An angel hovers over the cave.
The Virgin stands with her left hand resting on Jesus' head and behind her is a maidservant. Joseph, with a sack over his shoulder leads the clearly perturbed ass. In
Pseudo-Matthew 19, the travelers are accompanied by a retinue of formerly ferocious
lions and panthers. The illustrator of Ambrosian L58 sup. has given two pictures for
this story [Figure 4.19A, Figure 4.19B]. At folio 8vo, the family is in the same
position as in the prior image, however, the ass is visibly more perturbed. The next

4.E

And it came to pass on the third day of their journey, while they were walking, that Mary was fatigued by the excessive heat of the sun in the desert; and, seeing a palm-tree she said to Joseph, 'I should like to rest a little in the shade of this tree.' Joseph therefore led her quickly to the palm and made her dismount from her beast. And as Mary was sitting there, she looked up to the foliage of the palm and saw it full of fruit and said to Joseph, 'I wish it were possible to get some of the fruit of this palm.' And Joseph said to her, 'I am surprised that you say so, for you see how high the palm-tree is, and that you think of eating its fruit. I am thinking more of the want of water because the skins are now empty, and we have nothing with which to refresh ourselves and our cattle.' Then the child Jesus, reposing with a joyful countenance in the lap of his mother, said to the palm, 'O tree, bend your branches and refresh my mother with your fruit.' And immediately at these words the palm bent its top down to the very feet of Mary; and they gathered from it fruit with which they all refreshed themselves. And after they had gathered all its fruit it remained bent down, waiting the order to rise from him who had commanded it to bend down. Then Jesus said to it, 'Raise yourself, O palm, and be strong and be the companion of my trees which are in the paradise of my Father; and open from your roots a vein of water which is hidden in the earth and let the waters flow, so that we may quench our thirst.' And it rose up immediately, and at its root there began to gush out a spring of water exceedingly clear and cool and sparkling. And when they saw the spring of water, they rejoiced greatly and were all satisfied, including their cattle and their beasts and they gave thanks to God.

And on the day after, when they were setting out from there, and at the hour in which they began their journey, Jesus turned to the palm and said, 'This privilege I give you, O palm-tree, that one of your branches be carried away by my angels, and planted in the paradise of my Father. And this blessing I will confer upon you, that it shall be said to all who shall be victorious in any contest, "You have attained the palm of victory."' And while he was speaking, behold, an angel of the Lord appeared and stood upon the palm tree and, taking off one of its branches, flew to heaven with the branch in his hand. And when they saw this, they fell on their faces and were like dead men. And Jesus said to them, 'Why are your hearts possessed with fear? Do you not know that this palm, which I have caused to be transferred to paradise, shall be prepared for all the saints in the place of blessedness, as it has been prepared for us in this desert place?' And they were filled with joy; and being strengthened, they all arose.

The Gospel of Pseudo-Matthew 20–1

Figures 4.19 A and B The Miracle of the Lions and Panthers. Manuscript illuminations, fifteenth
century. Ambrosian Library, L58 sup., fols. 8 vo and 9ro. Photographs: Cartlidge.

folio (9ro) shows the lions and panthers, with an ox and ass, leading[61] the ass upon which Mary sits holding Jesus in her lap, and Joseph with his sack bringing up the rear. The ass strides along, now purposefully, but he still keeps a watchful eye on the crowd of predators before him.

The Holy Family arrive at the Egyptian town of Sotina; this arrival is one of the most common of the images in the cycle. Upon their entrance into the town, all the pagan idols in the city crumble and collapse. This miraculous event results in the conversion of the Egyptians, and the Family is greeted by Affrodisius, the pagan high priest (*Pseudo-Matthew* 22–24; *Arabic* 10–11) [see Figure 4.15]. The greeting is usually depicted in two stages. The arrival, fall of the idols and Affrodisius' coming out to meet the family. There is also a scene in which Affrodisius kneels before the mother and child and kisses Jesus' feet. That there was a complete cycle of the arrival which involved all these scenes is suggested by Weitzmann on the basis of an illustrated *Pseudo-Matthew* in Paris (Bibl. nat. cod. lat. 2688). It has no fewer than fifty-two quite impressive miniatures, one of them (Figure 10a) the scene of Affrodisius bowing down. The idols fall before the Virgin dismounts the ass and the scene of Affrodisius' kissing Jesus' feet follows.[62]

The Holy Family stays in Egypt 'for a little time' (*Pseudo-Matthew* 25) and returns to Nazareth after an angel – in Joseph's Third Dream – tells them the return is now safe. According to Albrecht Dürer, Joseph the carpenter pursued his occupation during the sojourn in Egypt [Figure 4.20]. Dürer's woodcut has the family in a city. Mary sits with a group of women, sewing, the child safely wrapped in a crib. Over the crib there leans a crowned figure, likely Affrodisius. Joseph is busy with an adze, cutting out a trough from a log. An angel guards the group of sewing women, and small angels (cherubs) help Joseph keep his workplace clean. Over the whole scene is the figure of God, keeping watch on this special place in His world.

The journey from Egypt to Nazareth was not without incident. On the way, the Family meet with robbers (*Arabic Infancy Gospel* 13; 23) [Texts 4.F; 4.G] There are two such stories. In the first, the brigands have attacked a caravan and taken its people captive. Jesus' approach is 'like the noise of a magnificent king going out of his city

---

4.F

Going out from there, they came to a place where there were robbers who had plundered many men of their baggage and clothes, and had bound them. Then the robbers heard a great noise, like the noise of a magnificent king going out of his city with his army, and his chariots and his drums; and at this the robbers were terrified, and left all that they had stolen. And their captives rose up, loosed each other's bonds, recovered their baggage, and went away. And when they saw Joseph and Mary coming up to the place, they said to them, 'Where is that king? When the robbers heard the magnificent sound of his approach they left us, and we have escaped safe?' Joseph answered them 'He will come behind us.'

The Arabic Infancy Gospel 13

Figure 4.20 Albrecht Dürer: The Sojourn in Egypt. Woodcut, *c.* 1501–2. Boston Museum of Fine Arts, Boston, MA, Maria Antoinette Evans Fund, 30.1167. Photograph: Boston Museum of Fine Arts.

4.G

And departing from this place, they came to a desert; and hearing that it was infested by robbers, Joseph and the Lady Mary decided to cross this region by night. But on their way, behold, they saw two robbers lying in wait on the road, and with them a great number of robbers, who were their associates, sleeping. Now those two robbers into whose hands they had fallen were Titus and Dumachus. Titus therefore said to Dumachus, 'I beseech you to let these persons go free, so that our comrades do not see them.' And as Dumachus refused, Titus said to him again, 'Take forty drachmas from me, and have them as a pledge.' At the same time he held out to him the belt which he had had about his waist, that he should not open his mouth or speak. And the Lady Mary, seeing that the robber had done them a kindness, said to him, 'The Lord God will sustain you with his right hand, and will grant you remission of your sins.' And the Lord Jesus answered, and said to his mother, 'Thirty years hence, O my mother, the Jews will crucify me at Jerusalem, and these two robbers will be raised upon the cross along with me, Titus on my right hand and Dumachus on my left; and after that day Titus shall go before me into Paradise.' And she said, 'God keep this from you, my son.' And they went from there towards a city of idols, which, as they came near it, was transformed into sand-hills.

The Arabic Infancy Gospel 23

with his army, and his chariots and his drums; and at this the robbers were terrified, and left all their plunder.' Thus, the child Jesus stages a hostage rescue operation. In the second story, as Joseph and his family attempt to cross a robber-laden territory, they are saved by two of the crooks. These two, the story says, will be the two crucified with Jesus. That, in this story, the two robbers are Titus and Dumachus (not the Gestas and Demas of the more familiar crucifixion narratives – such as in the *Gospel of Nicodemus*) gives tribute to the variety of early Christian legend-fashioning. Images of the episodes of the robbers occur on a sixteenth-century wood sculpture in the choir of the Church of S. Nicholas, Kalkar, Turkey.[63] There are two scenes in stone sculpture at the Church of Saint-Thiebaut, west portal, main tympanum, in Thann, Alsace. The latter carvings are from the fourteenth century.[64]

Jesus grows up

There are no canonical accounts of Jesus' childhood, aside from Jesus' early disputation with the leaders of the temple. In the apocryphal gospels, the childhood of Jesus in Bethlehem was not without incident. There, Jesus frequently displays his marvelous powers. In some of these, he appears to be out of control, at least by modern standards. The *Infancy Gospel of Thomas*, later paralleled by additions to the *Pseudo-Matthew* and in the *Arabic Infancy Gospel*, recounts in often hyperbolic and troublesome detail the earliest years of Jesus, portraying him in the form of a budding Greco-Roman divine man (*theios aner*). The form of this 'gospel' (although it is not named 'gospel' in the ancient texts)[65] is basically a collection of legends which display the raw power of the child Jesus. We will follow the text's lead and list the scenes relevant to our purpose.

In perhaps the most infamous scene in the *Infancy Gospel of Thomas* (4–5), Jesus causes a boy who has bumped into him in a crowd to die. That this scene was problematic in the church is witnessed by a Syriac variant in which Jesus defends his behavior: 'If these children had been born in wedlock they would not be cursed.'[66] We have found no iconic parallel to this scene (which does not exclude the existence of such an image), a lacuna in the tradition which is likely significant. However, in this and many other such cases (such as the episode of the birds, below) the villagers of Nazareth complain to Joseph about Jesus' behavior.

Jesus, while playing at a stream crossing, gathers pools of water from the running water, purifying the water at the same time. He takes clay and moulds sparrows from it. Jesus vivifies them and they fly away. The act receives disapproval from the religious leaders of the town; Jesus has done this on the Sabbath. That this type of incident throughout these gospels is an intentional anti-Semitism is doubtless (*Infancy Gospel of Thomas* 2; *Arabic* 36; *Pseudo-Matthew* 27) [Text 4.H] [Figure 4.21].

Christ carries water in his cloak, when his mother sends him to fetch water, and the jug is broken in the crowd (or, in some images, is broken by other children) (*Infancy Gospel of Thomas* 11; *Pseudo-Matthew* 33) [Figure 4.22]. Another version of this scene is in a fourteenth-century lectionary in the town library, Schaffhausen, Switzerland (ms. A. 8, fols. 27vo, 28ro) [Text 4.I].

4.H

When this boy Jesus was five years old he was playing at the crossing of a stream, and he gathered together into pools the running water, and instantly made it clean, and gave his command with a single word. Having made soft clay he moulded from it twelve sparrows. And it was the sabbath when he did these things. And there were also many other children playing with him. When a certain Jew saw what Jesus was doing while playing on the sabbath, he at once went and told his father Joseph, 'See, your child is at the stream, and he took clay and moulded twelve birds and has profaned the sabbath.' And when Joseph came to the place and looked, he cried out to him, saying, 'Why do you do on the sabbath things which it is not lawful to do?' But Jesus clapped his hands and cried out to the sparrows and said to them, 'Be gone!' And the sparrows took flight and went away chirping. The Jews were amazed when they saw this, and went away and told their leaders what they had seen Jesus do.

The Infancy Gospel of Thomas 2

Figure 4.21 Jesus vivifies clay birds. Wooden ceiling panel, *c.* 1120. Church of S. Martin, Zillis, Switzerland. Photograph: Peter Heman.

A child falls from a tower in a house, and Jesus raises him from the dead. (*Infancy Gospel of Thomas* 9; *Arabic* 44; *Pseudo-Matthew* 32). This scene is in the Ambrosian library manuscript which we introduced at the head of this chapter (ms. L58 sup. fol. 13vo) and in terracotta tablets in the British Museum and in the Victoria and Albert Museum which we discuss below (pp. 114–16) [Text 4.J].

Christ heals a woodcutter who has wounded himself with an axe (*Infancy Gospel of Thomas* 10) [Figure 4.23]. This scene also occurs on the terracotta tablets in the British Museum [Text 4.K].

Christ sows and reaps a miraculous harvest. The harvest is depicted in Ambrosian ms. L58 sup. fol. 15ro Jesus performs a miracle in respect to a harvest of wheat (*Infancy Gospel of Thomas* 12; *Pseudo-Matthew* 34 – which has evidently been expanded by its knowledge of the legends in the *Infancy Gospel of Thomas*) [Text 4.L]. This wheat harvest is often given in allusion in painting, especially images which are of the Flight to Egypt. An example is a sixteenth-century painting on the Altar of S. Anne in the Württembergische Staatsgalerie, nr. 1010, in Stuttgart. In the painting, the Holy Family travels toward Sotina. An idol falls off its pedestal on the upper left, and, in the upper right there are harvesters in a field. Schiller points out that such a detail reflects the story of the miraculous harvest.[67] As is the case with the Rest on the

4.I

When he was six years old, his mother gave him a pitcher and sent him to draw water and bring it into the house. But in the crowd he stumbled, and the pitcher was broken. But Jesus spread out the garment he was wearing, filled it with water and brought it to his mother. And when his mother saw the miracle, she kissed him, and kept to herself the mysteries which she had seen him do.

The Infancy Gospel of Thomas 11

4.J

Now after some days Jesus was playing in the upper story of a house, and one of the children who were playing with him fell down from the house and died. And when the other children saw it they fled, and Jesus remained alone. And the parents of the one who was dead came and accused him. But they threatened him. Then Jesus leaped down from the roof and stood by the corpse of the child, and cried with a loud voice, 'Zeno' – for that is what he was called – 'arise and tell me, did I throw you down?' And he arose at once and said, 'No, Lord, you did not throw me down, but raised me up.' And when they saw it they were amazed. And the parents of the child glorified God for the sign that had happened and worshipped Jesus.

The Infancy Gospel of Thomas 9

Figure 4.22 Jesus carries water in his cloak. Manuscript illumination, fifteenth century. Ambrosian Library, L58 sup., fol. 14vo. Photograph: Cartlidge.

4.K

After a few days a certain man was cleaving wood in a corner, and the axe fell and split the sole of his foot, and he was losing so much blood that he was about to die. And there was a clamour, a crowd gathered, and the child Jesus also ran there, forced his way through the crowd, and took the injured foot, and it was healed immediately. And he said to the young man, 'Arise now, cleave the wood and remember me.' And when the crowd saw what happened, they worshipped the child, saying, 'Truly the spirit of God dwells in this child.'

The Infancy Gospel of Thomas 10

Figure 4.23 Jesus heals a woodsman who cut himself with an axe. Manuscript illumination, fifteenth century. Ambrosian Library, L58 sup., fol. 14ro. Photograph: Cartlidge.

4.L

Again, in the time of sowing the child went out with his father to sow corn in their field. And as his father sowed, the child Jesus also sowed one grain of corn. And when he had reaped it and threshed it, he brought in a hundred measures, and he called all the poor of the village to the threshing-floor and gave them the corn, and Joseph took the residue. He was eight years old when he performed this sign.

The Infancy Gospel of Thomas 12

Flight to Egypt, the musical arts contribute to the continuation of the story. An English carol is based upon the 'Miraculous Harvest.'[68] The carol combines the miraculous harvest with the Massacre of the Innocents:

There's thousands of children young.
Which for his sake did die;
Do not forbid those little ones,
And do not them deny.

In the story of the dyer Salem (*Arabic* 37), Jesus goes into a dyer's shop and mischievously throws all the shopkeeper's pieces of cloth into a vat full of indigo dye. Upon the remonstrations of the dyer, Jesus begins to pull each piece of cloth from the indigo dye and, miraculously, each comes out dyed the appropriate color [Figure 4.24] [Text 4.M].

The tale of the child Jesus and the boys in the oven (*Arabic* 40) displays an element that we pointed out in the Introduction to this volume: there is an Arabian Nights flavor to the Arabic version. In this story, Jesus is shunned by those he seeks as playmates. They have hidden from him in an oven. Some women, in collusion with the boys insist that there are kids in the oven. Jesus calls them out and indeed they have become kids. In certain images evidently related to this story, the children become pigs (an anti-semitic variant?). Images related to the story are on terracotta tiles in the British Museum and a fourteenth-century manuscript in the British Library (Egerton 2781, fol. 88vo) [Text 4.N].

Christ stretches a plank in one of the more benign and charming stories (*Infancy Gospel of Thomas* 13; *Pseudo-Matthew* 37). Joseph the carpenter has cut one plank of a bed shorter than the other. Jesus grabs one end of the mis-measured plank and stretches it to the proper length [Figure 4.25] [Text 4.O]. A variant on the story has Jesus straightening out a bent beam to fit a plow. This version of the scene occurs on the terracotta tiles in the British Museum and the fourteenth-century lectionary in Schaffhausen, Switzerland (Stadtbibliothek, A. 8, Lectionary, fol. 27vo, 28ro).

Christ raises James, Joseph's son, who was bitten by a viper while James was working in the fields. (*Infancy Gospel of Thomas* 16; *Pseudo-Matthew* 41; *Arabic* 43). See Ambrosian ms. L58 sup. 17vo [Text 4.P].

Figure 4.24 Jesus and the dyer Salem. Manuscript illumination, fifteenth century. Ambrosian
Library, L58 sup., fol. 12ro. Photograph: Cartlidge.

4.M

One day, when Jesus was running about and playing with some children, he
passed by the workshop of a dyer called Salem. They had in the workshop
many cloths which he had to dye. The Lord Jesus went into the dyer's workshop, took all the pieces of cloth and put them into a tub full of indigo.
When Salem came and saw that the cloths were spoiled, he began to cry
aloud and asked the Lord Jesus, saying, 'What have you done to me, son of
Mary? You have ruined my reputation in the eyes of all the people of the
city; for everyone orders a colour to suit himself, but you have come and
spoiled everything.' And the Lord Jesus replied, 'I will change for you the
colour of any cloth which you wish to be changed', and he immediately began
to take the cloths out of the tub, each of them dyed in the colour the dyer
wished, until he had taken them all out. When the Jews saw this miracle
and wonder, they praised God.

The Arabic Infancy Gospel 37

4.N

On another day the Lord Jesus went out into the road, and seeing some boys who had met to play, he followed them; but the boys hid themselves from him. The Lord Jesus, therefore, having come to the door of a certain house, and seen some women standing there, asked them where the boys had gone; and when they answered that there was no one there. He said again, 'Who are these whom you see in the furnace?' They replied that they were young goats of three years old. And the Lord Jesus cried out and said, 'Come out, O goats, to your Shepherd.' Then the boys, in the form of goats, came out, and began to skip round him; and the women, seeing this, were very much astonished, and were seized with trembling, and speedily supplicated the Lord Jesus, saying, 'O our Lord Jesus, son of Mary, you are truly that good Shepherd of Israel; have mercy on your handmaidens who stand before you, and who have never doubted: for you have come, O our Lord, to heal, and not to destroy.' And when the Lord Jesus answered that the sons of Israel were like the Ethiopians among, the nations, the women said, 'You, O Lord, know all things, nor is anything hid from you; now, indeed, we beseech you, and ask you of your mercy to restore these boys, your servants to their former condition.' The Lord Jesus therefore said, 'Come, boys, let us go and play.' And immediately, while these women were standing by, the kids were changed into boys.

The Arabic Infancy Gospel 40

4.O

His father was a carpenter and made at that time ploughs and yokes. And he received an order from a rich man to make a bed for him. But when one beam was shorter than its corresponding one and they did not know what to do, the child Jesus said to his father Joseph, 'Lay down the two pieces of wood and make them even from the middle to one end.' And Joseph did as the child told him. And Jesus stood at the other end and took hold of the shorter piece of wood, and stretching it made it equal to the other. And his father Joseph saw it and was amazed, and he embraced the child and kissed him, saying, 'Happy am I that God has given me this child.'

The Infancy Gospel of Thomas 13

Figure 4.25 Jesus stretches a plank. Manuscript illumination, fifteenth century. Ambrosian Library, L58 sup., fol. 15vo. Photograph: Cartlidge.

4.P

Joseph sent his son James to gather wood and take it into his house, and the child Jesus followed him. And while James was gathering the sticks, a viper bit the hand of James. And as he lay stretched out and about to die, Jesus came near and breathed upon the bite, and immediately the pain ceased, and the creature burst, and at once James was healed.

The Infancy Gospel of Thomas 16

We mentioned above a series of ceramic tiles, probably from the fourteenth century, in the British Museum and the Victoria and Albert Museum, which contain scenes of Jesus' childhood. These tiles, probably church decorations, depict a whole series of these aretalogical stories which migrated from the *Infancy Thomas* into popular literature and legend.[69] The tiles in the British Museum contain the following scenes:

1   The pools (*Infancy Thomas* 1–3; *Pseudo-Matthew* 26). The Christ Child, not nimbed, makes two pools with a compass. A boy with a stick is wrecking the pools and falling headlong. The Virgin, crowned, admonishes the Christ child who is kicking a boy holding a stick.

2   A schoolmaster is seated on a bench. A boy, who is represented twice, is once on the back of Christ, and once falling down.

3   The Christ child, cross-nimbed, pulls a boy from a tower. (*Infancy Thomas* 9).

4   Christ confounds a teacher. The teacher (Levi) is seated on a bench, striking Christ, who is cross-nimbed and holding a book. Christ child is represented a second time, his hands raised. In a second scene, the teacher and another, both seated, are arguing with the Christ child. Two cripples are seated on the ground.

5   The miraculous harvest (*Infancy Thomas* 10). A boy is harvesting grain with a man placing a sheaf in a cart. Second scene. The Christ child opens an oven door. The parents stand beside him.

6   Tame lions (*Pseudo-Matthew* 35). The Christ child, cross-nimbed, points to three lions. Joseph and the Virgin, who is crowned, watch with several spectators. Second scene. A master and a workman are holding an axe. The Christ child, cross-nimbed, points to a bent beam.

7   (*Pseudo-Matthew* 42). A workman is holding an axe. Master and the Christ child, cross-nimbed, hold a bent beam. Second scene. A servant plows with a plow made from the bent beam.

8   A family feast (as in *Pseudo-Matthew* 42) or the miracle of Cana. Christ or the Christ Child, cross-nimbed, stands by three jars. An attendant is serving Joseph (?) and several others seated at a table.

The tiles in the Victoria and Albert Museum display: Tile 1. Jesus, cross-nimbed, raises some boys who fell on a hill. Jesus holds a book in his left hand and extends his right hand toward some kneeling boys. In a second scene, a boy with a pitcher in his hand stands beside a well; Jesus stands behind the well with a pitcher in his left hand and his right hand raised. Three boys each carry a pitcher. Tile 2. Three men remonstrate Joseph about Jesus' behavior. In a second scene, Jesus holds a book in his left hand and raises the boy who came to an end sliding on a sunbeam, after the boy had attempted to imitate Jesus' successful ride on a sunbeam. Three boys kneel.

Not only are the two sets of tiles interesting in themselves, but they point to the widespread variations upon the infancy gospels which transmitted, adapted and disseminated the stories of the boy Jesus' miracles. Among those medieval manuscripts which contain the text and images of these stories is that in the Bodleian Library, ms. Selden supra 38. It contains some sixty illustrations, including that of Jesus' sliding on a sunbeam and the demise of the child who imitates him (fol. 24ro). James mentions a number of such manuscripts, including British Museum, Egerton ms. 2781; Bodleian Library Douce 237.[70]

One of the features of a *bios* is the precocious wisdom and learning of the divine man. Several stories in the *Infancy Thomas* have Jesus the child confounding (and often irritating his teachers). On different occasions Jesus confounds his school-teachers (*Infancy Gospel of Thomas* 14, 15, 19; *Pseudo-Matthew* 31) [Text 4.Q]. The Ambrosian manuscript L58 sup. 16ro, 16vo and 17ro illustrates the story of the teacher who dies in a disagreement with Jesus' interpretation of 'the letters' and is raised again.

4.Q

And after some time yet another teacher, a good friend of Joseph, said to him, 'Bring the child to me to the school. Perhaps I by persuasion can teach him the letters.' And Joseph said to him, 'If you have the courage, brother, take him with you.' And he took him with fear and anxiety, but the child went gladly. And he went boldly into the school and found a book lying on the lectern and picked it up, but did not read the letters in it; instead he opened his mouth and spoke by the Holy Spirit and taught the law to those that stood around. And a large crowd assembled and stood there listening to him, wondering at the beauty of his teaching and the fluency of his words, that, although an infant, he made such pronouncements. But when Joseph heard it, he was afraid and ran to the school, wondering whether this teacher also was inexperienced. But the teacher said to Joseph, 'Know, brother, that I took the child as a disciple; but he is full of much grace and wisdom; and now I beg you, brother, take him to your house.'

The Infancy Gospel of Thomas 15

The narrative of Christ and the Doctors in the Temple is told in Luke 2:41–51 (and in *Infancy Gospel of Thomas* 19; *Arabic* 50). It is embellished, according to some interpreters, by reference to the *Infancy Thomas* 15, in which Jesus confounds his teachers in school with his interpretation of letters. This image in its iconic form adds to the canonical account by showing Jesus holding a book or a scroll in hand [Figure 4.26]. An ivory in Milan, a book cover, has a scene which Garucci and de Waal have interpreted as the scene from *Infancy Thomas* 15. Fabricius rejects this interpretation of the image, a picture which has also been interpreted as Jesus among the Doctors in the Temple (Volbach), Jesus before Pilate, and Jesus teaching an apostle. The image simply has to be listed as unidentified.[71]

The mission

The apocryphal gospels do not pass on narratives only about the infancy of Jesus. Some of them add to the main subject of the canonical gospels, that is, the message and mission of Christ the man. Many of these gospels, such as the *Coptic Gospel of Thomas*, *Evangelium Veritatis* and the *Coptic Gospel of Philip* are not good subjects for iconic narratives; sayings other than parables generally do not lend themselves to pictorial art. However, there are parallels for narratives of Jesus' mission and passion which occur in apocryphal versions of rhetoric which is both extra- and intra-canonical.

First, A. de Waal[72] suggests that the prevalence of four miracles on the early monuments of the church, namely, the healing of the man born blind, the raising of Lazarus, the man bent over from gout, and the haemorrhagia, were due to the influence of the *Gospel of Nicodemus (Acta Pilati)* 6. De Waal appears to be a school of one on this issue.

Figure 4.26 Jesus and the Doctors in the Temple. Wooden ceiling panel, *c.* 1120. Church of S. Martin, Zillis, Switzerland. Photograph: Peter Heman.

Second, we call your attention to our discussion in Chapter 3 of the mosaics in S. Apollinare Nuovo in which, in the mosaics which precede the Passion, and which are of miracles, Jesus is a beardless youth. In those mosaics which are of the Passion, Jesus is bearded. It is as if an expression of the epiphanic Christ (as Christ, the beautiful youth) were associated with the miracles of Christ.

The baptism

The baptism of Christ, which begins his ministry in the canonical gospels, is one of the central elements in the history of Christian art. Especially in the East, but certainly not confined to that region, there are details in the baptism which vary from canonical accounts. If one includes the church fathers' mentioning of these variants in the stories which led to the creation of both canonical and apocryphal gospels, they deserve mention here.

First, the Jordan is personified. Although this element of the images is not mentioned in either canon or apocrypha, it is worthy of mention to clarify the identification of the figure which is so often at the bottom of the stream in which Jesus is baptized. It is the depiction of the *persona* of the Jordan; he is usually a figure in the water itself. This variance is likely stylistic; it derives from this practice in Greco-Roman art in general. Such images occur in Jewish art as well. In the Vienna Genesis (sixth century) an illustration of Rebecca and Eliezer at the well (at Genesis 24:15–18) contains a figure of a water sprite.[73]

Second the water of the Jordan swirls up around Jesus; it 'defies gravity to rise to Christ's waist.'[74] The rising of the water is symbolic of the stillness of time; all has come to a halt at the moment of incarnation (Arian) or at the announcement of the incarnation. There are also usually angels present at the baptism, and, sometimes, there is a star shining over the scene. Ephraim of Syria, in his *Paschal Chronicles* mentions each of these phenomena. The angels occur more often than not in images of the baptism [Figure 4.27]. This image does not occur in any known Christian apocryphon as such. However, one can posit that Ephraim's use of the images represents the vast store of tradition which underlies the apocrypha. As such, we treat his version of the story as an apocryphon. As we will see in a following chapter, such stories also occur in regard to the Apostles. An example is the scene in which John the Evangelist is boiled in oil before the Porta Latina in Rome (see Chapter 6, below).

The correspondence with Abgar

Jesus, according to an early legend, was asked by Abgar, the king of Syria, to come to him.[75] An ill Abgar wants Jesus as a healer to come to Edessa and to restore his health. Jesus was unable to come, but he sent in his stead Thaddeus (Addai). There are images of Abgar's dictating the letter to Jesus and of his reading Jesus' reply. This correspondence was a favorite apocryphon in the early church. It is detailed in Eusebios, *Church History* I.13.5; II.1.6, and in several other manuscripts.[76] We have images from the sixth century which depict the scene of Abgar's reception of Jesus' correspondence [see Figure 3.1].

The Abgar legends are also illustrated in a fourteenth-century manuscript in the Pierpont Morgan Library, New York (cod. M.499). The manuscript has some twenty-one scenes which are about King Abgar's correspondence with Jesus in the hope that Abgar will be healed of his disease and with the legend of the Mandylion (discussed in Chapter 3, above).[77] An even earlier manuscript, mentioned in the previous chapter, an illustrated Pseudo-Matthew in Paris, contains both a collection of infancy stories and the Abgar legend (Chapter 3, note 4).

The passion

Some twenty passion scenes have been identified in early Christian art, up to the middle of the fifth century. This number does not include 'the passion by trope,' such as the sacrifice of Isaac, the Hebrew children in the fiery furnace, Daniel in the lion's den and the Jonah cycle.[78]

Once the crucifixion became included in the passion cycles, depictions of the resurrection itself soon followed. The resurrection and the ascension became part of the theological passion cycle of Christian art. By the early medieval period, church decorations and manuscript illuminations include full-blown, narrative depictions of the passion, approximately fifty scenes, if we include the deposition, the preparation for burial, and the entombment. Virtually every scene in the four canonical gospels is

Figure 4.27 The Baptism of Christ. Manuscript illumination, *c.* 980. The British Library, Benedictional of S. Aethelwold, ms. Add. 49598, fol. 25. Photograph: British Library.

represented, and the passion cycle in a given church or other locus is usually a kind of image-*diatessaron*, a harmony of the passion from the gospels. Christian apocrypha are included in this Gospel Harmony.

The passion by trope

On the sarcophagi of the early church, the passions of the apostles, first those of Peter and Paul, become replications of Jesus' passion. The famous sarcophagus of Junius Bassus is a case in point. In the very early church these crucifixions represented Jesus' crucifixion, which was, as far as we can tell from extant visual art, not shown. It is undoubtedly therefore not a happenstance that so many apostolic martyrdoms are pictured as some variation of crucifixion. We will discuss these pictorial images below, therefore it suffices now to mention that most of these martyrdoms of the apostles by crucifixion are paralleled in the Christian apocrypha.

In the earliest materials, Jesus' passion is usually represented by a scene of Christ before Pilate (which, in some cases, has only Pilate in the scene), of Jesus' arrest, or of the entrance into Jerusalem. It is in this last scene that the *Gospel of Nicodemus* first plays a part.

The entrance into Jerusalem

In our discussion of Thecla (Chapter 5) we mention the role that the late fourth, early fifth century pilgrim woman, Egeria's (a.k.a., Silvia; Aetheria) diary of her travels has played in our knowledge of the popularity of S. Thecla's cult in the early church. In Egeria's description of a Palm Sunday service in Jerusalem, she also lets us know that the *Gospel of Nicodemus*, in some form, was read:

> As the eleventh hour draws near, that particular passage from a Gospel is read in which the children bearing palms and branches came forth to meet the Lord, saying: *Blessed is He who comes in the name of the Lord*. The bishop and all the people rise immediately, and then everyone walks down from the top of the Mount of Olives, with the people preceding the bishop and responding continually with *Blessed is He who comes in the name of the Lord* to the hymns and antiphons.
> (Egeria, Diary of a Pilgrimage, *c.* 31)[79]

The element in this scene in which the children bear palms and sing 'Blessed is He who comes in the name of the Lord,' appears only in *Acta Pilati (Gospel of Nicodemus)* 1:3. There are several early scenes of the entrance into Jerusalem which parallel the text of the *Gospel of Nicodemus*, that is, they show children bearing palm-branches and spreading them before Jesus as he enters the city [Figure 4.28]. This iconography is widespread. In fact it is difficult to find any Byzantine or early Western image of the Entrance into Jerusalem in which there are not small, unbearded figures waving palms and placing garments under the feet of the ass ridden by Jesus. The scene has also entered other art-forms as well. It is commonly sung in the hymnology of many churches in a hymn-text by Jennette Threlfall (1821–80):

Figure 4.28 The Entrance into Jerusalem. Ivory. State Museum, Berlin, Stiftung Preussischer Kulturbesitz, Inv. Nr. 1590. Photograph: Foto Marburg/Art Resource, NY.

Hosanna, loud hosanna
The little children sang;
Through pillared court, and temple
The lovely anthem rang

. . .

From Olivet they followed
'Mid an exultant crowd,
The victor palm branch waving,
And chanting clear and loud . . .

Threlfall's hymn text thus proclaims not only the palm as a symbol of Jesus' triumphal entry into Jerusalem but also the palm as a symbol of the victory of martyrdom (*Pseudo-Matthew* 21).

In addition, note the popular hymn translated by the Rev. John M. Neale (1854) from a text by Theodulph of Orleans (*c.* 820); the hymn begins with the following stanza as an ascription and ends with it as a refrain

All glory, laud and honor
To Thee, Redeemer King,
To whom the lips of children
Made sweet hosannas ring. [Text 4.R]

4.R

Then Pilate called for the messenger and said to him, 'Why have you done this, and spread your scarf on the ground and made Jesus walk on it?' The messenger answered him, 'Lord governor, when you sent me to Jerusalem to Alexander, I saw him sitting on an ass, and the children of the Hebrews held branches in their hands and cried out; and others spread their garments before him, saying, "Save now, you who are in the highest! Blessed is he that comes in the name of the Lord!"'

The Gospel of Nicodemus: Acts of Pilate 1, 3

Jesus before Pilate

The earliest canonical scenes of Jesus before Pilate generally show the procurator seated on a chair or stool; he may have an attendant or two, one of whom carries a bowl in which he is to wash his hands [Figure 4.29]. According to the *Gospel of Nicodemus*, when Pilate sends a messenger to bring Jesus to him, the messenger is converted and lays his cloak at Jesus' feet; the Jews protest. When Jesus is brought into the presence of Pilate, the standard-bearers bow down, lowering their banners in obeisance to

Figure 4.29 The arrest of Jesus/Pilate washing his hands. Sculpture from the sarcophagus of Junius Bassus, *c.* 359. Museo Pio Cristiano, Vatican. Photograph: Art Resource, NY.

the Christian Messiah (*Gospel of Nicodemus* 1) [Figure 4.30]. It is possible that the earliest depiction of this scene is on a ciborium column, in San Marco, Venice (right forward column, zone 5, niche 3). In one niche, Christ is shown walking. In the next niche, on the next column, is the cursor sent to bring Jesus before Pilate. In the third niche, are two soldiers, dressed in dalmaticas and standing [Text 4.S].[80]

The crucifixion

The earliest scenes of the crucifixion which depict Jesus on the cross appear during the latter part of the fourth century. In every case, Jesus is wearing either a loin-cloth [Figure 4.31] or a colobium (an undershirt) [see Figure 4.32]. Christ is thus clothed in spite of the canonical gospels' indication that Jesus was crucified in the customary manner, that is, nude, a fact that many theologians have noted. The Fourth Gospel in particular (John 19:32) emphasizes that the soldiers have claimed Jesus' outer and under garments, implying that they left him naked. A naked crucifixion would have been the norm. Crucifixion was meant to be a particularly humiliating as well as excruciatingly painful death.[81]

Trexler suggests elements in the church's theology to explain why Jesus is depicted as at least partially clothed in every crucifixion scene in the church's early art. As crucifixion was death by asphyxiation and such a death often results in priapism at the moment of death, that alone would be reason enough to cover Jesus' genitalia. Further, the theological thrust of the fourth and fifth centuries tended to place the central locus of human sin and shame in the genitals:

> Representing the bare-chested Jesus in the mutilated state of the Passion, while
> rendering him sensually undesirable in the hardened contemplative, could not

Figure 4.30 Cursor lays his cloak before Christ. Manuscript illumination, thirteenth or fourteenth century. Biblioteca Nacional, Madrid, Illustrated Gospel of Nicodemus, Vit. 23–8 fol. 164vo. Photograph: Biblioteca Nacional, Madrid.

hide what could be expected of any male on the point of expiring on a cross: an erection, followed by an ejaculation. This embarrassingly public and uncontrollable *motus corporis* might be anticipated to stimulate male viewers to an erection.[82]

Thus, in spite of the fact that Jesus was undoubtedly crucified nude and both knowledge of the Roman customs of execution and of the canonical gospels show this, crucifixion scenes present a (lightly) clothed Jesus on the cross. It is in the *Gospel of Nicodemus* (10:1) that there appears a brief hint of what Jesus' death throes would have been. There, Jesus is covered with a loin-cloth while he is on the cross. Indeed there appears to have been a theological conundrum at play in the early church: the awful sacrifice of Jesus' death played against the belief in the power of God in Christ on the cross.[83] Johannes Molanus (mid-sixteenth century) shows that this argument continued in the church, saying that 'Christ was crucified naked, but I think it is pious to believe that his shameful organs were [then] veiled for decency.' Trexler's ironic comment is to the point: 'Christians are actually in a better state of grace if they believe the inverse of biblical fact: that Jesus' humiliation was not, after all, as complete as it might seem to have been.'[84]

4.S

Now when Jesus entered, and the ensigns were holding the standards, the images on the standards bowed down and worshipped Jesus. And when the Jews saw the behaviour of the standards, how they bowed down and worshipped Jesus, they cried out loudly against the ensigns. But Pilate said to them, 'Do you not marvel how the images bowed and worshipped Jesus?' The Jews said to Pilate, 'We saw how the ensigns lowered them and worshipped him.' And the governor summoned the ensigns and asked them, 'Why did you do this?' They answered, 'We are Greeks and servers of temples: how could we worship him? We held the images; but they bowed down of their own accord and worshipped him.'

Then Pilate said to the rulers of the synagogue and the elders of the people, 'Choose strong men to carry the standards, and let us see whether the images bow by themselves.' So the elders of the Jews took twelve strong men and made them carry the standards by sixes, and they stood before the judgement-seat of the governor. And Pilate said to the messenger, 'Take him out of the praetorium and bring him in again in whatever way you wish.' And Jesus left the praetorium with the messenger. And Pilate summoned those who had previously been carrying the images, and said to them, 'I have sworn by the salvation of Caesar that, if the standards do not bow down when Jesus enters, I will cut off your heads.' And the governor commanded Jesus to enter in the second time. And the messenger did as before and begged Jesus to walk upon his scarf. He walked upon it and entered. And when he had entered, the standards bowed down again and worshipped Jesus.

The Gospel of Nicodemus: Acts of Pilate 1, 5–6

Figure 4.31 Crucifixion of Christ. Wooden carving, *c.* 430. Door of the Church of S. Sabina, Rome. Photograph: Art Resource, NY.

It is also in the *Gospel of Nicodemus* that characters at the crucifixion receive names: Longinus, the soldier who stabs Jesus with a lance (that is, *lonche*, from which the soldier's name likely derives). The second soldier, who gives Christ the sponge, is pictured in the crucifixion images, but the origin of his name, Stephaton, is a mystery. In Chapter 9 of the *Gospel of Nicodemus* the two thieves crucified with Jesus are also first named: Demas (Dysmas) and Gestas. One of the earliest images of these namings is on an eighth-century icon at Mount Sinai (Icon B.36)[85] [Figure 4.32]. This icon is remarkable in several of its elements: it may be the first image of the crucifixion in which Jesus has his eyes closed and wears the crown of thorns; even more startling is that the thief on the left, the 'bad thief,' is apparently depicted as a female – or so Weitzmann judges on the basis of the thief's hair and gynomastic characteristics.[86]

The resurrection and Descensus ad Inferos

Depictions of Jesus' rising from the dead do not appear in early Christian art. It is not until the end of the period we call Late Antiquity and the beginning of the Carolingian period that we find images in which Jesus is shown coming out of the tomb or climbing from a coffin. In the earliest images, the Resurrection was signified by the women's coming to the tomb and their finding it empty. However, in

Figure 4.32 Crucifixion of Christ, with thieves named. Icon, eighth century. Monastery of S. Catherine, Mount Sinai, Icon B.36. Photograph: Michigan–Princeton–Alexandria Expedition to Mount Sinai.

such scenes, a trope is often employed: on the door of the empty tomb is a scene of the resurrection of Lazarus (for example see the ivory in the British Museum).[87]

The Eastern Church in particular, adopted as its depiction of the resurrection the Descensus ad Inferos (Anastasis; Harrowing of Hell), paralleled in the *Gospel of Nicodemus* 8–10, in the *Questions of Bartholomew* 6–20 and in the *Gospel of Peter* 39–42 [Text 4.T].[88] The iconography of the Anastasis was set early, especially if one can date the ciborium columns at San Marco as early as the sixth century.[89] The general scheme of the Anastasis has Christ standing on the broken-down doors of Hell, his hand reaching to pull Adam (in some cases Eve) from their coffins, and with the kings and prophets standing by; this may be derived from a pre-iconoclastic iconography. There are literary indices of the Anastasis by the beginning of the eighth century.[90] The earliest images 'date from the pontificate of Pope John VII (705–07),' and images appear twice in the frescoes of S. Maria Antiqua[91] and in mosaic in the Oratory of John VII in S. Peter's.[92] The Anastasis, as is the case with virtually all images, has developed several types. In this case, the usual definitions involve the relationship of

---

4.T

While Hades was speaking with Satan, the King of Glory stretched out his right hand, and took hold of our forefather Adam and raised him up. Then he turned to the rest and said, 'Come with me, all you who have died through the tree which this man touched. For behold, I raise you all up again through the tree of the cross.' With that he sent them all out. And our forefather Adam was seen to be full of joy, and said, 'I give thanks to your majesty, O Lord, because you have brought me up from the lowest Hades.' Likewise all the prophets and the saints said, 'We give you thanks, O Christ, Saviour of the world, because you have brought up our life from destruction'. When they had said this, the Saviour blessed Adam with the sign of the cross on his forehead. And he did this also to the patriarchs and prophets and martyrs and fore-fathers, and he took them and sprang up out of Hades. And as he went the holy fathers sang praises, following him and saying, 'Blessed be he who comes in the name of the Lord. Alleluia. To him be the glory of all the saints.'

Thus he went into paradise holding our forefather Adam by the hand, and he handed him and all the righteous to Michael the archangel. And as they were entering the gate of paradise, two old men met them. The holy fathers asked them, 'Who are you, who have not seen death nor gone down into Hades, but dwell in paradise with your bodies and souls?' One of them answered, 'I am Enoch, who pleased God and was removed here by him. And this is Elijah the Tishbite. We are to live until the end of the world. But then we are to be sent by God to withstand Antichrist and to be killed by him. And after three days we shall rise again and be caught up in clouds to meet the Lord.'

The Gospel of Nicodemus: Descensus ad Inferos 8–9

Figure 4.33 Anastasis. Manuscript illumination, *c.* 1230. Herzog August Bibliothek, Wolfenbüttel, Germany, Cod. Guelf 61.2. Aug 8, fol. 92ro., Miscellany. Photograph: Herzog August Bibliothek, Wolfenbüttel.

Figure 4.34 Anastasis. Stained glass, twentieth century. Transept of the Church of Hagios Giorgios, Knoxville, TN. Photograph: Cartlidge.

the image of Christ to that of Adam.[93] The Byzantine version was passed on in such images as that of the model book in Wolfenbüttel [Figure 4.33]. The image persists to the present day in the Eastern Orthodox churches [Figure 4.34].

In addition to the Anastasis, the *Gospel of Nicodemus* narrates a story of Dysmas (the 'good thief') in heaven, where the crucified Jesus promised he would be. There are, in addition, stories of the imprisonment and rescue of Joseph of Arimathea. These tales appear in iconic forms. Examples of the continuing story of Joseph of Arimathea and that of Dysmas are in the profusely illustrated, thirteenth-century manuscript of the *Gospel of Nicodemus* in the Biblioteca Nacional, Madrid (Vit. 23–8).

Whether there is a pictorial image corresponding in detail to the *Gospel of Peter's* resurrection narrative is problematic. Gertrud Schiller believes that a manuscript illumination in the Utrecht Psalter [Figure 4.35], which shows Jesus carried from the tomb by two figures is related to the *Gospel of Peter*; we may have some reservations on this judgment. It may also be that the huge image of Jesus in certain Anastasis scenes, such as the marvelous illumination in the Cotton Psalter, may be a parallel to the Gospel of Peter's description (British Museum, Cotton ms. Tiberius C. VI, fol. 14).[94]

Figure 4.35 Resurrection of Christ. Manuscript illumination, *c.* 830. Utrecht University Library, Utrecht, Netherlands, Utrecht Psalter, fol. 10vo; illustration to Psalm 10:12 (9:33). Photograph: Utrecht University Library.

Figure 4.36 The Ascension of Christ, with James and Peter. Ivory, late fourth or early fifth century. Bayerisches National Museum, Munich. Photograph: Foto Marburg/Art Resource, NY.

The Ascension

In the Lucan version of the Ascension of Jesus the whole group of apostles (save, of course Judas and Matthias) witness the event. In the *Acts of John* 102 and the *Apocryphon of James* this is not the case. In the former, John is isolated from the other disciples and, in the latter, Peter and James are given special instructions, apart from the other disciples. An ivory, one of the most famous in Christian art history, shows that at the Ascension Peter and James were the only witnesses [Figure 4.36]. (Cf. p. 222.)

As we mentioned above, there is no specific mention of the Virgin Mary's presence at the Ascension in the early literature. The church obviously assumed that she should have been there. There are few ascension scenes beginning with the early Middle Ages in which Mary is not present, usually she stands orans in the midst of the disciples with Jesus rising in a mandorla above the group. This holds true in the case of both ascension types, that is, the disappearing type in which only Jesus' feet are seen at the top of the frame, and the full-figure type.

5

PAUL, THECLA
AND PETER

On the inside bottom of a mid-fourth century terracotta bowl in the Metropolitan Museum of Art (52.25,1), Paul and Peter face each other. They are both seated, named and nimbed, but not bearded. Their hand gestures suggest that they are engaged in a spirited conversation. Above the two apostles and slightly above their heads is a small medallion which contains a Chi-Rho, a symbolic Christ keeping watch over and engendering the position of the two most well-known and influential of Jesus' apostolic successors.[1]

This scene is paralleled in several artifacts from the same general period. One is a gilt-glass bowl in the Metropolitan Museum (Rogers Fund, 11.91.4) also with the apostles not bearded, but with them named and seated facing each other in conversation. Their figures are more erect than in the terracotta bowl. In this image, there is a figure of Christ as a beardless youth, facing frontally, placed in the position of the Chi-Rho on the terracotta bowl. Around the figures is an inscription in the form of a toast: *DENGNETAS AMICORUM ELARES EN CRISTO* ('Worthy among your friends; rejoicing in Christ').[2] The Metropolitan has another gilt-glass bowl which exemplifies the more well-recognized iconography of Paul and Peter: they are bearded with the facial characteristics usually associated with the two apostles.[3] Among other scenes of Peter and Paul together there are bronze medallions in the Vatican,[4] which are busts of Peter and Paul, with the apostles named and facing each other. As is the more usual case, both of them are bearded.

It is not only in early church iconography that the two apostles were considered a pair. A fourth-century, pre-Constantinian graffito from the Via Appia, *Paule ed Petre petite pro Victore* ('Paul and Peter, pray for Victor')[5] attests to this pairing. Eusebios (*Church History* VII, 18, 4), in about 325 CE, mentions that there were early portraits of Paul and Peter (Eusebios mentions the images in that order) which served as cult images. He does not approve of these images 'because it was the custom of pagans of olden times to worship them as saviors.'

The pairing of Paul and Peter is also in a fresco in the Cemetery (catacomb) of Severo in Naples (*c.* 350–450). In the cubiculum on the back wall is an image of the deceased (small) flanked by Paul on the left and Peter on the right. Neither is named, but Peter and Paul bear their unmistakable facial characteristics: Paul is narrow-faced, with a receding hairline, and a long pointed beard. Peter is more broad-faced, with relatively short, curly hair and a shorter, rounded beard.

To those who are familiar with the early church's literature, this amicable and convivial pairing of the two apostles may strike a discord. First, there is the problem of the founder of the earliest congregation in Rome. In his Epistle to the Romans, Paul indicates that he is introducing himself to a congregation already in existence, but the epistle does not tell us who was the founder of that congregation. In the Lucan Acts, Paul goes to Rome to appeal to Caesar after his arrest, and he functions and works in an already established Christian community. Again we have no indication about whose evangelizing founded this church, even though it is established doctrine in the Eastern and Western Catholic traditions that the apostle who founded this church was Peter.

What is more intriguing about the iconic insistence upon the collegiality of Paul and Peter is that from early church literature we gain strong indications that there were considerable tensions between the two apostles and their followers. Paul himself reports this division in Galatians 1–2. The rift between the two appears to underlie the Lucan Acts' attempt to smooth over the difficulties (Acts 10–11; 13–16). There are indications that the problem of contention, which involved the co-existence of Christians who came from Judaism and those who came to the church from paganism, went on into the second and third centuries. The *Acts of Peter* begins with Paul in Rome, but the text takes considerable pains to make it plain that Paul was called away from Rome before Peter enters to engage in his dramatic contest with Simon the Magician. A set of documents which is a bit later than the *Acts of Peter*, the so-called *Pseudo-Clementine Homilies* and *Recognitions*, but which is apparently based on the same store of Peter-traditions which underlies the *Acts of Peter*, contains a polemic against Pauline theology. This set of documents, through the use of allusions to the Pauline epistles, appears to declare that, of the two, only Peter has the true doctrine and is the true inheritor of the 'chair of Moses.'[6] A comparison of the Pastoral Epistles and the *Acts of Paul* gives evidence that these materials were set over against each other as part of this struggle.[7]

There may be some iconographic remains of the rivalry between Paul and Peter. Certain monuments in Ravenna rely upon a tradition that the law was given by Christ (*traditio legis*) to Paul rather than to Peter.[8] One of these monuments is the 'Sarcophagus of the Twelve Apostles' (fifth century) in the Church of S. Apollinare in Classe.[9] In addition the same scene occurs on the 'Pietro Peccatore' sarcophagus in the Church of Santa Maria in Porta fuori le Mura in Ravenna.[10]

Most strikingly in contrast to the earliest documents, when one compares the rhetoric to the iconic scenes involving Paul and Peter, are those narrative, iconic images which depict Peter's contest with the arch-heretic, Simon Magus. Although in the *Acts of Peter* the contest is solely between the two Simons (Peter and Magus), on most of the extant iconographical evidence of the contest, Peter and Paul combine to defeat the magician. From the end of the fourth century through the medieval period, it is common to find cycles of Peter's and Paul's lives and acts joined in a sub-cycle which begins with the meeting of the two apostles in Rome and which continues with their contentions with Simon before the emperor, their both being involved in the several incidents of the contest – including the popular scene in which their prayers force the airborne Simon Magus to fall from the sky (or a tower). In addition, Peter is often shown as being present at Paul's execution. This scene is in direct contrast to the portion of the *Acts of Paul* known as the *Martyrdom of Paul*, that is, *Acts of Paul*, section 11[11] [Text 5.A].

5.A

Then Simon Magus went up upon the tower in the face of all, and, crowned with laurels, he stretched forth his hands, and began to fly. And when Nero saw him flying, he said to Peter, 'This Simon is true; but you and Paul are deceivers.' Peter said, 'Immediately you will know that we are true disciples of Christ; but that he is not Christ, but a Magician, and a malefactor.' Nero said, 'Do you still persist? Behold, you see him going up into heaven.' Then Peter, looking steadfastly upon Paul, said, 'Paul, look up and see.' And Paul, having looked up, full of tears, and seeing Simon flying, said, 'Peter why are you idle? Finish what you have begun; for already our Lord Jesus Christ is calling us.' And Nero hearing them, smiled a little, and said, 'These men see themselves lost already, and are gone mad.' Peter said, 'Now you shall know that we are not mad.' Paul said to Peter, 'Do at once what you must do.'

And Peter, looking steadfastly against Simon, said, 'I adjure you, angels of Satan, who are carrying him into the air, to deceive the hearts of the unbelievers, by the God that created all things, and by Jesus Christ, whom on the third day He raised from the dead, no longer from this hour to keep him up, but to let him go.' And immediately, being let go, he fell into a place called Sacra Via, that is, Holy Way, and was divided into four parts, having perished by an evil fate.

Pseudo-Marcellus, *Passio Sanctorum Apostolorum Petri et Pauli* 75–7

Herbert Kessler has looked closely at the iconographic evidence of these Peter–Paul cycles.[12] It is an historically accidental irony that the joining of the Pauline and Petrine stories is first witnessed by a belt buckle[13] [Figure 5.1]. This piece of ivory – probably part of ecclesiastical garb – was found beneath the cathedral at Castellammare di Stabia; it is now in the Antiquarium in that city. Archaeological evidence indicates that the buckle is from the late fourth or early fifth centuries. The scene on the buckle shows Paul on the left and Peter on the right, each at the end of their rapid approach to an embrace. Their legs are just finishing a long stride and their cloaks still billowing behind them.

The earliest recorded church decoration involving this scene of the apostles' meeting is apparently, as Kessler notes, 'not in a Petrine ambience at all, but in a church dedicated to Paul, the basilica of St Paul's Outside the Walls of Rome.'[14] There were forty-two panels of the life of Paul on the north wall of the fourth-century basilica. The iconography of these panels is customarily assigned to be mid-fifth century, although Kessler would place it at about 400 CE.[15] These panels were destroyed by a fire in 1823 CE, but they are partially known by drawings. The image which was at S. Paul's of the embrace of Peter and Paul is preserved in watercolor copies from 1635 CE (Vatican, Biblioteca, Cod. Barb. lat. 4406, fol. 126ro). There is another scene of the meeting in the same codex, at fol. 54ro.[16] The whole narrative cycle on the

Figure 5.1 Paul and Peter meeting in Rome. Ivory belt buckle, fifth century. Antiquarium, Castellammare di Stabia, Italy. Photograph: Soprintendenza archeologica di Pompei.

panels at S. Paul's Outside the Walls begins with the creation and includes the mission of Moses and Aaron, who are also depicted in an embrace; after much fraternal discord 'Moses and Aaron work together to secure the liberation of God's Chosen People.'[17] In an analogous manner, the embrace of Paul and Peter serves to obliterate the Jewish–Christian against Gentile–Christian contentions in the early church. Certain of these images of the conjoining of Paul and Peter make it clear, however, that Peter is more equal than Paul; an example is at Müstair (eighth century) where the scene of the embrace is below one of Peter's receiving the law.[18]

Other church decorations follow those at S. Paul's Outside the Walls. Notable are the Norman mosaics in Sicily. Both the Cappella Palatina in Palermo[19] and the Cathedral of Monreale feature what Kessler calls 'the canonical histories of Paul and Peter.'[20] These histories continue with the images from the contest of the apostles with Simon Magus. At Monreale, on the south wall of the Peter Chapel, there are two panels. One above the door shows, on the left, Peter raising Tabitha. In the right side of the same panel is the embrace of Peter and Paul. Below this panel, partially divided by a door, we see, on the left, Peter, Paul and Simon before the emperor. On the right is the fall of Simon Magus, with Peter and Paul kneeling in prayer as the Magician falls from a tower; the doomed Magus is flanked by two winged angels.[21]

Kessler lists more than a dozen images of the meeting of Peter and Paul along with the locations of the images' publication. These images are in virtually all of the standard media, including textiles, frescoes, icons and ivories. The geographical range of the pictorial version of the two apostles' meeting stretches from the East to the West and from Coptic to Byzantine traditions.[22]

In our discussion of this combination of Peter and Paul in the contest with Simon Magus, we have so far emphasized where the iconography does not parallel the most familiar early Christian apocrypha, that is, the *Acts of Peter* and the *Acts of Paul*. There are, however, literary parallels for these scenes; the narratives occur in literature which is succedent to the iconographical appearance of the narrative: the Latin *Passion of the Holy Apostles Peter and Paul* (Pseudo-Marcellus) and a Greek version the *Acts of the Holy Apostles Peter and Paul*.[23] They are documents which are usually assigned to, or shortly after, the sixth century. This does not rule out, however, that there were earlier literary or oral prototypes.[24] In the extant witnesses to the narrative of this apostolic collegiality, however, the iconic form of the story precedes the rhetorical.

The pairing of Peter and Paul is likely akin to another iconographical event which Georg Stuhlfauth and Erich Dinkler discuss in detail.[25] They present strong evidence that the appearance of certain images of Peter at the beginning of the Constantinian period was due to a push, Stuhlfauth calls it a *Petrussturm*,[26] in which the Western church proceeded to establish the primacy of Peter.[27] Crucial to this push is the scene of Peter's striking the rock (also known as 'Peter's water-miracle') which was very common during the fourth century and then began to fade. We will discuss this image below. The Western Church thus joined the Eastern Church which had already considered Peter the first in the rank of the apostles. The close-joining of Peter and Paul (for Catholics) or of Paul and Peter (for Protestants) is a *terminus ad quem* which has affected iconographical studies of the very earliest images of the two apostles. The Petrine primacy is a monument which has cast its shadow (or light) over the pre-Constantinian images of Paul and Peter.

Portraits of Paul and Peter

The early image-types of Peter, of Paul or of any other Christian figure, either in rhetoric or in iconic form, are not what we would call in modern terms 'likenesses' of the apostles. We expect a portrait to look like the subject. Most of us would expect any excellent modern portrait, whether it is in a painting or a photograph, to give us much more than, say, a passport photo would. We expect the artist's vision of the personality of the subject. Nevertheless, after viewing a portrait, we would expect to recognize the image's subject if we met him or her in the street.

Along with virtually every other aspect of its pictorial language the early church took over the customs of portraiture which were in the iconographic vocabulary of the Imperial Period. Many such portraits exist for philosophers and royal personages. The purpose of a portrait in Greco-Roman terms was not to show a 'likeness' in the contemporary sense that the image 'looks just like him or her.' If any excellent portrait is basically to present the dignity, power and virtue of the person portrayed, ancient portraiture concentrated heavily on that latter aspect.[28] The ancient portrait, in both its rhetorical and iconic forms was intended to show us the *arete* of the person depicted. This 'divine power' (which is to be distinguished from 'deity') was expressed in dress and accessories, in gestures, and in the portrayal of the subject's carriage as well as in the physical characteristics of the image. He or she often carried an artifact which was a sign of his prowess: a sceptre, a sword, or, in the case of a philosopher–teacher, a scroll. In addition, the famous hierarchical style of the images of the Imperial period also was employed to demonstrate the main subject's *arete*; the image of Constantine's handing out largesse on the Arch of Constantine in Rome is a good example.[29] In the case of these two most famous of the apostles, we can say that their dress and facial characteristics most likely spoke to early Christian viewers, 'this person is a great teacher and a true bearer of the *logos*.'

We have mentioned in the course of the previous discussion the facial characteristics of Paul and Peter, features which became fixed in the church during the fourth century and which endure to this day. In the case of Paul, this physiognomy is well-recognized as its being parallel with early Christian apocrypha. The face of Peter is more of a mystery.

The *Acts of Paul* 3 contains a physical description of Paul [Text 5.B]. It has long been recognized that there is a certain if not exact relationship between this rhetorical description and early church's standard iconography of the apostle: a man with a narrow face, a pointed beard and a receding hairline. This iconography was set in the church early enough that, with few exceptions, Paul is always portrayed this way; this convention continues. In addition, Paul very often carries a sword, the symbol of his martyrdom. According to *The Martyrdom of the Holy Apostle Paul* 5, the apostle was beheaded at the behest of Nero[30] [Figure 5.2]. Paul's features in both the rhetorical and iconic images are likely based in turn on the descriptions of Socrates, which have a history which begins during the lifetime of the philosopher.

5.B

And a certain man, by name Onesiphorus, hearing that Paul was to come to Iconium, went out to meet him with his children Simmias and Zeno and his wife Lectra, in order that he might entertain him. Titus had informed him what Paul looked like, for he had not seen him in the flesh, but only in the spirit.

And he went along the royal road to Lystra and kept looking at the passers-by according to the description of Titus. And he saw Paul coming, a man small in size, bald-headed, bandy-legged, of noble mien, with eyebrows meeting, rather hook-nosed, full of grace. Sometimes he seemed like a man, and sometimes he had the face of an angel.

The Acts of Paul 2–3

The rhetorical portraiture of Socrates is in Aristophanes' *The Clouds*; the playwright's treatment of Socrates is a caricature through and through. It has, as Zanker put it, 'long been recognized that this description of Socrates' physical appearance is as much a conventional topos as the caricature of his supposed teaching.'[31] Socrates is described in the rhetorical portraits as 'strikingly ugly.'[32] He was compared to Silenus and Marsyas. This judgment of Socrates' physical characteristics may be the reflection of an historical fact or, perhaps, an exaggeration. The portraits of Socrates, which are mostly bust portraits and are Roman copies of a Greek original of *c.* 380 BCE, show a man with receding hair and a pointed beard.[33] He is also, to put it mildly, not comely. A full-figured scene at Pompeii assigns the same basic iconography to Socrates.[34] The Socratic iconic tradition therefore differed considerably from the customary portraiture of a good and great man. Socrates' *arete* was certainly not

Figure 5.2 Portrait of Paul. Stained glass window, twentieth century. New Providence Presbyterian Church, Maryville, TN. Photograph: Cartlidge.

Figure 5.3 Portrait of Peter. Icon encaustic, *c.* 700. Monastery of S. Catherine, Mount Sinai, Icon B.5. Photograph: Michigan–Princeton–Alexandria Expedition to Mount Sinai.

visualized by the figure of a man who was handsome and dignified, with an athletic body.

Paul, therefore, stands in the early church, at least in respect to his physical depictions, as the church's Socrates. There has been a certain amount of expurgation of the portrait in its transfer from Socrates to Paul. The Pauline face is not 'satyr-like.' Nevertheless, Paul is depicted in rhetoric and iconography as martyr to the cause of the truth, and, in spite of his physical characteristics, at least according to the *Acts of Paul*, he is seductive in his message. His opponents in the *Acts of Paul*, however, take a more earthy view of his seduction.[35]

But whence the Peter-type; the broader-faced man with the short, curly hair, and the rounded, curly beard? [Figure 5.3]. He certainly does not look to be a fisherman from the far-flung provinces. Rather, he is the replica of 'philosophy' or of 'the teacher' from pagan monuments [see Figure 1.1].

The earliest clearly identifiable image of Peter, and the only one which is prior to the Constantinian period, according to Dinkler,[36] is on the Baptistery of Dura Europos. It shows Peter without a beard; the scene is Peter's attempt to walk on water (Matthew 14:29). There have been attempts to push images of Peter (such as those on medallions) back into the second century. Dates earlier than the fourth century are now considered doubtful. Wilpert attempted to derive the Peter-type from bearded Good Shepherds, using as his argument John 20, in which Jesus tells Peter to 'feed my sheep.' This stretches the evidence beyond the snapping point.[37]

Dinkler, Stuhlfauth and others are probably correct in their suggestion that it was to depict Peter as the teacher above teachers which caused the early church to depict the apostle as the bearded teacher, dressed in a philosopher's tunic and with a scroll or book.[38]

An intriguing suggestion from Christopher Matthews does not look for the 'origin' of the Peter-type, but for a point which more closely matches our purpose, namely, a rhetorical parallel. Matthews argues that there was a description of Peter in the *Acts of Peter* much like that of Paul in the *Acts of Paul* and that the description fits the accustomed iconography of Peter. The description is given by the thirteenth-century church history of Nicephorus Callistus:

> The divine Peter was of moderate stature and he stood quite erect. His face was pale yellow and very fair. The hair of his head and beard was woolly and thick, but not flowing. He presented eyes that were bloodshot and dark, and his eyebrows were raised. His nose was long but did not end in a point; he was flat-nosed as it were.[39]

On the basis of Nicephorus' prolific use of the apocryphal Acts in his writing and his fidelity to their wording in general and to the *Acts of Peter* in particular, Matthews argues that 'the contrasting images of Peter and Paul, so prominent in later Christian art-work, began as an intertextual development connected with these apostles' respective Apocryphal Acts.'[40] The arguments of Matthews do not exclude those of Dinkler and Stuhlfauth.

The distinctive images of Peter and Paul, and especially in the case of the former, have created some problems in respect to the iconography of the early church. Peter's image is so akin to that of the 'teacher' who appears in virtually all media and on both pagan and Christian artifacts, that there has been a tendency to identify any such image as that of Peter. For example, in 1919 a group of frescoes, busts of men, was discovered in the Hypogeum of Aurelii. Two of these figures were identified as Peter and Paul. But, as Dinkler points out, these are more likely portraits of members of the Aurelii society.[41]

It was common in the artistic vocabulary of the Greco-Roman world to portray the great teacher as a bearded man who wore the tunic in the style of the philosopher and often carried a scroll or had a vase or basket of scrolls at his feet. He was often shown seated before a small group of students. It is possible that early Christians, looking at such a figure, thought of 'Peter.' That cannot be demonstrated one way or the other. It is likely that the second- or third-century Christian would have seen in such images 'apostle ——' or 'noted teacher ——' or some other bearer of the logos. An analogy would be the employment of the pagan favorite, the Good Shepherd on oil lamps and other household and personal items, such as finger rings.[42] As we mentioned above (Finney, in Chapter 1) both pagans and Christians likely bought their household items from the same ateliers and from the same inventories.

The same purchasing pattern would have taken place in the hiring of a workshop to dig out and decorate a funereal site. The atelier had a certain product and Christians would have had to pick and choose from the inventory available.[43] Specifically Christian or biblical scenes would often have been adaptions which employed already available iconography. The classic example is that of Jonah under the gourd vine, always in a pose associated with that of Endymion. A further analogy is the several fresco images in the catacombs which picture a supper. These images often feature a central figure who is flanked by other diners. The knee-jerk reaction is to label such an image as 'The Last Supper' or a 'eucharist.' This could be a correct identification. On the other hand, the scene may be one of the particular family's celebrating a *refrigerium*. The crucial questions are what did the early Christian patrons intend to portray in the image and what did they 'see' when they beheld it? Those questions continue to require carefully qualified and tentative answers.

The purpose of this digression is simply that it is becoming more and more recognized throughout the iconographical world that one must be very cautious to identify an unnamed, pre-Constantinian figure as Peter or Paul because the image bears the look of the Petrus- or Paulus-type.

Paul in narrative

Although there are several early narrative or historical images of Paul which are parallel with the Lucan Acts,[44] the earliest extant Pauline images are not 'canonical' but are of Paul's arrest which leads to his martyrdom. The final arrest – in the sense of the apostle's being led to his death – of Paul and his beheading do not occur in the New Testament; they are in the final portion of the *Acts of Paul*, namely, the *Martyrdom of Paul* [Text 5.C]. An image portraying this scene is on one of the most famous of all early Christian art objects, the Sarcophagus of Junius Bassus[45] [Figure 5.4]. The sarcophagus is dated, and is therefore one of the very few pieces of art (along with the *terminus ad quem* of the frescoes at Dura Europos) from the early church which we can place precisely in an historical chronology. Junius Bassus, was a prefect of Rome, according to the inscription on his sarcophagus:

Junius Bassus, *vir clarissimus* [of senatorial rank],
who lived 42 years, 2 months,
in his own prefecture of the city,
newly baptized, went to God,
the 8th day from the Kalends of September,
Eusebius and Hypatius, consuls [August 25, 359].[46]

5.C

And turning toward the east, Paul lifted up his hands to heaven and prayed
at length; and after having conversed in Hebrew with the fathers during
prayer he bent his neck, without speaking any more. When the executioner
cut off his head milk splashed on the tunic of the soldier. And the soldier
and all who stood near by were astonished at this sight and glorified God
who has thus honoured Paul. And they went away and reported everything
to Caesar.

The Acts of Paul: Martyrdom 5

The image of Paul's arrest and his going to his martyrdom is in the lower register,
on the far right of the sarcophagus. It shows Paul – his image is a classic example of
the Paul-type – accompanied by two soldiers. Paul's hands are bound behind his back,
and one of the soldiers has his hand on the hilt of his sword. The Pauline physiognomy, the position of Paul's hands and the soldier's readiness with his sword are the
markers by which to identify this image. The image occurs on several sarcophagi.[47]
Among them are a fourth-century frieze sarcophagus at the Cemetery of S. Valentinus,[48] a fourth-century five-niche sarcophagus in the Museum of the city of Valence,[49]
and a seventh-century sarcophagus in the Church of S. Ambrose, Milan.[50] The scene
is almost always accompanied by that of the arrest for martyrdom of Peter. A notable
example is the so-called 'Tree sarcophagus' from the mid- to late fourth century.[51]
It is in the Museo Pio Cristiano in the Vatican (formerly Lateran 164) [Figure 5.5].
To the right of a symbolic resurrection (a Chi-Rho under which soldiers are asleep)
is Paul, his hands bound, accompanied by one soldier who has partially drawn his
sword; to the left of the Chi-Rho is the arrest of Peter.

Medieval scenes of Paul's execution employ a different iconography. By the middle
ages, the church had long since shifted from the paleo-Christian style of 'abbreviated
representation' to a more naturalistic style.[52] Church art became more representational.
Thus medieval images of Paul's climactic martyrdom usually show the actual
beheading of the apostle. His head lies on the ground (still nimbed) and his headless
torso is kneeling. The executioner stands with his sword raised. A Paul and Peter
window in Chartres, Notre Dame,[53] a fresco in the Church of S. Maria in Sylvis, in
Sesto al Reghena, Italy,[54] and the polyptych assigned to Giotto are examples.[55] The
mosaic in the Church of San Marco, Venice, has a double scene in the north aisle of

144

Figure 5.4 The arrest of Paul. Sculpture from the sarcophagus of Junius Bassus, *c.* 359. Museo Pio Cristiano, Vatican. Photograph: Art Resource, NY.

the martyrdoms of both Peter and Paul. The mosaic is one of those in the church that were thoroughly reworked in the Baroque period.[56] Our example is in the *Benedictional of S. Aethelwold*, fol. 95vo, where the executions of both Paul and Peter are depicted [Figure 5.6].

In paleo-Christian art, narrative images of Paul alone which are paralleled in Christian apocrypha are not prolific, other than those of Paul's martyrdom. This is not the case for scenes of Paul in the accompaniment of the virgin, Thecla. There is a collection of ivory plaques in the British Museum (56, 6–23, 8, 9, 10) which feature acts of Paul and Peter[57] [Figure 5.7]. These plaques are from the early half of the fifth century, *c.* 430 CE. The images appear to be Roman in style, but they are not

Figure 5.5 Tree sarcophagus from the Via Salaria with the arrest of Peter and the arrest of Paul. Sculpture, fourth century. Museo Pio Cristiano, Vatican (formerly Lateran 164). Photograph: Art Resource, NY.

Figure 5.6 The Martyrdoms of Paul and Peter. Manuscript illumination, *c.* 980. The British Library, Benedictional of S. Aethelwold, ms. Add. 49598, fol. 95vo. Photograph: British Library.

Figure 5.7 Saints Paul and Thecla and the stoning of S. Paul. Ivory, fifth or sixth century. The British Museum, London. Photograph: Art Resource, NY.

connected with the extensive Pauline cycle which is reported to have existed on the walls of the Church of S. Paul's Outside the Walls, Rome. The scenes 'likely . . . originated in an extended narrative cycle, perhaps a now lost illustrated apocryphal text.'[58] One of the plaques has two Pauline scenes: (1) On the left is Paul preaching or reading from a book and Thecla, his companion in the *Acts of Paul*, listening from a tower (*Acts of Paul* 7); (2) On the right, Paul is stoned. The latter scene, says Kessler, is a 'legend'[59] and 'elaborates the report of Acts 14:19.'[60] It is more likely a variation on the story in *Acts of Paul* 21, especially in the light of its pairing with the Thecla-scene. A sarcophagus now in Marseilles has the image. Destroyed frescoes which were on the walls of S. Paul's also picture the occasion of Paul's being stoned.[61]

Thecla of Iconium

The earliest extant Thecla image illustrates both Thecla's singular importance and her ties to Paul. The image is pre-Constantinian, a plaque which is either a gravestone[62] or a sarcophagus fragment (Musei Capitolini, Sala II, inv. nr. 67)[63] [Figure 5.8]. The iconography is intriguing but its interpretation is somewhat illusive. Paul, named and bearded, stands on a single-masted ship. He holds the tiller in his left hand and the mainsheet in his right. There is a figure in the bow of the ship, which is partially broken. A third figure sits on shore. The ship is named 'Thecla' by an inscription on the gunwale. Whether the plaque is a gravestone for a Thecla or part of a sarcophagus intended to illustrate the link between Thecla and Paul, its visual connection between Paul and Thecla certainly argues for our considering it a parallel with the *Acts of Paul*.

What an early Christian would have understood the message of this image to be is difficult if not impossible to determine. It is safe to say that by the end of the fourth century, Christians would have associated the ship's name with Thecla of Iconium, if only because of her burgeoning popularity in the church. Modern viewers,

Figure 5.8 Thecla ship. Sarcophagus fragment, fourth century. Musei Capitolini, Rome, Sala II, inv. nr. 67. Photograph: Graydon F. Snyder.

however, are inclined to echo the dichotomy of Thecla's historic position in the early church. On one hand, Paul is clearly in command of the Good Ship Thecla's course; he handles the tiller and the mainsheet. Thecla's dependence on the Pauline message and her attraction to his preaching of 'celibacy and the resurrection' (*Acts of Paul* 5f.) are emphasized in the rhetorical narrative. On the other hand, it may well be that the ship parallels the rhetorical narrative's ambiguity: Thecla is both dependent upon Paul and an independent pursuer of her baptism and of the faith. In the end, she is an independent teacher, preacher and female martyr; yet her story emphasizes her carrying the message of Paul that 'there is no male or female in the church' (Galatians 3:28). In contemporary meetings of scholars in which the image is discussed, it has been our observation that both views are strongly debated, and the debate tends to divide along gender lines, usually to the amusement of those in these groups. This reaction illustrates the dynamic of the Thecla-narrative to carry on purposes which appear to be embedded in the tale. MacDonald, for example, argues persuasively that the legends as they appear in the *Acts of Paul* still carry the hallmark of their having been stories transmitted by and for Christian women.[64] The reader of the narrative can hardly fail to notice the consistency of the male versus female sub-text which permeates the story.

To those who are acquainted with the *Acts of Paul*, the apostle Paul and Thecla of Iconium are almost as closely linked as are Paul and Peter. The longest continuing narrative in the *Acts of Paul* features the virgin Thecla and her adventures as she accompanies the apostle throughout Asia Minor. She is so prominent in the narrative that many refer to the section as *Acts of Paul and Thecla* or even *Acts of Thecla*. Thecla is not on official lists of apostles (nor are any other females, in spite of Romans 16), but in the service for her feast-day (September 24) and in a canon for that holy service attributed to John of Damascus (*c.* 675–749) she is named 'Protomartyr and equal of the apostles.' After Paul 'ordains' her (*Acts of Paul* 21), she performs as an apostle in everything but the title.

A silver reliquary, which has been dated as early as the beginning of the fifth century, has on it a medallion in which Peter and Paul face each other with a cross between them.[65] Flanking the medallion are two identical panels with S. Thecla. She stands orans, with beasts at her feet. Thus the conjoining of Peter and Paul is, in this image, inclusive of Thecla. The piece is in the Eski Eserlei Museum in Adana, Turkey.[66]

Thecla's story in both rhetorical and iconic form has recently gained considerable interest in academic and ecclesiastical circles. A renewed interest in the Christian apocrypha and the relatively recent attention given to the roles of women in the church, both then and now, have contributed to Thecla's renaissance in church studies. But, more than these interests, the story of Thecla itself draws attention simply because it is attractive and romantic. The tale is full of marvelous adventures, centering on the struggles of a beautiful and persistently faithful woman; it may well be the most novelistic of all the many stories of converted women in the apocryphal Acts. It certainly reads more like the Greco-Roman romances, such as Achilles Tatius and Longus, than any of the other apocryphal Acts. As with the Lucan Acts, the story of Thecla is intended to 'profit with delight.'[67] Among the heroines of the apocryphal Acts, such as Mygdonia in the *Acts of Thomas* and Drusiana in the *Acts of John*, Thecla became the most prominent and she remains so, both in the iconic and rhetorical versions of her story.

Thecla's adventures were certainly well-known and venerated in the early church; they became the focus of a wide-spread cultus to the point that her story 'was indeed *hieros logos* for celibate women in ecclesiastical authority.'[68] Thecla as a symbol for the possibility of women's power in the church received negative notice (from Tertullian, *de baptismo* 17, 5) as well as accolades. The latter is attested by the pilgrim woman, Egeria, who made a visit to a central shrine of Thecla in Seleucia where 'a prayer was said at the shrine and the complete *Acts of Saint Thecla* were read.'[69] Whether this reading was of the *Acts of Paul and Thecla* which we now have or of some other document is not clear. There is a *Life and Miracles of St. Thecla* from the fifth century.[70] Further, the origins of Thecla's story were likely oral traditions which go back to the late first or early second century.[71] A document of the sixth century contains a homily which is a panegyric to Thecla.[72] Her cult flourished from the late fourth through the seventh centuries. Iconic records of her veneration stretch from the Near East virtually to the western boundaries of Europe and Africa [Text 5.D].

As is the case with the officially listed apostles, the images of Thecla concentrate on portraits – with Thecla usually standing orans – her contentions with men (and her sisterhood with other females) and her martyrdoms. In addition to the ivory plaques in the British Museum (mentioned above), the 'seduction' of Thecla away from her ordinary life to the freedom afforded in Christian celibacy appears in manuscript illuminations, for example, at Mount Athos (Pantokrator 234, fol. 63ro).[73] Paul is seen preaching to Thecla, and apparently writing an epistle. Thecla, as is the common iconographic element, is watching and listening from a tower. At the necropolis at El Bagawat, Egypt, on the dome of the 'Peace Chapel' (Chapel 80) there is a fresco scene (sixth to eighth century) of Paul and Thecla seated, facing each other on folding stools [Figure 5.9]. It is likely intended to be a depiction of Paul's teaching Thecla.[74] Another scene, of Paul's teaching Thecla is in Chapel 25. This fresco is badly deteriorated; it is published by Fakhry who has attempted to reconstruct the picture in a drawing. Our judgment about the subject of the original fresco is therefore dependent upon Fakhry's reconstruction.[75]

The images of Thecla tend to contain strong visual reference to her martyrdoms. The portraits of Thecla's standing, usually orans, most often depict her in the fire or flanked by beasts [see Figure 5.10]. These references are strong to the point that one could consider that the images are not just portraits but that they are actually narratives. A more portrait-like image is a fifth-century bust in the Eski Eserlei Museum, Adana, Turkey, which was the capital on a column. It shows Thecla, wearing a necklace and framed by palms, one of the standard symbols of martyrdom in early church iconography.[76]

The martyrdoms of Thecla involve first the attempts of her jilted fiancé, Thamyris, and her outraged mother (with the complicity of officialdom and scheming by two of Paul's opponents, Demas and Hermogenes) to punish her apparent seduction by Paul and her elopement with the apostle; the lamb has jumped the fence and must pay for it. A carving in the Brooklyn Museum (40.300) illustrates Thamyris' rage at the defection of Thecla.[77] A woman flees a man who is on horse-back. He carries a sword, plunged at her like a dagger. If this scene is a Thecla-scene,[78] it does not parallel a rhetorical description in the *Acts of Paul*. However, there is such a narrative described in Pseudo-Chrysostum's *Thecla Homilies*.[79] The description of Thamyris' palpable anger (and his association with the villains Demas and Hermogenes,

5.D

And while Paul was speaking in the midst of the church in the house of Onesiphorus a certain virgin named Thecla, the daughter of Theoclia, betrothed to a man named Thamyris, was sitting at the window close by and listened day and night to the discourse of virginity, as proclaimed by Paul. And she did not look away from the window, but was led on by faith, rejoicing exceedingly. And when she saw many women and virgins going in to Paul she also had an eager desire to be deemed worthy to stand in Paul's presence and hear the word of Christ. For she had not yet seen Paul in person, but only heard his word.

As she did not move from the window her mother sent to Thamyris. And he came gladly as if already receiving her in marriage. And Thamyris said to Theoclia, 'Where, then, is my Thecla (that I may see her)?' And Theoclia answered, 'I have a strange story to tell you, Thamyris. For three days and three nights Thecla does not rise from the window either to eat or to drink; but looking earnestly as if upon some pleasant sight she is devoted to a foreigner teaching deceitful and artful discourses, so that I wonder how a virgin of her great modesty exposes herself to such extreme discomfort.

'Thamyris, this man will overturn the city of the Iconians and your Thecla too; for all the women and the young men go in to him to be taught by him. He says one must fear only one God and live in chastity. Moreover, my daughter, clinging to the window like a spider, lays hold of what is said by him with a strange eagerness and fearful emotion. For the virgin looks eagerly at what is said by him and has been captivated. But go near and speak to her, for she is betrothed to you.'

And Thamyris greeted her with a kiss, but at the same time being afraid of her overpowering emotion said, 'Thecla, my betrothed, why do you sit thus? And what sort of feeling holds you distracted? Come back to your Thamyris and be ashamed.' Moreover, her mother said the same, 'Why do you sit thus looking down, my child, and answering nothing, like a sick woman?' And those who were in the house wept bitterly, Thamyris for the loss of a wife, Theoclia for that of a child, and the maidservants for that of a mistress. And there was a great outpouring of lamentation in the house. And while these things were going on Thecla did not turn away but kept attending to the word of Paul.

The Acts of Paul 7–10

Figure 5.9 Paul and Thecla. Fresco, sixth–eighth century. Necropolis of El Bagawat at the Kharga Oasis, Chapel 80 (Peace Chapel). Photograph: after an image by Ahmed Fakhry.

cf. 2 Timothy 1:15; 4:9–10) at Paul's causing women to leave their husbands (*Acts of Paul* 15–16) certainly underlies the legend of his murderous pursuit of Thecla.

In the *Acts of Paul*, Thecla's first trial is to be tied naked to the stake, to be burned. A miraculous rain with a hail-storm puts out the flames. Thecla's fire-martyrdom is pictured at the necropolis of El Bagawat. In the 'Exodus Chapel' (Chapel 80) there is an abbreviated fresco showing Thecla tied to the stake and surrounded by flames[80] [see Figure 2.8]. Thecla is named. Again, this image appears to come from about the sixth century. One of the more picturesque images of Thecla's martyrdom at Iconium is in the early twelfth-century Pamplona Bibles, (Bibliothèque de la Ville, nr. 108, Picture Bible-Vitae Sanct. fol. 237ro).[81] The scene has two registers; in the upper right center is Thecla, veiled, facing frontally, in the fire and surrounded by flames at Iconium. On the left, the King and executioner watching. Another executioner is on the right [Text 5.E]. The lower register is the martyrdom at Antioch; it shows Thecla stretched out and being bound, made ready for drawing and quartering. Four executioners are binding her. Alexander is on the far left, watching.

5.E

And the boys and girls brought wood and straw in order that Thecla might be burned. And when she came in naked the governor wept and admired the power that was in her. And the executioners arranged the wood and told her to go up on the pile. And having made the sign of the cross she went up on the pile. And they lighted the fire. And though a great fire was blazing it did not touch her. For God, having compassion upon her, made an underground rumbling, and a cloud full of water and hail overshadowed the theatre from above, and all its contents were poured out so that many were in danger of death. And the fire was put out and Thecla saved.

The Acts of Paul 22

The classic example of the depictions of Thecla's martyrdom at Antioch, and certainly one of the most interesting visually of all the Thecla images, is the fifth–eighth century roundel now in the Nelson-Atkins Museum of Art in Kansas City (48.10) [Figure 5.10]. The sculpture is rather large, almost thirty inches in diameter and over three inches thick. It is likely that it was at one time part of a church or chapel decoration. A beautiful and almost mischievously posed Thecla is shown bound, with her upper torso nude; she is clad in a flowing skirt. At her feet are a bear and a lioness (the lioness who defended Thecla to the death against the other beasts). The sculpture bears the marks of its being of Eastern, perhaps Egyptian origin, in that it preserves the sexuality of Thecla in its voluptuous figure and it has the drilled eye pupils typical of the Eastern style. A unique characteristic of this figure is the two winged angels which accompany Thecla.[82]

Figure 5.10 S. Thecla with wild beasts and angels. Limestone carving, fifth–eighth century. The Nelson-Atkins Museum of Art, Kansas City, Missouri (Purchase: Nelson Trust). Photograph: The Nelson-Atkins Museum of Art.

The 'Eastern Thecla,' of the type in the Nelson-Atkins roundel, is known on a number of pilgrims' souvenirs, in the form of flasks and oil lamps. These also show Thecla among the beasts. Typical is the terracotta ampulla in the Louvre (Ant. Grec. MNC 1926) with Thecla among the beasts on one side and S. Menas on the other.[83] There were monasteries of both Thecla and Menas near each other in Egypt; hence the pairing of the two on a number of pilgrims' reliquaries. Elizabeth Willis has presented persuasive iconographic evidence to demonstrate that the model for Thecla in these images was that of Mediterranean mother-goddesses, particularly that of Cybele. She argues that the development of the legends of Thecla in both rhetorical and iconic form

> was a result of a need to Christianize the popularity of the Cybele cult in Asia Minor and to satisfy or to fill the gap caused by a loss of the Mother Goddess brought about by a rejection of pagan religion necessitated by a person's conversion.[84]

Thecla also had to face an attempt to draw and quarter her. Alexander is notably persistent in his attempts to punish Thecla for her having humiliated him in her resistance of his amorous advances (*Acts of Paul* 26). After he has her thrown to the beasts, and she has been saved by the lioness who fights to the death for Thecla, the Saint throws herself into a pool of 'man-eating sea lions' (some texts have sea-serpents), and thus baptizes herself. A bolt of lightning hits the pool, killing the beasts but sparing Thecla. Alexander then decides to have bulls pull Thecla apart. Fires are applied to the bulls' testicles to enrage them and start them pulling on the ropes, but a burning flame from these fires miraculously sears through the ropes, and Thecla is saved again [Text 5.F]. (Is there any doubt in the reader's mind about the story's ability to entertain the early Christian reader?) Weitzmann has theorized that a streak of red in the image at Mount Sinai is from a depiction of that fire.[85] Alexander's seemingly limitless determination and invention to kill Thecla is halted by the governor of the city, and Thecla is freed. She is also baptized and can now proceed on her own mission.

5.F

And Thecla, having been taken from the hands of Tryphaena, was stripped and received a girdle and was thrown into the arena. And lions and bears were let loose upon her. And a fierce lioness ran up and lay down at her feet. And the multitude of the women cried aloud. And a bear ran upon her, but the lioness went to meet it and tore the bear to pieces. And again a lion that had been trained to fight against men, which belonged to Alexander, ran upon her. And the lioness, encountering the lion, was killed along with it. And the women cried the more since the lioness, her protector, was dead.

Then they sent in many beasts as she was standing and stretching forth her hands and praying. And when she had finished her prayer she turned around and saw a large pit full of water and said, 'Now it is time to wash myself.' And she threw herself in saying, 'In the name of Jesus Christ I baptize myself on my last day.' When the women and the multitude saw it they wept and said, 'Do not throw yourself into the water!'; even the governor shed tears because the seals were to devour such beauty. She then threw herself into the water in the name of Jesus Christ, but the seals, having seen a flash of lightning, floated dead on the surface. And there was round her a cloud of fire so that the beasts could neither touch her nor could she be seen naked.

But the women lamented when other and fiercer animals were let loose; some threw petals, others nard, others cassia, others amomum, so that there was an abundance of perfumes. And all the wild beasts were hypnotized and did not touch her. And Alexander said to the governor, 'I have some terrible bulls to which we will bind her.' And the governor consented grudgingly, 'Do what you will.' And they bound her by the feet between the bulls and put red-hot irons under their genitals so that they, being rendered more furious, might kill her. They rushed forward but the burning flame around her consumed the ropes, and she was as if she had not been bound.

And Tryphaena fainted standing beside the arena, so that the servants said, 'Queen Tryphaena is dead.' And the governor put a stop to the games and the whole city was in dismay. And Alexander fell down at the feet of the governor and cried, 'Have mercy upon me and upon the city and set the woman free, lest the city also be destroyed. For if Caesar hear of these things he will possibly destroy the city along with us because his kinswoman, Queen Tryphaena, has died at the theatre gate.'

And the governor summoned Thecla out of the midst of the beasts and said to her, 'Who are you? And what is there about you that not one of the wild beasts touched you?' She answered, 'I am a servant of the living God and, as to what there is about me, I have believed in the Son of God in whom he is well pleased; that is why not one of the beasts touched me. For he alone is the goal of salvation and the basis of immortal life. For he is a refuge to the tempest-tossed, a solace to the afflicted, a shelter to the despairing; in brief, whoever does not believe in him shall not live but be dead forever.'

When the governor heard these things he ordered garments to be brought and to be put on her. And she said, 'He who clothed me when I was naked among the beasts will in the day of judgement clothe me with salvation.' And taking the garments she put them on.

And the governor immediately issued an edict saying, 'I release to you the pious Thecla, the servant of God.' And the women shouted aloud and with one voice praised God, 'One is the God, who saved Thecla', so that the whole city was shaken by their voices.

The Acts of Paul 33–8

Just as the rhetorical images of Thecla grew and expanded into aretalogies and further feats of faith, so does the iconic record. A fresco in the Church of Staro Nagoricino, in the former Yugoslavia, is a scene in which Thecla is actually mauled by a lion. She lies back to the right, with the lion's jaws clamped on her left shoulder. Warns suggests that this scene reflects the legends in Pseudo-Chrysostom's *Homilia de Sancta Thecla* (Migne, *Patrologia Graeca* 50, 748ff.) and ms. G of the *Acts of Paul*. According to the texts, some men come to despoil Thecla, 'like lions.' They are outraged at her preaching chastity for women. Chrysostom declares that the lion is actually a demon.[86]

Thecla escapes from her attackers and finds refuge in a cleft in a rock. This becomes her 'hermitage' for the rest of her life. Two manuscript illuminations, one of the twelfth century (Menologion in Biblioteca Marciana, Venice) and the other of the fourteenth century (Oxford, gr. th. f.1, fol. 10vo), preserve what were undoubtedly earlier images of this Thecla-event.[87]

Of the making of apocrypha there is no end.[88] Thecla's legends went on and, in certain regions, continued into the modern age. The *locus classicus* is the Eastern part of Spain, specifically in Tarragona. Thecla was the patron saint of the region and the cathedral of Tarragona is dedicated to her. There are as well many legends about

Thecla which are specific to that area.[89] The church decorations of the cathedral are mainly dedicated to her, and they are both a Romanesque (on the altar antependium) and a Gothic recounting (on the retable) of Thecla's prominence. On the antependium of the high altar, there are several scenes. The zones on the left are of Thecla in Iconium; on the right she is in Antioch and Selucia. All of the scenes are Thecla-scenes. In the center zone there are the dove of the Holy Spirit and a Hand of God, nimbed, above Paul, who is nimbed. Paul is large, seated on folding stool decorated with animal heads, and in a mandorla. Paul's right hand is extended toward Thecla; she is veiled and kneeling before the apostle. The smaller zones of the antependium are as follows: (1) Top left. Unidentified ornament of foliage and fantastic animals; four men are present, with the arm of the foremost grasped by a woman, possibly Thecla. (2) Top, second from left. Thecla hears Paul preach – she is within a building from which come figures. Paul is nimbed and holds an open codex in his hand. (3) Bottom left. Thecla is before the governor. The governor is sitting on a backed chair, and holds a sword in his hand. Thecla is held by a man. (4) Bottom left. Thecla is tortured; there is a bust of Christ in upper left. Thecla kneels, nude, facing the bust (left); a male figure (bust) is in the upper left. A Hand of God is in the upper right. (5) Upper right. Thecla is among the beasts. She stands orans, facing frontally, flanked by beasts. On her left two lions are fighting. On her right are bears. (6) Thecla with Tryphena, who is apparently taking her home. The altar-images thus preserve in iconic form one of the most touching and woman-oriented stories in the *Acts of Paul and Thecla*. During her trials at Antioch, Thecla is taken under the wing of a high-born woman, Tryphena, who houses her and loves her as if she were her daughter. (7) Lower right. Thecla, nude, kneels, facing frontally. She is surrounded by birds and toads, who appear to be attacking her. (8) Far right, lower. Thecla's death; her soul is borne to heaven from within a building; there are two angels supporting the soul of Thecla, which is represented as a dove.

It is noteworthy that the Romanesque carvings on the altar antependium preserve much of the earlier iconography of Thecla. Her figure is full and beautiful, and the representations resemble in dress the Egyptian and Syrian images in which her upper body is nude in the martyrdom scenes. The Gothic retable shows how the iconography of Thecla becomes much more like that of other virgin martyrs. She is clad in a long robe and veiled. Nevertheless, on the retable her important status is clearly stated. Three large figures hold prominent places on the retable, each in its own niche: on the left is Thecla; in the middle is the Virgin as Queen of Heaven, holding the Christ-child; on the far right is Paul. All three are standing.

Thecla images appear in stained glass as well. An example is in the Church of S. Francesco, Assisi, in the Catherine's Chapel, lower window of window 1. Thecla stands, facing frontally, her hands clasped in prayer.[90] Another fourteenth-century image, a manuscript illumination (Coll., R. von Gutman, *Vita Hedwiges*, fol. 82vo) at the New Pearl Farm collection (near Victoria, British Columbia) shows S. Hedwig of Silesia visited by saints. Among these saints in Hedwig's vision is Thecla who is nimbed with a wreath and holds a book and a vessel.[91] One would expect Thecla to be important in the East, and she is. There are a number of images, usually portraits of Thecla, in some of the oldest churches in Asia Minor and Cappadocia. An example is in the tenth-century church at the Hermitage of the Monk Symeon, Chapel of S. Symeon, Göreme in Cappadocia.[92]

Figure 5.11 El Greco: Madonna and Child with Saint Martina (or S. Thecla) and Saint Agnes. Oil on canvas, *c.* 1600. National Gallery of Art, Washington, DC, Widener Collection, 1942.9.26. Photograph: The National Gallery of Art.

In about 1600 CE, an easterner exiled to Spain, El Greco, included Thecla in his work which is alternatively titled 'The Virgin with Saint Agnes and Saint Thekla (or Saint Martina),' which hangs in the Washington National Gallery [Figure 5.11]. There is some question as to whether the figure is Thecla or S. Martina. The National Gallery, in its descriptions, at first leaned toward Thecla; it now bends toward S. Martina, because Martina is the feminine name of the founder of the Chapel of S. Joseph in Toledo. It was this chapel for which El Greco was commissioned to paint this picture, along with one of S. Martin, next to which it originally hung. However, as the museum's commentary puts it, 'It is also possible . . . that she is Saint Thekla, who appeared to Saint Martin in visions.'[93] The figure in question is painted with short hair, in a blue robe, and with an adoring lioness at her feet. The iconography is thoroughly consistent with traditions about Thecla, especially Thecla's short hair and the adoring lioness at her feet. In our mind there is little doubt that the museum's original identification is correct; it is Saint Thecla.

Thecla was the patron saint of the town of Este in northern Italy. No less a painter than Giovanni Battista Tiepolo was commissioned in about 1758 to produce a painting to hang above the altar in the cathedral. The image is of Thecla saving the town of Este from the plague of 1638. A preparation (*modello*) for the painting itself, which is in Este, hangs in the Metropolitan Museum of Art [Figure 5.12]. It shows Thecla, nimbed, with short hair, dressed in monk's cloth tunic with a light blue apron; she kneels in prayer in the lower left. She faces half-right, her face lifted toward a gray-bearded male figure in clouds, upper right, with four winged angels clustered around him. Dark gray figures (demons of the plague), some winged, are in the air in center and far left. Victims of the plague, a child and woman, lean in an anguish of mourning over a dead man in the bottom right; one veiled-in-black figure kneels at far left of Thecla. The city is in the background, at a distance.

The martyrdom of Thecla in early Christian art was depicted in all its realism. The beasts were ferocious, the flames were hot, and Thecla's willingness to sacrifice herself stands out in most of these images. During the nineteenth century, however, Sarah Paxton Ball Dodson, in 1891, painted 'Une Martyre (Sainte Thechla)' in highly romantic terms (Washington National Gallery, Museum of American Art, 1923.8.1). Her Thecla stands in profile, drawn from the waist up, looking to the left, veiled and wimpled. Her hands are joined at her breast; she clutches a palm branch, the symbol of her martyrdom, to her left breast. Her arms are bare. Her eyes are virtually closed as if in resignation or meditation. There is some sort of cloth or a fold of her clothing draping over her left forearm. The background is plain, with square panels suggesting an architectural wall.

The iconography of a particular scene or person continues to evolve, just as does the rhetoric of the stories about the figure. This evolution always is both inventive (especially after the Renaissance) and conservative. The contemporary artist, Warrington Colescott, in his 'Anita Ekberg as S. Thecla,' has painted a martyrdom of Thecla which does not appear in the *Acts of Paul* [Figure 5.13]. Thecla hangs, completely nude, nimbed, on a cross, facing frontally. She is attacked by three wolves, two on right, one on left. The wolves are black and gray. Above and to the right of Thecla is a pale, winged angel. The presence of wolves as well as the crucifixion of Thecla are innovative. Although these elements are a good example of what iconographers deem the corruption of traditional iconography, at least one traditional element

Figure 5.12 Giovanni Battista Tiepolo: Saint Thecla Praying for the Plague-stricken. Oil on canvas, *c.* 1750. The Metropolitan Museum of Art, New York, Rogers Fund, 1937.37.165.2. Photograph: The Metropolitan Museum of Art.

Figure 5.13 Warrington Colescott: Anita Ekberg as S. Thecla. Print, twentieth century. Edwin A.
Ulrich Museum of Art, Wichita State University, Wichita, KS, Endowment
Association Art Collection. Photograph: Edwin A. Ulrich Museum

remains. The model for the early images of Thecla is clearly that of Mediterranean
mother-goddesses.[94] Colescott has said that his model for Thecla was an image of the
actress Anita Ekberg (see Fellini's ground-breaking motion picture, *La dolce vita*).[95]
The element of Thecla, as mother-goddess, which appears in early images of Thecla
may have re-asserted itself in Colescott's painting.

Peter

As we stated above, the earliest image of Peter, at least the one which can be positively identified, is the fresco in the baptistery of the house church at Dura Europos,
which narrates Peter's attempt to walk on water. The identification of Peter is by
virtue of the figure's context in the scene's subject. Aside from the figure's attempting
to walk on water and his perilous position, there is no hint of the so-called Peter-
type in the image. As Dinkler points out, the image is not really a portrait of Peter;
it is an image of the lost human who is saved by Christ.[96] But almost equally early
are Petrine scenes which are paralleled in early Christian apocrypha.

As part of the early fourth-century Peter-storm which Stuhlfauth and Dinkler
describe (see p. 138, above), there appeared a number of images of the apostle, the
most notable of them being scenes which occur prolifically:

Peter, striking the rock, also known as Peter's water miracle;
Peter's denial of Christ;
Peter's arrest; and
Peter, teaching.

On several of the earliest sarcophagi – namely, the frieze-sarcophagi of the early fourth century – the first three of these Peter images are combined with certain depictions of Jesus' miracles, e.g. the wedding feast at Cana, the feeding of the thousands, and the healing of the blind man. After this first period, when the zoned and niched sarcophagi begin to appear, the Peter scenes begin to scatter.[97] Most of the teaching scenes which involve Peter-types are generic; they are not necessarily tied to a particular Christian text. They are iconographically derived from the visual vocabulary of the Greco-Roman world. When the teaching scene consists of Peter's teaching soldiers, as it does on a sarcophagus in the Musée Réattu in Arles,[98] all but Peter's denial are paralleled in Christian apocrypha.

The teaching scene in which the apostle is instructing the soldiers is part of the cycle of Peter's water miracle. The texts for the water miracle and Peter's arrest for his martyrdom are found in Pseudo-Linus, *Martyrium beati Petri apostoli a Lino episcopo conscriptum* V.[99] Peter, as he is being jailed before his martyrdom, converts his military escort and is asked by the soldiers to baptize them. There being no water in the jail cell, Peter strikes the rock walls of the prison and water gushes forth: . . . *fonte precibus et ammirabili signo crucis de rupe producto, in sanctae trinitatis nomine baptizasti.* This scene occurs at least thirty-two times[100] on the sarcophagi of the fourth and early fifth centuries.[101] The text occurs at least a century, perhaps two, after the appearance of the images. The significance of the images is clear. The water miracle bestows Moses' mantle on Peter. This transference is part of the campaign to give Peter the title of the church's Moses. In that sense, the striking of the rock image is parallel with those in which Christ gives the law to Peter (*traditio legis*).

After the sixth century, the water miracle scene disappears.[102] During the fourth century, however, the scene was well enough known to be recognizable in allegorical form. On the sarcophagus of Junius Bassus, on a spandrel, between two niches, is a lamb who strikes a rock and a second lamb drinks the water which pours from it. Another example of this Peter scene is on the so-called 'Dogmatic Sarcophagus' in the Museo Pio Cristiano (formerly Lateran 104).

The scene in which Peter brings forth water from the rock does not occur as often in the catacombs. There as on the sarcophagi it is sometimes difficult to tell whether the subject is intended to be Peter's water miracle or that of Moses (Exodus 17:1–7). There are cases in which on both the sarcophagi and in the catacombs the iconographic context helps to decide if the artist intended us to see Peter or Moses. In the Cemetery of Cyriaca, the scene of a man with a wand striking a rock is accompanied by one of Moses taking off his sandals; this figure is likely intended to be Moses. Sometimes the context does not help. In the cemetery of Domitilla, on the dome of a vault, a beardless figure strikes the rock. The scene is accompanied by scenes of the miracle of the loaves and fishes (with a beardless Jesus), Abraham's sacrifice of Isaac, and the three Hebrew youths in the fiery furnace. Is this Peter or Moses performing the water miracle?

A famous example of this image on an artifact other than sculpture or fresco is on the so-called Podgoritza plate. This shallow glass plate was found near Doclea in

Dalmatia; it is now in the Hermitage in St Petersburg (Reg. no. Omega 73). It is assigned to the late fourth or early fifth century. The plate has in its center medallion Abraham's sacrifice of Isaac. Around the perimeter are scenes in frieze-style: Jonah; Adam and Eve; the raising of Lazarus; Peter, striking the rock; Daniel and the lions; Susanna. The inscriptions all have to do with the depicted as the recipients of salvific acts:

DIVNAN DE VENT/RE QVETI LIBERATVS EST
ABRAM ETET EV/AM
DOMNVS/LAIARUM/rsuscit/at
Petrus uirga perq/uouset/fontis cipe/runt quore/re
DANIEL DE LACO/LEONIS
TRIS PVERI DE ECNE/CAMI
SVSANA/DE FALSO CRI/MINE[103]

On a late fourth- or early fifth-century sarcophagus in Fermo there is a puzzling pair of Peter scenes [Figure 5.14]. The monument is a five-niche, columnar sarcophagus, with alternating arched and rounded niches. It contains the following scenes, from left to right: (1) A figure who appears to be Peter, who is flanked by a man and a female. A third female kneels and touches Peter's garment. (2) A man is center, facing slightly to the left; he grasps a woman's wrist (she is on his left). Another man stands to the right. Both of the men are bearded and of the Peter-type in their facial characteristics. (3) Christ beardless and long-locked stands between two apostles, or, the scene may be Christ's arrest. (4) Three soldiers, one of them asleep, outside Peter's prison cell, guarding him. (5) Peter is in prison with another figure (either an angel or an unidentified man).

It is the two left-hand niches (1 and 2) on this sarcophagus which are problematic. That they feature Peter is doubtless.[104] Garrucci[105] suggests that both scenes are of the raising of Tabitha (Acts 9:39–41). He is joined by von Sybel.[106] De Waal interprets this scene as Peter with Eubola in Jerusalem and with Xanthippe, Livia and Agrippina in Rome.[107] Styger, on the other hand, sees the scenes as related to the story of Peter's raising of the paralyzed daughter – in the Coptic fragment of Codex Berol 8504.2 (a fragment of the *Acts of Peter*)[108] [Text 5.G]. Stuhlfauth argues that the mysterious scenes are a conflation of two rhetorical narratives from the *Acts of Peter*: one in which Peter restores the sight of the widows (*Acts of Peter* 20–21) and the other in *c.* 23ff. in which Peter raises Nicostratus, a senator's son – this in a confrontation with Simon Magus.[109] Stuhlfauth subsequently points out that 'Nicostratos' mother fell at the apostle's feet; Peter lifted her up and comforted her by holding her hand, while the other mother remains standing.' There are two mothers in the rhetorical story. 'The artist has combined in the first niche the Senator's mother and in the second the lower-born mother.' Then one of the mothers says '*qui mihi manum porriget?* (who has given me his hand?).' In the second field the apostle holds the hand of one of the two mothers.[110] Fabricius follows Stuhlfauth.[111] The jury is out on the identification of the scenes, and it is likely to be sequestered indefinitely. We present the scenes under the strong possibility that Stuhlfauth and Fabricius have correctly identified them as parallels with the scene of Peter and the widows in the *Acts of Peter*.

Figure 5.14 Peter and the widows (two left niches). Sarcophagus, fourth or fifth century. The Archaeological Museum, Fermo, Italy. Image: Cartlidge, after a photograph by P. Styger.

5.G

But on the first day of the week, which is the Lord's Day, a multitude gathered together, and they brought many sick people to Peter for him to cure them. And one of the multitude was bold enough to say to Peter, 'Peter, behold, before our eyes you made many blind see and deaf hear and the lame walk, and you have helped the weak and given them strength; why have you not helped your virgin daughter, who has grown up beautiful and believed in the name of God? For behold, one of her sides is completely paralysed, and there she is helpless in the corner. We can see those whom you have cured, but you have neglected your own daughter.'

But Peter smiled and said to him, 'My son, God alone knows why her body is sick. Know that God is not unable or powerless to give his gift to my daughter. But in order that your soul may be convinced and those present believe the more'– he looked at his daughter and said to her, 'Arise from your place with the help of none except Jesus, and walk naturally before those present and come to me.' And she arose and came to him. The multitude rejoiced at what had taken place. And Peter said to them, 'Behold, your hearts are convinced that God is not powerless concerning the things which we ask of him.' They rejoiced the more and glorified God. Then Peter said to his daughter, 'Return to your place, sit down there and be helpless again, for it is good for me and you.' And the girl went back, lay down in her place and became as before. The whole multitude wept and besought Peter to make her well.

Peter said to them, 'As the Lord lives, this is good for her and for me. For on the day on which she was born to me I saw a vision and the Lord said to me, "Peter, this day has been born for you a great affliction, for this daughter will harm many souls, if her body remains well!" I, however, thought that the vision mocked me.

'When the girl was ten years old she became a stumbling-block to many. And a very rich man, Ptolemy by name, when he saw the girl bathing with her mother, sent for her to take her for his wife, but her mother did not consent. He often sent for her, for he could not wait . . .

. . .'Ptolemy brought the girl, and leaving her before the door of the house went away.

'When I saw this, I and her mother went downstairs and found the girl with one side of her body paralysed from head to foot and dried up. We carried her away, praising the Lord that he had kept his servant from defilement and violation and . . . This is the reason why the girl remains thus to this day. But now you shall hear what happened to Ptolemy. He repented and lamented night and day over that which had happened to him, and because of the many tears which he shed he became blind. Having decided to hang himself, behold, about the ninth hour of that day, whilst alone in his bedroom, he saw a great light which illuminated the whole house, and he heard a voice saying to him, "Ptolemy, God has not given the vessels for corruption and shame; it is not right for you, as a believer in me, to violate my virgin, whom you are to know as your sister, as if I had become one spirit to both of you – but arise, and speedily go to the house of the apostle Peter and you shall see my glory. He will explain the matter to you." And Ptolemy did not delay, but ordered his servants to show him the way and bring him to me. When he had come to me, he told all that had happened to him in the power of Jesus Christ, our Lord. And he saw with the eyes of his flesh and with the eyes of his soul, and many people set their hope on Christ; he did good to them and gave them the gift of God.

'After this Ptolemy died; he departed and went to his Lord. When he made his will, he left a piece of land in the name of my daughter because through her he became a believer in God and was made whole. I, however, who was appointed trustee, have acted carefully. I sold the acre, and God alone knows that neither I nor my daughter have kept anything from the money of the acre, but I sent the whole sum to the poor. Know, therefore, O servant of Christ Jesus, that God cares for his people and prepares for each what is good – even when we think that God has forgotten us. Now then, brethren, let us mourn, be watchful, and pray, and God's goodness will look upon us, and we hope for it.'

And Peter delivered other speeches before them, and glorifying the name of the Lord Christ he gave of the bread to all of them, and after distributing it he rose and went into the house.

The Acts of Peter from Codex Berol. 8502.4 (fragmentary)

The whole of the *Acts of Peter* is in the context of the church versus Simon Magus. We have discussed above the iconography in which both Peter and Paul take on the heinous Magician. There are, however, images which allude to the contest of Peter and Simon Magus in which Peter alone carries on the conflict, as is the situation in the *Acts of Peter*. A sarcophagus from southern Gaul, now lost and known by a drawing from Le Blant, shows Peter faced by a dog; the dog's paw is lifted as if in greeting or the giving of a message.[112] Le Blant places this image in the fourth century[113] [Figure 5.15]. Another sarcophagus of the late fourth century is in the crypt of the Church of S. Giovanni in Valle, Verona. Dubbed the 'Sarcophagus of Sts. Simon, Judas and Thaddeus' it also shows the scene in the *Acts of Peter* 9–12 in which a dog carries messages back and forth between Peter and the Magician. Of interest also is a scene on this latter sarcophagus in which a male figure faces a serpent. This scene is identified by Klauser and Deichmann as Daniel and the 'Babylonian dragon.'[114] The scene, however, could also represent one of the apostles confronting a serpent who has become the lover of a woman (Paul, Thomas, John). The identifications of that scene will likely remain diverse.

Figure 5.15 Peter and Simon Magus' dog. Sarcophagus, late fourth or early fifth century. Southern Gaul, now lost. Image: Cartlidge, after a drawing by Le Blant.

In the middle ages, as we have already mentioned, the contest with Simon Magus is usually conducted by both Peter and Paul. However, at Troyes there are windows devoted to Peter (Cathedral of S. Pierre, Bay II, Bay IV) in which Peter and Simon attempt to raise a dead man (Peter succeeds), and both face Nero. An earlier scene, on what is possibly a seventh-century ivory diptych, at Musée Cluny, Paris, shows Simon's having fallen, lying supine on the ground with a winged demon diving at him. This niche is accompanied by another niche which may be of the scene from the *Acts of Peter* in which Peter reads to the widows. The apostle sits behind a desk, lecturing, with a book open in his hand. Two women and a man are seated on the floor to his right, listening. A third niche pictures the upside-down crucifixion of the apostle. A fourteenth-century manuscript illumination in Queen Mary's Psalter, fol. 305vo (British Museum, Roy. 2 B. VII) has Simon in the middle, falling headlong and escorted down by two winged demons. Nero is on the left, sitting on a stool and observing, while Peter, nimbed, is on the right, kneeling in prayer. There are three observers on the far right, none of them nimbed.

The arrest of Peter, namely, the arrest which leads directly to his martyrdom, is paralleled in the *Acts of Peter*. There are numerous depictions of this scene on the sarcophagi. Stuhlfauth divides these scenes into four types; each represents a separate incident in the apostle's arrest and martyrdom:[115]

Ia Peter arrested (Verhaftung). This scene is marked (according to Stuhlfauth) by Peter's being flanked by two soldiers who grasp Peter by the arms. The apostle's head is turned, usually to the left, as if he were startled. Examples of the many sarcophagi which contain this scene are the former Lateran 173, Lateran 175 and Lateran 104. All in all, Stuhlfauth lists some forty-three sarcophagi upon which the arrest of Peter is of this type.

Ib Peter taken to prison (Gefangenführung). Here, Peter is again flanked by his guards. However, his head faces in the direction in which he is being led by the guards. An example of this type is the former Lateran 161, in the Vatican.

Stuhlfauth's second example is one of the most famous of the early sarcophagi, the so-called 'Jonah Sarcophagus' in the Vatican (formerly Lateran 119) [Figure 5.16] which has been identified in two ways and is thus also a classic illustration of the difficulties in some cases of the identification of an image's subject. The sarcophagus is generally considered to be *ante pacem*.[116] If so, it is possibly the earliest scene of the arrest of Peter. Above the main Jonah-scene are two smaller images. One is of a man striking the rock and water is pouring forth. To the immediate right is a man, seemingly struggling; he is held by the arms by two men. The portrayal may be of Moses' water miracle or that of Peter. It may also be that of Peter's arrest or of Moses' being hassled by the Egyptians.[117] We would, with Stuhlfauth, prefer that they be Peter-scenes.

IIa Peter led to his sentencing before the execution (zu der Richtstätte). In certain images, Peter is flanked by the soldiers and he is carrying a cross, or, as in the case on the sarcophagus in the Museo Pio Cristiano (former Lateran 151), in the second niche, the soldier carries the cross.

IIb Peter led to the execution itself (auf der Richtstätte). In these scenes, Peter stands, facing fully frontally, his figure appears to be one of acceptance, even of peace. The most well known of this type is the image on the Sarcophagus of Junius Bassus [see Figure 5.17]. A second illustration of this 'arrest of Peter' is on the sarcophagus, inventory number 174, in the Vatican, in the second niche. There, Peter stands with his hands partially outstretched, a younger man is behind him, partially obscured by a column. Stuhlfauth interprets this as Peter at the point of his execution. This identification is not as sure as is the one on the Junius Bassus sarcophagus.[118]

Stuhlfauth's four categories of the arrest of Peter and martyrdom of Peter may be somewhat too close a reading of the iconography. Nevertheless, he has certainly identified four types of iconography of the narrative.

In the earliest Christian art, Peter's martyrdom is represented by the arrest scenes. It is only in later periods that we begin to get images of the actual crucifixion of Peter, which has theological concern in the *Acts of Peter*. A sixth- or seventh-century ivory at the Musée Cluny appears to be one of the earliest of these images. The scene of Peter's inverted crucifixion begins to appear in numbers in the early middle ages and thoroughly replaces the scenes of his arrest. An intermediate stage is that of Peter's carrying his cross, such as on a sarcophagus in Ravenna (Sarcophagus Barbatianus, of the fifth or sixth century) in which it appears that Paul is receiving the law.[119] A similar pattern is on the so-called 'Sarcophagus of the Twelve Apostles' (fifth century) in Ravenna, at the Church of S. Apollinare in Classe.[120]

On the sarcophagi, Peter's arrest (and Paul's) often accompanies a scene of Christ's arrest and of Pilate's washing his hands. The arrest of Peter (as well as that of Paul) is therefore a trope for the passion of Christ. Of course, artistic representations in any medium can hardly ever be said to represent only one thing. Even if we assume that the earliest Christians who gazed upon any given scene knew exactly what its subject matter was, certainly it was the intent of a strong group within the early church to merge the figures of Moses and Peter, as we discussed above. It is possible that, for example, the striking the rock scene and the arrest scene in the Jonah sarcophagus recalled the narratives of both Moses and Peter to those early Christians who beheld it.

Figure 5.16 Peter striking the rock/Peter's arrest (top center). Sarcophagus, late third or early fourth century. Museo Pio Cristiano, Vatican (formerly Lateran 119). Photograph: Art Resource, NY.

Figure 5.17 The arrest of Peter. Sculpture from the sarcophagus of Junius Bassus, *c.* 359. Museo
Pio Cristiano, Vatican. Photograph: Art Resource, NY.

Further, the scenes of trial which are the majority of paleo-Christian art's narrative
images must have pointed not only to the sacrifice of Christ in the eyes of early Christian
beholders. They pointed to the actual portrayed figures (Peter, Paul, Susanna, Daniel,
Jonah and Thecla) as well as to those of the faithful who had endured, with the promises
of God, to the end. To Christians who were trained in the narrative complex of the
tradition-matrix in their world, the abbreviated forms of the paleo-Christian images
were well suited to be 'seen' with multiple meanings.[121] To them, there was no high
fence to prevent their looking at what we now call 'extra-canonical.'

6

APOSTLES AND
EVANGELISTS

Ulrich Fabricius finds no extant narrative images of the apostles prior to the year
1000 CE to which he can attribute the influence of Christian apocrypha upon early
Christian art – other than those of Peter and Paul.[1] Fabricius seeks the influence
of Christian apocrypha upon art rather than the existence of parallels. Further, as
Fabricius' purpose is basically to make a survey of pictorial art extant before the year
1000 CE, he does not consider medieval images in order to hypothesize that early
Christian models of these images once existed.

Art historians often hypothesize that many medieval images derive from early
church antecedents and that a number of illustrated versions of early Christian apocrypha were those antecedents. For a particular text to gain illumination it had to be
both popular and have a story-telling quality which lent itself to illustration.[2] There
are strong indications that such images did exist in works that were popular and
story-worthy. Weitzmann takes care to list the apocryphal acts and gospels as such
texts.[3] The nature of the medieval images parallel with early Christian apocrypha
supports the judgment that they were derived from illustrations that were created –
likely in early Byzantine workshops – when the texts became popular enough for the
production of illuminated editions, that is, from the end of the fourth century.

That precious few early illustrated copies of the canonical books have survived[4] is
indicative of what would be an even lower chance that illustrated apocryphal materials
would have come down to us. As Weitzmann points out:

> Apocryphal texts have their peculiar difficulties. Like folk tales and fairy tales
> they evade the establishment of canonical text versions, and they undergo constant
> change and accretions. . . . While no illustrated Greek apocryphal manuscripts
> have survived, reflections in other languages suggest that they must once have
> been widespread and that only because they were not officially accepted were they
> circulated neither among the learned upper classes around the court nor among
> the monasteries, i.e. the two institutions in whose libraries illustrated as well as
> non-illustrated books had the best chances of survival.[5]

In view of the long history of the church's transmission of texts and the interac-
tion of these texts with each other, it would be unlikely that a particular image of
an apostle's deed or a cycle of such deeds was copied directly from a fifth-century illuminated apocryphal acts to a medieval church decoration or to a miniature. It would
be equally unlikely that the artists or patrons had in hand the 'original' texts of the

apocryphal acts as modern scholarship has reconstructed them. The rhetorical tales journeyed from text to text and interacted with oral folk tales. In addition, there were both intra- and inter-familial interactions of the iconic versions and the rhetorical versions of these narratives in this long history; these interactions are an integral part of the fuel mixture which powers *traditio*. The stories were excerpted from the acts into homilies, menologia, and liturgical texts (such as lectionaries which included readings for the saints' feast-days). There were collections of the aretalogical acts of Christian heroes. These stories were then reassembled into later 'acts of the apostles' which became extremely popular in the church: Pseudo-Abdias, Hegesippus, Pseudo-Melito, the *Acta Sanctorum*, and the like, and in what is perhaps the most popular compendium of these tales, Jacobus de Voragine's *Golden Legend*, which was published in the mid-thirteenth century. William Granger Ryan states that Abbé Roze has identified 130 such sources for the *Golden Legend*.[6] Among these sources are, of course, various versions of apocryphal acts and gospels. Each of these works has its own history; the result is a very complex history of tradition, and, unfortunately, this history has gaps many and wide.

The iconic images migrated as well, sometimes in concert with the rhetorical narratives and often under their own impetus. The family of iconic images traveled to wall, to manuscript, to glass bowl, to plate, to window, and they did so in diverse orders of migration. These images re-emerged in early medieval church decorations and in miniatures; sometimes those in charge of a monument's construction would employ the texts of a later recension of the 'acts' of an apostle or of a liturgical text derived from an 'acts' and, at the same time, use another church decoration, an ivory, an icon or a model book from an atelier as a model for the images themselves [see Figure 4.33].

The tradition both in words and pictures was thus both evolutionary and conservative. Each discrete story or episode in rhetoric and picture has its own itinerary, and students of these journeys are constantly attempting to trace them. The complexity of these interactions creates an historical narrative which is sublimely hypothetical in the case of virtually every image in both rhetoric and in pictorial representations. It is for this reason that we risk redundancy to repeat the general program of this study: we are not proposing to demonstrate the source of iconic versions of the apostle's acts, but to point out parallels between the acts in their very diverse pictorial and rhetorical versions. Above all, our purpose is to acquaint the reader with often unknown iconic narratives that from the beginning have been powerful in the church.

Portraits

In the case of Paul and Peter, we can affirm (see Chapter 5) that the iconography of their portraits began to become traditional during the Constantinian period. This affirmation does not hold as clearly true in the case of the remainder of the apostles. By the middle Byzantine period, however, there do appear to be traditions which have established the physiognomy of several of the apostles. Andrew usually has long gray and rumpled hair, Philip and Thomas are often shown as beardless youths, Bartholomew has brown, curly hair and a full, brown beard, and John the Evangelist is pictured as either an old man or a beardless, ascetic-looking youth.[7] It may well be, as Grabar points out, that the images derive from the fashion of Greco-Roman group portraiture: '. . . in principle all ages are represented, beginning with the old men and going down to the youngest, shown beardless. Thus Philip and Thomas as youths end the line of the twelve apostles.'[8]

Can we locate rhetorical parallels for the iconic portraits of other apostles as we can for Paul and, possibly, for Peter? There are few physical descriptions in early Christian rhetoric of any Christian hero or heroine. There is a rhetorical description of Bartholomew in *The Passion of Bartholomew*, which text, according to Elliott, may have originated in the fifth or sixth century.[9] However, the pictorial portraits of Bartholomew do not seem to parallel this description: '[h]e has black curly hair, white skin, large eyes, straight nose, his hair covers his ears, his beard long and grizzled . . . middle height.'[10]

Andrew is usually portrayed with white dishevelled hair and beard. There is no rhetorical equivalent of this iconic portrait. His extremely rumpled look, however, may refer to the story of Andrew's being dragged through the streets by his enemies (*Acts of Andrew and Matthias* 26, 28) and this may be reflected in his portraits [Text 6.A]. Two further examples of this portrait style may be mentioned – one is a sixth-century mosaic of the apostle in the Church of Panagia Kanakaria, Cyprus. According to Beckwith, this portrait is stylistically very close to those at Mount Sinai and S. Apollinare Nuovo, Ravenna. The apostle faces frontally with white dishevelled hair and beard.[11] The other is a fresco portrait in S. Maria Antiqua in Rome (eighth century) which bears these same characteristics.[12] That text and iconic art are parallel in this case is pure speculation on our part, if not wishful thinking.

6.A

The crowds ran to him, seized him, and said, 'What you have done to us we shall do to you.' They deliberated among themselves saying, 'How shall we kill him?' They said to each other, 'If we behead him, his death will not be agonizing for him.' Still others said, 'If we burn him with fire and give his body to feed our superiors, this death is not painful for him.'

Then one of them whom the devil had entered and possessed said to the crowd, 'As he has done to us, let us do to him. Let us invent the most heinous tortures for him. Let us go, tie a rope around his neck, and drag him through all the avenues and streets of the city each day until he dies. When he is dead, let us divide his body for all of the citizens and distribute for their food.'

Hearing this, the crowds did as he had said to them. They tied a rope around his neck and dragged him through all the avenues and streets of the city. As the blessed Andrew was dragged, his flesh stuck to the ground, and his blood flowed on the ground like water. When evening came, they threw him into the prison and tied his hands behind him. He was utterly exhausted.

Early the next morning, they brought him out again, tied a rope around his neck, and dragged him about. Again his flesh stuck to the ground and his blood flowed. The blessed Andrew wept and prayed, 'My Lord Jesus Christ, come and see what they have done to me your servant. But I endure because of your command which you commanded me when you said, "Do not respond in kind to their unbelief." Now Lord, observe how many tortures they bring upon me, for you, Lord, know human flesh. I know, Lord, that you are not far, from your servants and I do not dispute the command which you gave me. Otherwise, I would have made them and their city plunge into the abyss. But I shall never forsake your command which you commanded me, even to the point of death, because you, Lord, are my help. Only do not let the enemy mock me.'

As the blessed Andrew said these things, the devil was walking behind him saying to the crowds, 'Hit his mouth to shut him up!'

At nightfall they took Andrew, threw him again into the prison, tied his hands behind him, and left him again until the next day . . .

The next morning they again fetched Andrew, tied a rope around his neck, and dragged him. Again his flesh stuck to the earth, and his blood flowed on the ground like water. As he was dragged, the blessed Andrew wept, saying, 'Lord Jesus Christ, these tortures are enough; I am exhausted. Look at what the enemy and his demons have done to me. Remember, O Lord, that you spent three hours on the cross and you weakened, for you said "My Father, why have you forsaken me?" Look, Lord, for three days I am dragged around in the avenues and streets of this city. Lord, especially because you know that human flesh is weak, command my spirit to leave me, my Lord, so that at last I may attain rest. Lord, where are your words which you spoke to us to strengthen us, telling us, "If you walk with me, you will not lose one hair from your head?" Therefore, Lord, look and see that my flesh and the hairs of my head stick to the ground, for I have been dragged around in heinous tortures for three days, and you, my Lord, have not revealed yourself to me to fortify my heart. I am utterly exhausted.' The blessed Andrew said these things as he was dragged about.

The Acts of Andrew and Matthias 25–6, 28

There is a description of John the Evangelist in the *Acts of John*, in a narrative of Lycomedes' commissioning a portrait of the apostle, a painting which the apostle rejects (*Acts of John* 26–9). In the *Acts of John* 24, John raises Lycomedes from the dead. Lycomedes treats John as a divinity (an action of which John disapproves) and gets a painter to paint the apostle's portrait (*c.* 27), a 'crowned picture of an old man, and candlesticks and an altar before it.' John is given a mirror – it is evidently a sign of his ascetic nature that he has never previously looked at even a mirror-image of himself – and declares that the portrait is his likeness but 'the picture resembles me, child, but is not like me, only the image of my body.' (*c.* 28). At this point the text becomes obscure;[13] Elliott's reconstruction says 'if the painter . . . will paint me, he would now lack the colours given to you as well as tables and opportunity (?) and access (?) and carriage and form and age and youth and everything visible.'[14] The narrative is intended to make a theological point, and it is very consistent with the ascetic tendencies of the whole text of the *Acts of John.*

There is another description of John in a Syriac version of John's acts; he is described as 'a youth in his body but exalted beyond the whole garland of his brethren' (Syriac *The History of the Son of Zebedee*).[15] Whether John's early portraits, which show him sometimes as a bearded man and sometimes as a youth, depend upon the same traditions as these textual descriptions is again pure speculation. In the middle ages, some cycles of the life of John employ these two different images of the apostle to distinguish John prior to his exile to Patmos and his later missions after his return to Ephesus. This is not a consistent convention. In the *Paris Apocalypse* (Bibliothèque nationale, ms. fr. 403), John is bearded throughout.

Portraits of the evangelists composing their gospels are legion. They head up the illuminated manuscripts of the majority of 'their' gospels. This practice begins with some of the earliest illuminated gospels. John is customarily pictured, if he is not alone, with his legendary amanuensis, Prochoros [Figure 6.1]. Images of John's writing his gospel are readily recognizable. He has a long pointed white beard and relatively long white hair, with a receding hairline. His head is often cocked back over a shoulder toward an arc in heaven; he is listening to the *logos*. Prochoros, shown as a beardless youth, sits before him, writing down the dictation. The point of the iconic images is certainly congruent with that of the rhetorical descriptions of John; he is an ascetic youth and a wise theologian. There is enough shared in the texts and in the pictorial images to suggest that the iconic versions of John and the rhetorical descriptions reflect traditions which at least serve parallel purposes of their demonstrating the wide range of John's holy attributes: John is evangelist, theologian, ascetic saint, and martyr.

Iconographic types of other apostles did appear in both the East and the West. There appears to have been a standardization of these portraits by the so-called middle Byzantine period. But, with the exceptions we have already named, and, as we stated above, it is not clear as to what was the origin of these types.[16]

Narrative images

The emphasis of the church upon certain aretalogical deeds of the apostles and upon their martyrdom was the main component of an ecclesiastical filter through which the legends about the apostles passed. Passions of the apostles and collections of their miraculous deeds were the fuel of the church's progress in both the rhetorical and pictorial versions of liturgical praxis. The popularity of the cult of the martyrs was virtually always connected with the chief martyrs, the apostles and early saints who lived out the words of Jesus, 'Come, follow me.' Thus, when we begin to look at the earliest medieval cycles of the apostles' lives, a common pattern emerges. The apostle is called to follow Christ by his pursuit of a Christ-delivered mission; this calling always leads to violent contentions with the enemies of the faith, and these contentions result in the martyrdom of the saint. In many cases, it is the latter two categories which prevail in the extant images of the apostles. One unfortunate aspect of the apostles' enemies is that frequently they are depicted as Jews. Thus the anti-semitism

Figure 6.1 John the Evangelist and Prochoros. Manuscript illumination, eleventh century.
Monastery of Dionysiou, Mount Athos, Greece, Gospel Lectionary, cod. 587m, fol. 1vo.
Photograph: Ekdotike Athenon.

which is already strong in the church's early rhetoric is carried on and even heightened in the iconic versions of the narratives.

One of the most venerable of Christian art-works, the Church of San Marco in Venice, provides an entrance for us to consider the iconic deeds or 'acts' of the apostles. The church was built, in the basis of its present form, by about 1100 CE, and therefore San Marco contains in mosaic and other media some of the earliest examples of cycles and individual pictures of the acts of the apostles. The mosaics, the sculptured carvings in the ciborium columns and the icons on the famous altar piece, the Pala d'Oro, all contribute early examples of cycles of Jesus, the Virgin, and the lives of the apostles and evangelists.

In addition to San Marco's early cycles of the Life of the Virgin and of John the Evangelist (in the north dome; see p. 180), there is a series of scenes from the deeds of the apostles (on the north and south walls and vaults of the Cathedral); the series begins and ends on the outer nave walls.[17] The first series is comparatively late; its images were thoroughly reworked in the Baroque period, but they likely followed the themes of the medieval originals in most cases. Each image is inscribed; the plate or figure numbers are references to the images in Demus:[18]

1   Peter and Paul: (*Passion of SS. Peter and Paul*) (fig. 42) The scene shows Nero, enthroned on the left, Peter stands, pointing above where Simon Magus falls headlong, escorted by two demons. Paul, nimbed, kneels on Peter's left, facing him. On the right are the scenes of Peter's inverted crucifixion and Paul, about to be beheaded.

2   John the Evangelist: John is boiled in oil before the Porta Latina (*Acts of John in Rome*), Rome; he says his last mass; he enters his grave alive (fig. 39). These scenes are in addition to the scenes of the North vault, described below.

3   James Major (James the Great): James disputes with high priests (left); he is beheaded (right) (fig. 39). In both images, James is bearded and long-haired (Acts 12:1–2; Pseudo-Abdias, IV).[19]

4   Andrew: The apostle is crucified on the X-shaped cross (fig. 40) (*Acts of Andrew* 51) [Text 6.B]. Demus also hypothesizes that a scene of Andrew in dispute before Aegeates (Egeas) also existed.[20]

5   Thomas: Thomas is shown before King Gundaphorus; he is transfixed with a lance in India (fig. 40) (*Acts of Thomas* 17f., 168). Thomas is before the king; probably the image refers to his taking his fee for the palace he designed for Gundaphorus and giving the money to the poor. In the second image, on the right, an idol topples from its pedestal in the background, while Thomas in the right foreground is pierced through with a lance (not four, as in the text of the *Acts of Thomas*).

The second series of mosaics in San Marco is one which Demus entitles 'original (that is restored but still authentically medieval)':[21]

6   James Minor (James the Less): the Saint is pushed from the roof of the temple in Jerusalem; he is then beaten and killed with a fuller's club; he is buried (Pseudo-Abdias VI). The image at San Marco contains several of the versions of the James stories, including the attempt of some of the people to stone him. At the burial

6.B

Early in the morning, Aegeates summoned Andrew from prison and said to him, 'The time to complete my judgement against you has arrived, you stranger, alien to this present life, enemy of my home, and corrupter of my entire house. Why did you decide to burst into places alien to you and corrupt a wife who used to please me in every way and never slept with another man? She has convinced me that she now rejoices in you and your God. So enjoy my gifts!'

He commanded that Andrew be scourged with seven whips. Then he sent him off to be crucified and commanded the executioners not to impale him with nails but to stretch him out tied up with ropes, [and] to leave his knees uncut, supposing that by so doing he would punish Andrew even more cruelly.

This matter became known to everyone, for it was rumoured throughout Patras that the stranger, the righteous one, the man who possessed God, was being crucified by the impious Aegeates, even though he had done nothing improper.

The Acts of Andrew 51

---

      scene, James is tonsured – he is considered the first Bishop of Jerusalem (pl. 1, 8).

7   Philip: the Saint destroys the idol of Mars; he raises men poisoned by the breath of a dragon; the apostle is venerated; he is buried (Pseudo-Abdias X) (pl. 1, 8).

8   Bartholomew: the Saint is shown preaching; he is flayed (Ps-Abdias VIII). The Greek version has Bartholomew flayed (pl. 1, 79).

9   Matthew: Matthew baptizes the king of Ethiopia and his family; he is killed with a sword while he celebrates mass (*Passion of Matthew*) (pl. 1, 80).

10   Simon: the scene shows Simon pointing upward toward the top of a column from which the idol of the sun falls. Soldiers, one with a sword drawn (an allusion to the Saint's martyrdom), face the Saint from the other side of the column (*Passion of Simon and Jude*) (pl. 1, 361).

11   Jude (Thaddeus): This scene is a mirror-image of the Simon mosaic (pl. 1, 362).

Each of these images illustrates the mission, with the apostle's contending against the adversaries of the faith and with an emphasis upon the martyrdom and/or the burial of the apostle. We have also seen this pattern in respect to Paul, Thecla and Peter. The mosaics in San Marco are a useful example of the selectively reduced iconic versions of the acts of the apostles. Says Otto Demus, who has written definitively on San Marco's decoration:

The model [of these series] was not an Acts [by this Demus means the Lucan Acts] source but must have illustrated a menologion or synaxarion [Eastern liturgical books containing saints' lives] *based on apocryphal sources*, or else illustrations of a specific collection of apostles' legends.[22]

Such models would have derived from works such as *The Passion of Philip* and *The Passion of Simon and Jude*, among other sources. But they undoubtedly came to Venice by way of the sources which Demus indicates; the images were already set in their iconography by the time they appear in the menologia and liturgical texts.[23] The settling of this iconography probably began with illustrated apocryphal acts, in some form. The rhetorical acts and martyrdoms which were illustrated ultimately, through a number of recensions, sprang from the legends, oral and written, which the early church produced about these heroes of the faith.

The images demonstrate that they both followed the trail of the texts' evolution and, at the same time, struck out on their own. Although the iconography of the images appears to have been fixed early, both in the East and the West, the scenes migrated, as we have pointed out previously, to church decorations, to lives of the saints and to various liturgical books. The iconography of the early church worked under a rule of conservatism, but the location of the pictures was under constant change and revision.

John the Evangelist (the theologian)

In the north dome of San Marco, the iconic life of an apostle in more full form first appears to us in the cycle of John the Evangelist. The images of John's acts are among the finest mosaics in the church, and they represent, with few alterations, their early twelfth-century origin. The cycle contains the following scenes: (1) In the center, John, as a bearded elderly man, nimbed, stands orans in a frontal position. The other scenes are arranged in a ring around the portrait of John. (2) John, with his right hand outstretched, raises Drusiana, who is named, center, on a litter. On the right, there are witnesses to the scene, three visible and three with only the top of their heads visible (*Acts of John* 80). (3) John raises Statheus (Stachys; Stacteus). John is on the left, bearded, an old man, with his right hand outstretched toward a litter upon which Statheus lies, wrapped in grave cerements. Statheus' mother kneels behind the litter, her hands outstretched toward John. On the right stands a group of six witnesses (*Virtutes Iohannis* VII[24]) [Text 6.C]. (4) John fells the temple of Artemis, whose chief priest is Aristodemus.[25] John is on the left, bearded, nimbed. The temple is center, its top falling [Text 6.D]. There are again witnesses as in the previous scenes (*Acts of John* 37–47; *Virtutes Iohannis* VIII. 5). John is on the left, drinking the poison cup [Text 6.E]. Aristodemus is on the right; two criminals drop dead in the center. (6) John is on the right, nimbed, bearded, his right hand outstretched. Aristodemus and witnesses are on the left. Two criminals arise in the center (*Virtutes Iohannis* VIIIff.). Cycles of John's deeds which feature the saint facing frontally, often orans, and then accompanied by scenes of his acts evidently existed earlier, for example in the Chapel of John VII, in Rome (previously they were in St Peter in Rome). These mosaics have been lost; they are known by drawings.[26]

6.C

While the apostle John was speaking, behold there was brought to him by his widowed mother a young man who thirty days before had married a wife. And all the people who were waiting upon the burial came with the widowed mother and cast themselves at the apostle's feet with groans, weeping, and mourning, and besought him that in the name of his God he would raise up this young man as he had done with Drusiana. And there was such great weeping that the apostle himself could hardly refrain from crying and tears. He therefore cast himself down in prayer and wept a long time; and rising from prayer he spread his hands to heaven and, for a long period prayed within himself. And when he had so done three times, he commanded the body which was swathed to be loosed, and said, 'Young Stacteus who for love of your flesh have quickly lost your soul, youth which knew not your creator, nor perceived the Saviour of men, and were ignorant of your true friend, and therefore fell into the snare of the worst enemy: behold, I have poured out tears and prayers to my Lord for your ignorance, that you may rise from the dead, the bands of death being loosed, and declare to these two, to Atticus and Eugenius, what great glory they have lost, and what great punishment they have incurred.' Then Stacteus arose and worshipped the apostle.

Pseudo-Abdias, Virtutes Iohannis 7

The Johannine cycle on the dome of San Marco is from the Ephesian period of the saint's life, that is, after he has returned from exile in Patmos. Their style is a neatly blended mixture of the Byzantine and Western styles of decoration.[27] This leads Demus to suggest that the exemplar of the cycle was an Ephesian church, perhaps a 'templon beam.'[28]

A charming twelfth-century cycle of selected illustrations of John's acts is on a single leaf preserved from a Gospel Book of the Abbot Wedricus (Metz ms. 1151) which was destroyed in World War II [Figure 6.2]. The leaf is now in Avesnes-sur-Helpe, library of the Société archéologique et historique. The scenes in this mini-cycle are from John's life prior to his exile to Patmos. John is seated, writing in the center zone. The image has eight medallions, four on the corners and two on each frame. The medallions in the top center frame and bottom center frame are smaller than the others. The corner medallions carry scenes of the life of John. From upper left corner, clockwise, (1) John before Domitian. Domitian is left, crowned, enthroned, with a sword in his left hand, his right hand points admonishingly toward John, who is on the right. John is nimbed in gold, beardless, facing Domitian. John is held by a bearded man in red (to far right) and a beardless man partially hidden behind John. (2) A Hand of God extends into the center zone, holding a dove which is whispering in John's ear as he writes. (3) Unidentified. John, nimbed and beardless, steps to the right into what appears to be green water (?); he pushes aside a blue curtain with his left hand, in his

6.D

And John answered them, 'If you do not wish to die, let me convince you of your idolatry. And why? So that you may desist from your old error. Be now converted by my God or I will die at the hands of your goddess. For I will pray in your presence to my God, and ask him to have mercy upon you.'

After these words he prayed, 'God, who are God above all so-called gods, who to this day have been despised at Ephesus, you induced me to come to this place, which I never had in view. You have abrogated every form of worship through conversion to you. In your name every idol, every demon, and every unclean spirit is banished. May the deity of this place, which has deceived so many, now also give way to your name, and thus show your mercy on this place! For they walk in error.'

And with these words of John the altar of Artemis suddenly split into many parts, and the oblations put up in the temple suddenly fell to the ground, and its glory broke, and so did more than seven of the idols. And half of the temple fell down, so that when the roof came down, the priest also was killed at one stroke. And the people of the Ephesians cried, 'There is only one God, that of John, only one God who has compassion for us; for you alone are God; now we have become converted, since we saw your miraculous deeds. Have mercy upon us, God, according to your will, and deliver us from our great error.'

The Acts of John 40–2

right hand is a book. Behind John is the gray-bearded man dressed in red. A plant grows up on the right. Is this John in the bathhouse (?) (*Syriac History of John*; *Acts of John Prochorus*).[29] (4) The Abbot Wedricus, in the medallion, holds out to John, in the center frame, the inkwell into which John dips his quill. (5) John, nimbed, dreams on Patmos. He reclines to the left, a book in his left hand, his head supported by his right hand. A Hand of God extends from the top of the medallion. A winged, nimbed angel hovers at the right. (6) Domitian, in a small medallion, crowned, enthroned, sits facing medallion seven on the left. (7) In this medallion, John sits, nude, nimbed, beardless, being boiled in oil. Two executioners flank the crucible containing John; the one to the left, gray-bearded, is dressed in red. The other to the right pumps a bellows into the fire under the cauldron. (8) The eighth medallion holds the symbol of John the Theologian, that is, an eagle, nimbed, perched on a scroll.[30]

Later iconic cycles of John's acts give us a more complete picture of the intersecting passage through the church's history of both the iconic and rhetorical *Acts of John*.[31] During the twelfth and thirteenth centuries John was arguably the most popular of the apostles; no other apostle has such a volume of stories and images.[32] The medieval period's emphasis upon ascetic devotion often combined with an other-worldly eroticism popular in the twelfth and thirteenth centuries helps to account for John's

6.E

And John turned to him and said, 'Tell me, Aristodemus, what can I do to take away the anger from your soul?' And Aristodemus said, 'If you want me to believe in your God, I will give you poison to drink, and if you drink it, and do not die, it will appear that your God is true.' The apostle answered, 'If you give me poison to drink, when I call on the name of my Lord it will not be able to harm me.' Aristodemus said again, 'First I wish you to see others drink it and die straightway, so that your heart may recoil from that cup.' And the blessed John said, 'I have told you already that I am prepared to drink it, that you may believe in the Lord Jesus Christ when you see me whole after drinking the cup of poison.' Aristodemus therefore went to the proconsul and asked of him two men who were to undergo the sentence of death. And when he had set them in the midst of the market-place before all the people, in the sight of the apostle he made them drink the poison; and as soon as they had drunk it, they gave up the ghost. Then Aristodemus turned to John and said, 'Hearken to me and depart from your teaching with which you call away the people from the worship of the gods; or take and drink this, that you may show that your God is almighty if, after you have drunk, you can remain whole.' Then the blessed John, with those who had drunk the poison lying dead, like a fearless and brave man took the cup and, making the sign of the cross, said, 'My God, and the Father of our Lord Jesus Christ, by whose word the heavens were established; unto whom all things are subject, whom all creation serves, whom all power obeys, fears, and trembles, when we call on you for succour; upon hearing whose name the serpent is still, the dragon flees, the viper is quiet, the frog is still and strengthless, the scorpion is quenched, the serpent vanquished, and the spider does no harm; in a word, all venomous things, and the fiercest reptiles and troublesome beasts are covered with darkness, and all roots hurtful to the health of men dry up. I say, quench the venom of this poison, put out its deadly workings, void it of the strength which it has in it, and grant in your sight to all these whom you have created eyes that they may see and ears that they may hear and a heart that they may understand your greatness.' And when he had said this, he armed his mouth and all his body with the sign of the cross and drank all that was in the cup. And after he had drunk, he said, 'I ask that those for whose sake I have drunk be turned to you, O Lord, and by your enlightening receive the salvation which is in you.' And when for the space of three hours the people saw that John was of a cheerful countenance, and that there was no sign at all of paleness or fear in him, they began to cry out with a loud voice, 'He whom John worships is the one true God.'

Pseudo-Abdias, *Virtutes Iohannis* 8

Figure 6.2 Life cycle of John the Evangelist. Manuscript illumination, *c.* 1147. Library of Société archéologique et historique, Avesnes-sur-Helpe, France, Gospel Book of Abbot Wedricus, Metz ms. 1151. Photograph: Library of Société archéologique et historique.

popularity. Another and very strong reason for the prolific appearance of Johannine images and rhetorical legends of this period is his association with the Apocalypse and its popularity during the period. About the end of the eighth century, Beatus of Libana produced in Spain a commentary, or gloss, on the Apocalypse of John. *The Beatus Apocalypse* was apparently created as a picture book; only illustrated copies of the book are extant.[33] There remain some thirty manuscripts of this Apocalypse, of which the earliest is in the Pierpont Morgan Library in New York (ms. 644). That so many copies of this work are extant is a tribute to its popularity. These works were produced until the early twelfth century (the latest being British Museum, Add. 11 695).[34] The images in these illuminated Apocalypses concentrated on scenes of the Apocalypse itself.[35]

The next phase of these illuminated Apocalypses was the appearance of versions in which there are included scenes from John's acts. Illustrated versions of the *Acts of John* and/or Pseudo-Abdias, *Virtutes Johannis* may have been the source of these additional images in the second stage. The Apocalypses containing pictures of John's deeds sometimes sandwiched the text or gloss of Revelation with scenes from the life of John the Evangelist. The arrangement of these manuscripts is to divide the life of John the Evangelist into three sections: (1) John's work before his exile to Patmos; (2) John on Patmos, receiving the revelation from God; this is followed by the text or gloss of the Apocalypse, with illustrations; (3) The life of John from his return to Ephesus until his assumption (metastasis). The earliest extant copy of these Apocalypses *cum* pictorial acts of John is the *Trinity College Apocalypse* (Trinity College, Cambridge, ms. R.16.2; thirteenth century – between 1230 and 1250 CE). In addition to its being the first extant apocalypse to include the scenes from the life of John, the *Trinity College Apocalypse* is an extremely handsome and sumptuously illuminated book. Another of these apocalypses, and one of the most charmingly illustrated of these thirteenth-century works, is the so-called *Paris Apocalypse* (Paris, Bibliothèque nationale, fr. 403).

John's popularity during the twelfth and thirteenth centuries appears to have triggered a revival of scenes from his 'acts' not only in manuscripts, but in other media as well. This revival is illustrated in stained glass as well as in the illuminated Apocalypses. At Notre Dame de Chartres, a large portion of a window (in the nave; the first window on the right after entering the Royal Portal, i.e. the west portal) is given over to scenes from John's deeds: Panel 4: Death of Statheus (and, presumably, his revivification is implied). Panel 5: John is sent into exile on Patmos. Panel 6: On Patmos, John writes the apocalypse. Panel 7: John before Aristodemus, the priest of the temple of Artemis. Panel 9: John raises Drusiana. Panel 10: John drinks the cup of poison. Panel 11: John and the philosopher, Craton. The scene shows the youths who are disciples of Craton crushing gems [Text 6.F]. Panel 12: John restores the gems. Panel 13: Christ appears to John. Panel 14: John changes the sticks to gold and the stones into precious gems. Panel 15: Youths hold the gems and the sticks converted to gold. Panel 16: John, ascension; metastasis. John gets ready to be taken to God. John is in his grave, looking up to the heavens. Panels 17, 18: Two angels pay John homage. The window follows the order of the Feast of St John, December 27.[36]

Other thirteenth-century windows which are testaments to the popularity of John in that century are at the Church of St-Julien-du-Sault,[37] and the Cathedral at Bourges.

At the Cathedral of St-Etienne, Auxerre there is a window devoted to John and the Apocalypse, in which 'the union of the Evangelist with a detailed account of the Apocalyptic vision therefore must be related to manuscript painting.'[38] At Troyes, in the Cathedral, there is also a window devoted to the life of John.[39]

There are few or no narrative images of John extant before the late Carolingian or early medieval periods, with the exception of his appearance at the crucifixion. There he appears both as a beardless youth and as an old man. His presence at the cruci-fixion is based on a canonical reference. However, his presence at Jesus' death is also reinforced by the narratives which assume that John cared for the Virgin until her death, as in the *Transitus Mariae*. A ninth-century fresco in the Church of S. Maria Egiziaca, formerly the Temple of Fortuna Virilis, shows John greeting the apostles at the door of the Virgin's house.[40]

The iconic 'Acts of John' as handed down in the *Trinity College Apocalypse* and in thirteenth-century stained glass differs from reconstructed texts of the rhetorical *Acts*

6.F

Now on the next day Craton, a philosopher, proclaimed in the marketplace that he would give an example of the contempt of riches; and the spectacle was in this manner. He persuaded two young men, the richest of the city, who were brothers, to spend their whole inheritance and each of them buy a jewel, and these they broke in pieces publicly in the sight of the people. And while they were doing this, it happened by chance that the apostle passed by. And calling Craton, the philosopher, to him, he said, 'That is a foolish despising of the world which is raised by the mouths of men, but long ago condemned by the judgement of God. For as that is a vain medicine whereby the disease is not extirpated, so is it a vain teaching by which the faults of souls and of conduct are not cured. But indeed my master taught a youth who desired to attain to eternal life, in these words, saying that if he would be perfect, he should sell all his goods and give to the poor, and so doing he would gain treasure in heaven and find the life that has no ending.' And Craton said to him, 'Here the fruit of covetousness is set forth in the midst of men, and has been broken to pieces. But if God is indeed your master and wills that the sum of the price of these jewels should be given to the poor, cause the gems to be restored whole, that what I have done for the praise of men you may do for the glory of him whom you call your master.' Then the blessed John gathered together the fragments of the gems and, holding them in his hands, lifted up his eyes to heaven and said, 'Lord Jesus Christ, to whom nothing is impossible; who, when the world was broken by the tree of concupiscence, restored it again in your faithfulness by the tree of the cross; who gave to one born blind the eyes which nature had denied him; who recalled Lazarus, dead and buried, after the fourth day to the light, and have subjected all diseases and all sicknesses to the word of your power – so also now do with these precious stones which these men, not knowing the fruits of almsgiving, have broken in pieces for the praise of men: recover them, Lord, now by the hands of your angels, that by their value the work of mercy may be fulfilled, and make these men believe in you the unbegotten Father through your only-begotten Son Jesus Christ our Lord, with the Holy Ghost the illuminator and sanctifier of the whole Church, world without end.' And when the faithful who were with the apostle answered and said 'Amen', the fragments of the gems were forthwith so joined that no sign at all that they had been broken remained visible. And Craton, the philosopher, with his disciples, seeing this, fell at the feet of the apostle and believed immediately and was baptized, with them all, and began himself publicly to preach the faith of our Lord Jesus Christ.

Those two brothers, therefore, of whom we spoke, sold the gems which they had bought by the sale of their inheritance and gave the price to the poor; and thereafter a very great multitude of believers began to be joined to the apostle.

Pseudo-Abdias, *Virtutes Iohannis* 5

---

of John. This variance is to be expected, given the migratory instincts of the stories in the rhetorical acts.

The pictorial version of the *Acts of John* follows the common pattern, which begins with the call of the apostle. This pattern emerges not only in the illustrated Apocalypses but in a series of stained-glass windows and frescoes: S. Francis at Assisi (the upper church), Notre Dame de Chartres, Bourges, Sainte-Chapelle in Paris, Tours, Troyes, Rheims, Lyons. The iconographic programs of each of these iconic 'lives of John' is outside our purpose. What follows is an outline of this life, extracted from the various cycles of painting, manuscript illumination and stained glass; we employ the general order of the *Trinity College Apocalypse*, with the exception of the first two images.

A reconstruction of the original rhetorical *Acts of John* is, as is the case with the other apocryphal acts, the result of years of textual criticism which takes under consideration a host of Johannine texts.[41] In the course of the search for the 'original' version of the *Acts of John* there has arisen a general agreement that the currently reconstructed version of the text is missing what would amount to about its first eighteen chapters (the system of chapters and verses is a relatively modern invention). There are several hypotheses as to what were the contents of this missing, opening section. Junod and Kaestli suggest, on the basis of John's prayer in *Acts of John* 113, that the missing portion contained a story of the apostle's calling, and that this calling was away from marriage and an ordinary life to a celibate apostleship[42] [Text 6.G]

A manuscript illumination may lend strength to Junod and Kaestli's hypothesis.[43] The image [Figure 6.3] is a hapax among John the Evangelist depictions. It illuminates a prayer to S. John in a twelfth-century copy of Anselm of Canterbury's *Prayers and Meditations* in the library of the Benedictine Monastery at Admont (Stiftsbibliothek, lat. 289, fol. 56ro).

6.G

'You who have preserved me also till the present hour pure to yourself, and free from intercourse with a woman; who, when I inclined in my youth to marry, appeared to me and said, "I am in need of you, John"; who prepared for me beforehand my bodily weakness; who, on the third occasion when I wished to marry, prevented me immediately, and said to me at the third hour on the seas, "John, if you were not mine, I would let you marry"; who for two years blinded me, letting me mourn and be dependent on you; who in the third year opened up the spiritual eyes, and give me back my visible eyes; who, when I regained my sight, disclosed to me the repugnance of gazing upon a woman; who delivered me from temporary show, and guided me to eternal life; who separated me from the foul madness of the flesh; who snatched me from bitter death, and presented me only to you.'

The Acts of John 113

Figure 6.3 John the Evangelist leaves his betrothed. Manuscript illumination, *c.* 1160. Bibliothek Benediktinerstift Admonten, lat. 289, fol. 56ro. Photograph: Cartlidge.

Figure 6.4 John the Evangelist warned by Christ away from marriage. Manuscript illumination. Imperial Public Library, St Petersburg, Russia, 'Les Louanges de Monseigneur St. Jean Evangeliste', vol. I, pl. XI. Photograph: Cartlidge.

The Admont image is constructed from two formerly discrete pictures. On the left John leaves his betrothed. It shows the apostle as he strides away to the right from a woman. He is clearly in haste and leaves her with determination. The woman stands frontally in a pose of resignation at his departure. On the right is an image which is the first extant in a large group of statues and paintings of depictions which were very popular in the south of what is now Germany: John the Evangelist resting on the bosom of Christ.[44] This scene has a long history; it began in a eucharistic context at scenes of the Last Supper.

John's celibacy is emphasized as well in a fifteenth-century manuscript in the imperial library of St Petersburg. This manuscript is in a facsimile edition, *Les Louanges de Monseigneur St. Jean Evangeliste* [Figure 6.4]. One illumination in the manuscript shows a couple, a man and a woman, close together on the left. On the right, Jesus is drawing John away from the scene. Although the theme is that expressed in the *Acts of John* 113, the iconography is totally different from that of the Admont miniature. Its style is much later than that of the Romanesque miniatures in the Admont Anselm, and the composition is a unified one. A third image which may be relevant to *Acts of John* 113 is a window in the choir of the parish church at Twycross in Leicestershire, England. It was originally in the Church of Ste-Chapelle, Paris. It shows John, trailed by a woman. Another image in the third lancet of that window has a man seated on a throne, his hand raised in greeting (Aristodemus?). Both of the Twycross images are iconographically enigmatic and cannot be definitely identified.[45]

Figure 6.5 Life cycle of John the Evangelist: John preaches; the baptism of Drusiana; John before the Magistrate of Ephesus. Manuscript illumination, *c.* 1230–50. Trinity College Library, Cambridge, ms. R.16.2, fol. 1ro. Photograph: Trinity College.

The Admont illumination, however, serves as an example of the possibility of the iconic version of an apocryphal acts aiding us in the reconstruction of the rhetorical text. It joins scenes of the baptism of Drusiana, an incident which also does not occur in the rhetorical acts, but which, as M. R. James has suggested, represents a lost bit of narrative from the *Acts of John*.[46]

We pick up the story of the picture version of the *Acts of John* in the images of the *Trinity College Apocalypse*. Each image contains a heading in which the scene is described, e.g. 'Ici cum sein Johan le evangeliste preche la parole deu as mescreaunz,' that is, 'Here is John the Evangelist preaching the Word of God to the sinners' (fol. 1ro). Within the images there are banners which further describe the content of the picture-story. The iconic story of John is therefore similar to a modern comic strip. The pictures are placed in a vertical row of three on each folio (with the exception of fols. 2ro and fol. 31vo). This arrangement, with the images clustered together and separated from the text of the acts is a good sign that their exemplars were originally an illustrated copy of some version of the *Acts of John*.

1   Folio 1ro [Figure 6.5] contains three scenes.

   (a) John preaches to the miscreants. John is usually shown preaching to a group, some of them dressed as royalty, with Drusiana (often named) present. Andronicus, who wishes to marry Drusiana, is one of the high-born characters. In the *Trinity College Apocalypse*, the figures are not named. The manuscript's placing John in the center, orans and separated from his audience by a peaked enclosure, is reminiscent of the mosaic on the north dome of San Marco. The more usual iconography has John standing at the left with his audience on the right, facing him, as in *The Paris Apocalypse* (Bibliothèque nationale, ms. fr. 403) *The de Quincy Apocalypse* (Lambeth Palace Library, 209, London) and *The Lenin Apocalypse* (Lenin Library, 1678).

There was a sixth-century mosaic of the apostle preaching and baptizing on the south wall of the Church of the Apostles, Constantinople.[47] According to Künstle, who gains his information from Wilpert,[48] there was a seventh-century cycle in the Church of San Giovanni Laterano. Virtually every pictorial life of John the Evangelist has an image of John's preaching. The baptism of Drusiana is also a popular scene. Examples of the scene are in Paris, Bib. Nat. fonds néerlandais 3; Paris, Bibliothèque nationale, fr. 403 (*The Paris Apocalypse*); Oxford, Bodleian Auct. D.4.17; Saint-Julien-du-Sault, Saint John the Evangelist window.

   (b) John baptizes Drusiana. This is a common scene in the iconic version of the *Acts of John*. It occurs in *The Paris Apocalypse* (Bibliothèque nationale, ms. fr. 403, fol. 1ro) and the Apocalypse at Eton College (ms. 177, Miscellany), among others. It does not, however, appear in the rhetorical form.[49] As we indicated above, the pictorial version of the Acts may indicate the contents of a missing text in the *Acts of John*[50] or of a legend about John and Drusiana which was lost or omitted when oral tradition took its written form.

   (c) John is brought before the provost of Ephesus who sends John to Domitian. At this point, the iconic version's most direct parallel is to Pseudo-Abdias, *Virtutes Iohannis* V–VIII.[51]

2 Folio 1vo [Figure 6.6]: Three scenes.

(a) John is taken to the ship/John is put on board the ship. This image has what appears to have been two discrete scenes that have been merged into one frame: (i) John's being taken away under guard from the provost; (ii) John put aboard the ship. Such conflation of scenes is not unusual. This double scene indicates the possibility of the iconic tradition's formerly presenting these narratives as discrete images. This, in turn, indicates a fully illuminated version of some form of the *Acts of John*. In the *Trinity College Apocalypse* the illumination of this scene demonstrates good humor as well as the honor of the apostle. As the apostle is placed on the ship by the provost's minions, one of the apostle's traveling companions is already seasick and hanging over the gunwale.

(b) John is brought before Domitian. The emperor sits on his throne as John is brought to him by a soldier and a prosecutor.

(c) John is put into boiling oil/John emerges from the boiling oil. Again, we have a double scene, with John depicted twice, once entering and once exiting his 'bath' of oil. In *The Paris Apocalypse*, John is shown in the cauldron and standing outside the boiling pot, being led away (ms. fr. 403, fol. 2). As is the case with fol. 1, this effect may represent the conflation of what were at one time discrete scenes, each with its own frame.

The scene of John's martyrdom by boiling oil is early in Christian rhetoric. Tertullian (*c.* 160–210 CE) knows the story (*de praescriptione* 36). This scene also occurs in a Western spin-off of the *Acts of John* (cf. also Ps.-Abdias V,2), namely, *The Acts of John in Rome*. Tertullian may have received the story by oral tradition, or, he may have knowledge of an early form of the *Acts of John*. In addition to the popularity of this scene in illuminated apocalypses and church windows, it is one of the few scenes which appears early in the church's art, at least according to some art historians. There was a fresco of this scene in the Church of S. Giovanni in Laterano, Rome, baptistery vestibule, old entrance hall. The fresco was lost but appears to have been partially recorded by Barbarini (Biblioteca Vaticana, Barb. lat. 4423, fol. 18).[52] In the scene in S. Giovanni, John is depicted nude, nimbed, and being beaten by his arrestors. At the far left are a pair of scissors cutting John's hair (in a separate scene) as a humiliation before he is thrown in the cauldron of oil. Künstle believes this image to be part of a cycle and places it in the seventh century.[53] Kaftal assigns it to the twelfth century.[54] Both Künstle and Kaftal refer to Wilpert as their source for this image.[55] Waetzoldt, however, believes it to be an image of the martyrdom of S. Philomena.[56]

According to church tradition, John the Evangelist died a peaceful death. In the church, however, 'witness' (martyrdom) was a necessary attribute for sainthood; witness does not necessarily mean 'witness unto death.' So John's martyrdom before the Porta Latina became a necessary component of virtually every cycle of John's life and mission. The scene migrated to virtually every medium: glass (Bourges Cathedral, Joan of Arc Chapel; Lincoln Cathedral, South Aisle, East Window, 3a (Lafond nr. 37)); embroidery (Musée royal des beaux-arts, Brussels; Vestment (orphrey; embroidery: 1081–4; 1772)); psalters and martyrologies (Liégeoise Psalter, Pierpont Morgan Library,

Figure 6.6 Life cycle of John the Evangelist: John is taken to a ship, John boards the ship; John before the Emperor; John boiled in oil. Manuscript illumination, *c.* 1230–50. Trinity College Library, Cambridge, ms. R.16.2, fol. 1vo. Photograph: Trinity College.

ms. 183, fol. 12vo). Albrecht Dürer includes the scene in his illustrations of the Apocalypse (Bartsch, B.61).

3   Folio 2ro [Figure 6.7]: Two scenes.

    (a) Domitian exiles John to Patmos. As Domitian has had no success in his attempt to execute John, he decides to be rid of the apostle and exiles him to Patmos. In the first scene, John is being hustled by two captors away from Domitian's throne.

    (b) John is on the ship to Patmos.

Figure 6.7 Life cycle of John the Evangelist: John is exiled; John aboard ship. Manuscript illumination, *c.* 1230–50. Trinity College Library, Cambridge, ms. R.16.2, fol. 2ro. Photograph: Trinity College.

(In the *Trinity College Apocalypse* the scenes of the revelation to John and illustrations of the text of the Apocalypse occupy the central portion of the book.)

4 Folio 28ro [Figure 6.8]: Three scenes.

(a) The Emperor comes to a violent end. One of the most dramatic images in the *Trinity College Apocalypse*, the emperor is thoroughly dispatched.

(b) John, at the death of the Emperor, returns from his Patmos exile to the people of Ephesus. The scene shows John's disembarking from the ship to be greeted by the people.

(c) John meets the funeral procession of Drusiana, and he raises her from her pallet. In the *Acts of John* 80, the apostle raises Drusiana from her tomb and under a considerably different set of contextual circumstances. However, there appear to be legends about Drusiana which have been lost or misplaced.[57] This is a popular scene in medieval art. It occurs in virtually all of the church windows which we mentioned above, in other apocalypses, and in fresco cycles (such as that of Giotto in the Chapel Peruzzi, Church of S. Croce, in Florence).

5 Folio 28vo [Figure 6.9]: Three scenes.

(a) Craton preaches/John confronts Craton. The complex of stories of John and his engagement with the philosopher Craton are found in Pseudo-Abdias *Virtutes Iohannis* V–VIII,[58] and, in a different version, in the Irish traditions of the *Acts of John*.[59] In the *Trinity College Apocalypse*, on the left Craton oversees the destruction of gems to drive home his point that worldly riches are bad. On the right, John confronts Craton and tells him that the riches should have been given to the poor.

(b) Again, a double scene. John preaches to Craton and his disciples and, on the right, the philosopher and his followers are baptized. A discrete scene of John's baptizing Craton, of the early twelfth century, is on the baptismal font in the Church of S. Barthélemy, Liège. It is one of several scenes of Christian heroes (John the Baptist, Peter) baptizing. In the image, John baptizes Craton and in the apostle's hand is a book with an inscription from Matthew 28:19.

(c) On the left, the monies are given to the poor. On the right, John is preaching to two rich young men who are upset because the poor are living better than the formerly rich.

6 Folio 29ro [Figure 6.10]: Three scenes.

(a) The young men have brought a bundle of sticks (in the Irish *Acts of John* II, 12–13, it is hay) and pebbles. John turns the sticks into gold and the pebbles into precious gems.

(b) John raises a young man from the dead. On the right the young men who have the precious stones and gold are told by the raised youth that they have missed far greater riches in heaven.

(c) John tells these young men to repent.

Figure 6.8 Life cycle of John the Evangelist: the assassination of the Emperor; John arrives in Ephesus; John raises Drusiana. Manuscript illumination, *c.* 1230–50. Trinity College Library, Cambridge, ms. R.16.2, fol. 28ro. Photograph: Trinity College.

Figure 6.9 Life cycle of John the Evangelist: Craton preaches, John confronts Craton's disciples; John converts Craton and his disciples; he baptizes them. Manuscript illumination, *c.* 1230–50. Trinity College Library, Cambridge, ms. R.16.2, fol. 28vo. Photograph: Trinity College .

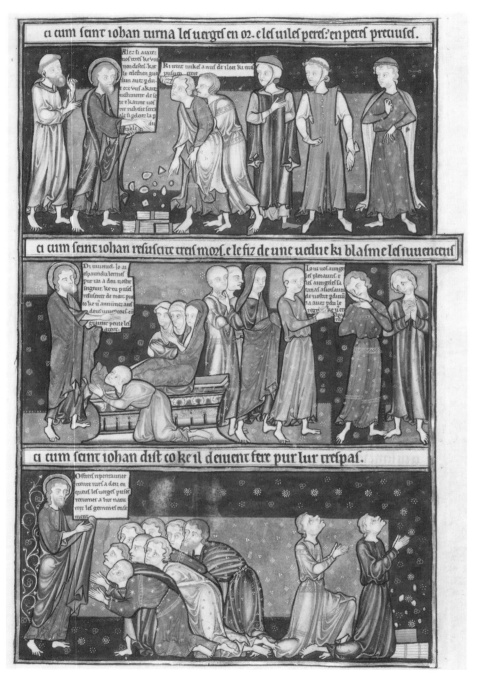

Figure 6.10 Life cycle of John the Evangelist: the miracle of pebbles and sticks; John raises a youth, the youth tells of the treasures in Heaven; John tells the youths to repent. Manuscript illumination, *c*. 1230–50. Trinity College Library, Cambridge, ms. R.16.2, fol. 29ro. Photograph: Trinity College.

Figure 6.11 Life cycle of John the Evangelist: the youths dispose of the sticks and pebbles; John
topples the idol of Mars; John confronts Aristodemus. Manuscript illumination,
c. 1230–50. Trinity College Library, Cambridge, ms. R.16.2, fol. 29vo.
Photograph: Trinity College.

7 Folio 29vo [Figure 6.11]: Three scenes, the first of which is a continuation of the miracle of the sticks and the pebbles; each with title inscription.

(a) John instructs the two youths to return the rods. On the right a youth carries a bundle of sticks on his shoulder, the other scatters pebbles at the foot of two trees.

(b) John enters into contest with Aristodemus, priest of the temple of Artemis. John destroys the temple of Artemis; he is shown pointing to the crumbling temple. The Aristodemus stories are preserved in Pseudo-Melito.[60]

(c) The next scenes are of the conversion of Aristodemus, who is the chief priest of Artemis. The story that follows concerns the poisoned drink which kills two criminals but does not harm John. This story was very popular, to the extent that John is often depicted in a portrait with a cup. In some of these images, the cup has been identified as a sign of John's saying Mass (Canterbury Cathedral, Nave W, Great West Window – in which John holds the cup and seems to pass his left hand over it). In other images, the cup is clearly that from the story of the confrontation with Aristodemus (Canterbury Cathedral, North-west Transept N. XVIII – in which the cup contains a serpent).

8 Folio 30ro [Figure 6.12]: Three scenes.

(a) On the left the two criminals drink the poison and drop dead. On the right, John has given Aristodemus his cloak which the priest places over the two dead men; they are instantly resuscitated. A particularly striking version of this scene of the criminals drinking the poison is in the Paris Apocalypse, in which the collapse of the criminals is an evocative composition [Figure 6.13].[61]

(b) Aristodemus is converted and kneels before John. On the right, Aristodemus is baptized. The baptism of Aristodemus occurs at Saint-Julien-du-Sault, Saint John the Evangelist window (thirteenth century); a manuscript illumination in Biblioteca Vaticana, lat. 8541; Passional, p. 23 (fourteenth century); the fresco cycle in the Church of S. Maria Donnaregina, Loffredo Chapel, Naples (fourteenth century).

(c) The beginning of the story of the robber youth. It is a very popular cycle in the iconic acts of John. In addition to the *Trinity College Apocalypse*, scenes appear on the cycle of the fourteenth-century vestment in the Musée royal des beaux-arts, Brussels (orphrey; embroidery: 1081–4; 1772), the early thirteenth-century window in Ste-Chapelle (apse, bay I, lancet 1) and in Biblioteca Vaticana, lat. 8541, Passional, p.24, an early fourteenth-century manuscript. The story appears as well in the Apocalypse in the British Museum add. 35166 and in numerous other locations. The story of the Robber Youth has a very early rhetorical anchor, that is, Clement of Alexandria's *Quis dives salvetur?* 42, in which Clement appears to know this story by the end of the second or beginning of the third century. In this scene, John brings the youth to the Bishop; the Bishop converts the youth; the Bishop baptizes the youth.

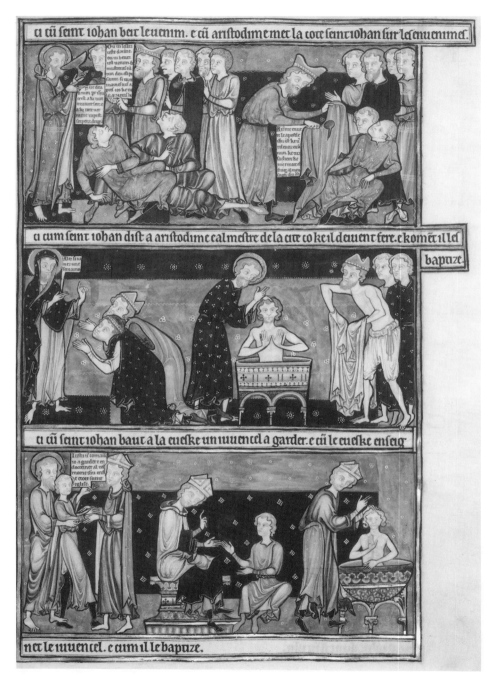

Figure 6.12 Life cycle of John the Evangelist: the episode of the poison cup; Aristodemus is converted and baptized; John converts the robber youth. Manuscript illumination, *c.* 1230–50. Trinity College Library, Cambridge ms. R.16.2, fol. 30ro. Photograph: Trinity College.

Figure 6.13 Life cycle of John the Evangelist: criminals drink from the poison cup; John's last Mass, John's Assumption. Manuscript illumination, thirteenth century. Bibliothèque nationale, Paris, ms. fr. 403, fol. 44vo. Photograph: Bibliothèque nationale.

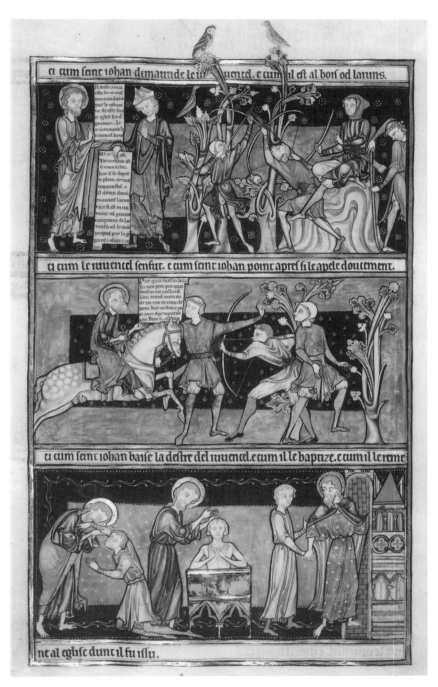

Figure 6.14 Life cycle of John the Evangelist: the Bishop informs John of the youth's recidivism, the youth robs and pillages; John pursues the robber youth; the youth repents and is baptized. Manuscript illumination, *c*. 1230–50. Trinity College Library, Cambridge, ms. R.16.2, fol. 30vo. Photograph: Trinity College.

Figure 6.15 Life cycle of John the Evangelist: the end of John's Life; he is presented with a church; his grave is dug. Manuscript illumination, *c*. 1230–50. Trinity College Library, Cambridge, ms. R.16.2, fol. 31ro. Photograph: Trinity College.

9 Folio 30vo [Figure 6.14]: Three scenes.

   (a) John, bearded, nimbed, with an inscription in hand faces the mitered bishop and asks to see the youth. The Bishop informs John that the youth's rehabilitation has failed; he returned to the other robbers. On the right is the robber band, with archers shooting at birds in trees; the youth, with quiver and bow is seated on mount.

   (b) John pursues the robber youth on horseback.

   (c) After he has recovered the back-sliding youth, John bearded, nimbed, baptizes the nude youth, who is in a font, orans. On the right, John bearded, with a decorated nimbus, leads a youth. He is bringing him back to the church. They are at the door of a church.

10 Folio 31ro; 31vo [Figure 6.15]: These last four scenes appear to be unfinished.

   (a) John kneels with the robber youth before an altar; second scene of top, John presents youth (on the left) with a key.

   (b) John kneels before Christ who gives to him a church with open doors – the apostles are present.

   (c) John stands before draped altar, celebrating his last Mass, and he delivers farewell speech – behind him is a fosser digging John's grave.

   (d) Folio 31vo [Figure 6.16]: The people stare at an empty grave. The scene is of John's translation to heaven. (*Metastasis* (*Acts of John* 115f.)) The taking up

Figure 6.16 Life cycle of John the Evangelist: John says his last Mass, John's grave is miraculously empty. Manuscript illumination, *c.* 1230–50. Trinity College Library, Cambridge, ms. R.16.2, fol. 31vo. Photograph: Trinity College.

of John to heaven is also, as one would expect, a popular scene in medieval art. The image allows for both rhetorical and pictorial imagination. Giotto's fresco in the Church of S. Croce, Chapel Peruzzi, shows Christ leaning out of heaven with his arms outstretched to receive John, while two witnesses stare, puzzled, at the empty grave. In an eleventh-century fresco in the Old Lateran Palace, Rome, Oratory of St Gregory the Great, John lies in his grave while manna flows from it.[62] In a fifteenth-century fresco by Vincenzo Foppa in the Oratorio di S. Maria di Castello, Savona, Italy, John is in the center, nimbed, kneeling with his hands folded in prayer. He ascends from his coffin, surrounded by misty clouds. Rays of light stream out of the coffin.[63]

The parable of the partridge

The apostles are depicted as wanderers; some of the episodes in rhetorical and iconic art also perigrinate. A fourteenth-century vestment in the Musée royal des beaux-arts in Brussels contains several of the common scenes which feature John:[64]

the apostle before Domitian and John's being boiled in oil;
the vision of Christ on the island of Patmos;
John's conversion of the Robber Youth; and
John, Aristodemus and the episode of the poison cup.

6.H

One day John was seated and a partridge flew through the air and was playing in the sand before him. John looked at this with amazement. And a priest, one of the hearers, came to John and saw the partridge playing before him. He was offended and said to himself, 'Such a great man rejoices over a partridge playing in the sand!' But John perceived his thoughts and said to him, 'It would be better if you, too, my son, would look at a partridge playing in the sand, and not contaminate yourself with disgraceful and impure acts. He who expects the repentance and conversion of all has brought you here for this purpose. For I have no need of a partridge playing in the sand. The partridge is your soul.'

When the old man heard this and perceived that he was not unknown, but that Christ's apostle had said everything which was in his heart, he fell to the ground and said, 'Now I know that God dwells in you, blessed John. And blessed is he who has not tempted God in you! He who tempts you, tempts him who cannot be tempted.' And he asked him to pray for him. And he instructed him, gave him commandments, dismissed him and praised God who is over all.

The Acts of John 56–7

On the vestment there is a more rare scene among the usual images, a depiction of the parable of the bow and the partridge [Text 6.H]. This scene occurs in rhetoric in de Voragine, *The Golden Legend*, but it also appears in one manuscript ('Q' – ms. Paris gr. 1468) of the *Acts of John*. Reconstructions of the text of the acts have the story in diverse places.[65]

We have mentioned above other illuminated Apocalypses which contain scenes paralleled in the *Acts of John*: the Paris, Lenin and de Quincy apocalypses. *The de Quincy Apocalypse* contains the following scenes: (1) fol. 40vo. Upper: John Preaching. Lower: The baptism of Drusiana. (2) fol. 41ro John is sent to Domitian. (3) fol. 41ro John boards a ship. (4) fol. 41vo. John before Domitian in two scenes. (5) fol. 42ro Upper: John is boiled in oil and exits the cauldron, in two scenes. (6) fol. 42vo. John boards a ship and arrives at Patmos, in two scenes. (7) fol. 43ro. John raises Drusiana and John confronts Craton and the youths with the hay and stones; this is in two scenes. (8) fol. 43vo. Upper: John is on the left, facing the two youths whose hay and stones have been turned to gold. Lower: John topples the idols. On the far right stands Aristodemus, hatted. (9) fol. 44ro. Upper: The two criminals have drunk from the poison cup. Lower: John drinks from the poison cup. (10) fol. 44vo. Upper: John, on the right, hands his cloak to Aristodemus. Lower: Aristodemus spreads the cloak over the two dead criminals. One criminal is rising, the other is still on the ground. (11) fol. 45ro. Upper: John before an altar, saying Mass. A Hand of God is over the altar, extending from an arc in heaven. Lower: John lies in his coffin with his hands raised in prayer. Two angels from an arc in heaven carry up John's soul in a napkin. Mourners are at the far left.[66]

M. R. James has supplied us with a list of Apocalypses with manuscript illuminations (both with and without scenes from the life of John). He also records some twenty-one of these works which have pictures from John's acts. Unfortunately, he does not list individual scenes. He also records Apocalypses which contain scenes from the iconic *Acts of John* in other media. An example of the latter are thirteenth-century sculpture scenes on the south-west portal of the Cathedral at Rheims and the scene of John's drinking from the poison cup in the window in the Cathedral of Auxerre.[67]

John the Evangelist and the Virgin

John the Evangelist is very closely associated with the Virgin Mary. In this case, there is a canonical impetus to the stories in which John cares for the Virgin after the crucifixion of her son (John 19:25–7 – under the hypothesis that the 'beloved disciple' is John the Evangelist). In the iconic and rhetorical versions of the Virgin's life after Jesus' resurrection and ascension, she stays with John. Several scenes reflect this association. A famous portrait of Peter [see Figure 5.3], which is indeed, in Weitzmann's words, 'one of the masterpieces' at Mount Sinai (Icon B.1), shows, above Peter, Christ Pantocrator, flanked by the Virgin and John. Weitzmann identifies the group's significance by a comparison with contemporary imperial portraits: 'Christ takes the place of the emperor . . . and the Virgin that of the empress . . . John that of the proconsul . . . The basic idea of the icon seems then to be that S. Peter holds the highest office under the reign of Christ and the Virgin, with the assistance of a co-administrator . . . (i.e. John the Evangelist).'[68]

In a scene in a thirteenth- or early fourteenth-century Miscellany (Cambridge University Library, St John's College, K.21. Miscellany, Fol. 61vo), John escorts the Virgin to the temple. There are four scenes on the page, each with a descriptive text in French: (1) Christ blesses the apostles; (2) the Ascension; (3) Pentecost; (4) John and the Virgin in the temple. This scene is illustrative of John's caring for the Virgin after Jesus' death and prior to her own.[69]

At the Church of St-Père de Chartres (St-Père de Chartres, window, nave, Bay 24) John presents the palm of martyrdom to the Virgin, 'The palm . . . was a rare attribute of St John during the transitional period, but never served any other apostle. It clearly derives from the apocryphal text of Pseudo-Melito, *De Transitu Beatae Mariae*, in which the palm, given by the angel Gabriel to the Virgin at the annunciation of her death, is carried by John in her funeral cortège'[70] [Text 6.I].

6.I

And behold, suddenly, while Saint John was preaching at Ephesus, on the Lord's day, at the third hour, there was a great earthquake, and a cloud raised him up and took him out of the sight of all and brought him before the door of the house where Mary was. And he knocked at the door and immediately went in. When Mary saw him she rejoiced greatly and said, 'I pray to you, my son John, remember the words of my Lord Jesus Christ wherewith he commended me to you. For behold, on the third day I am to depart out of the body and I have heard the counsels of the Jews who say, "Let us wait until the day when she who bore that deceiver shall die, and let us burn her *body* with fire."' So she called Saint John and took him into the secret part of the house and showed him her grave-clothes and that palm of light which she had received from the angel, and charged him to cause it to be borne before her bier when she should go to the tomb.

Pseudo-Melito, *The Assumption of the Virgin 4*

John greets the apostles when they come to the house at the death of the Virgin. This scene is in the Church of S. Maria Egiziaca. It is a ninth-century fresco. There are three paintings in the cycle, all of the Dormition: (1) Christ announces to the Virgin her impending death. (2) Three apostles are raised on clouds. (3) John the Evangelist greets the apostles before the Virgin's house.[71]

John and the Virgin are also connected in the stories of John's metastasis into heaven. An early fourteenth-century manuscript illumination in a Gradual in Zurich (Landesbibliothek, Gradual, fol. 161vo) depicts John's ascending in a mandorla, supported by Christ and the Virgin.

James Major and Josias

All of these scenes depicting James Major and Josias are paralleled only in *Pseudo-Abdias*. James Major is associated with Josias in the text, and the iconic life-cycle features the usual aretalogical deeds (confrontation with the authorities; contentions with demons; the conversion of an important person – Hermogenes) and martyrdom. In the case of James Major, he is crucified and beheaded (with Josias). James Minor (see below) is pushed off a temple and crucified.

The Baroque reworkings of the Martyrdom of James Major in San Marco parallel scenes which are in Acts 12:1–2. However, other images, which often team James and Josias, are paralleled only in Pseudo-Abdias. Those images which show James in a contest with the magicians Hermogenes and Philetus (Filetus) feature James alone. It is after he has converted the two magicians that the apostle converts the scribe, Josias, and they both go to their martyrdoms.

James Major and Josias are teamed in illustrations of the Pamplona Bibles (*c.* 1197). On the copy of the Pamplona Bible in Amiens [Figure 6.17],[72] James and Josias are falling, beheaded, their heads are descending behind them. Behind the apostles is an executioner with a sword in his right hand. On fol. 207ro, James has confronted two demons, sent to him by the magician, Hermogenes. In a two-zone miniature, the upper zone shows two winged demons pleading with James for mercy. In the lower zone is James' baptism of Josias, the scribe. Another set of scenes, from the fourteenth century, are in a polyptych in the Church of S. Silvestro, Venice, which shows James preaching; he stands in a pulpit. His preaching is under pressure; two men are tying nooses around his neck. The second scene shows James and Josias beheaded[73] [Text 6.J]. Again, these scenes are from Pseudo-Abdias and the *Golden Legend*, as are scenes in a fresco in the Basilica del Santo, Cappella di S. Giacomo in Padua: (1) Hermogenes the magician sends his disciple Philetus to debate with James. (2) James, leaning out from his position in a pulpit, debates with Philetus. (3) Hermogenes orders his demons to fetch James. (4) The demons, under James' command, instead bring Hermogenes to him. In this series, the demons turn against the magician, as they do in the text.[74]

Andrew and Matthias

Andrew and Matthias, as is the case with James Major and Josias, are linked in both rhetorical and pictorial art. In respect to the iconic versions of the acts of Andrew and of Matthias, their parallels in the texts of the earliest Andrew material (*Acts of Andrew*; *Acts of Andrew and Matthias*) are filtered down to us through the *Epitome* of Gregory (*Liber de Miraculis Beati Andreae Apostoli*) and several Byzantine texts.[75] This textual material is further and deeply affected by the sources which culminated in the mid-thirteenth century in the *Golden Legend*.

The textual tradition connects both Andrew and Matthias, although the major literature places its emphasis on Andrew. This is the case in the iconic versions as well. In the *Acts of Andrew and Matthias* 1, Matthias is called to the city of Myrmidonia, where his eyes are gouged out. His sight is miraculously restored by an epiphanic Christ, but Matthias is still condemned to death. Andrew is called upon to rescue him. This story is depicted in fresco in the Cathedral of Parma, although the frescoes appear to indicate that it is Andrew who restores Matthias' sight. This latter version

Figure 6.17 The Martyrdoms of James and Josias, with Andrew praying before a cross. Manuscript
  illumination, *c.* 1197. Bibliothèque municipale d'Amiens, ms. 108; Picture Bible-
  Vitae Sanctorum, fol. 208ro. Photograph: Bibliothèque municipale d'Amiens.

6.J

Abiathar, who was the high priest of that year, incited an uprising among the people, and put a rope around James' neck and had him brought before Herod Agrippa. At Herod's command he was led away to be beheaded. Along the road there lay a paralysed man who called out to James, begging him to cure him. James said to him, 'In the name of Jesus Christ, for whose faith I am led to execution, stand up cured and bless your Creator!' The man stood up and blessed the Lord.

The scribe who had put the rope around James' neck, and whose name was Josias, saw this, knelt at the apostle's feet, asked for his pardon, and requested that he be made a Christian. Observing this, Abiathar had him held and said to him, 'Unless you curse the name of Christ, you will be beheaded with James!' Josias answered, 'Cursed be you and all your days, and blessed be the name of the Lord Jesus Christ forever!' Abiathar ordered him to be punched and sent a messenger to Herod to obtain an order for his beheading. While the two were waiting to be executed, James asked the jailer for a jug of water. He then baptized Josias, and both of them had their heads struck off and thus achieved martyrdom.

Jacobus de Voragine, 'Saint James the Greater'
from *The Golden Legend*

may reflect the *Acts of Andrew and Matthias* 21, in which Andrew restores the sight of several men in prison [Text 6.K]. The fifteenth-century frescoes then abandon Matthias and concentrate on the acts of Andrew.[76] In fourteenth-century stained glass at the Chapel Goeweigerhof, in Stein an der Donau, it is Christ who heals Matthias before Andrew arrives.[77] This latter window is basically dedicated to Matthias; it depicts his martyrdom in which he is stoned and struck in the head with an axe.

A representative iconic cycle of Andrew's deeds is in a fourteenth-century Passional in the Vatican Library (Biblioteca Vaticana, Passional, lat. 8541, pp. 16–20). The cycle begins with Andrew's *vocatio* and extends to posthumous miracles. The cycle contains the following scenes, many of which are also found in earlier depictions: Page 16: (1) Andrew is called. (2) Andrew, decorated, is twice shown. Once he is in a barred window of prison (perhaps reflective of Gregory, *Epitome* 18; *Acts of Andrew and Matthias* 19–22, 26), his hand grasped by a saint or an angel; the second image of Andrew has him emerging from the portal of the prison, his arm grasped by a nimbed angel. (3) Andrew is beaten by a man with a club. (4) (Gregory, *Epitome* 12) Andrew is in a burning building. A youth has a vessel in his hand with which he miraculously puts out the fire [Text 6.L]. Page 17: (The following images are of the story of Sostratus, who is incestuously pursued by his mother (Gregory, *Epitome* 4)). (1) A judge sits on a throne. Andrew is on the left. A veiled woman, behind Sostratus is kneeling with hands raised. Sostratus is pointed to by his mother who is veiled and kneeling. (2) Andrew

6.K

Then Andrew looked into the middle of the prison and saw the prisoners naked and eating grass like dumb beasts. Andrew beat his breast and said to himself, 'O Andrew, look and see what they have done to people like you, how they nearly reduced them to the state of irrational beasts.'

Then Andrew began rebuking Satan saying to him, 'Woe to you, Devil, enemy of God and his angels. These wretches and strangers did you no harm, so why have you brought this punishment upon them? O rogue, how long will you war with the human race? From the beginning you caused Adam to be expelled from paradise. God caused him to sow a diet of grain on the earth, but you turned his bread on the table into stones. Later, you entered into the minds of the angels, made them to be defiled with women, and made their unruly sons giants, so that they devoured the people of the earth, until the Lord raged against them and brought a flood on them in order to obliterate every structure the Lord had made on the earth. But he did not obliterate his righteous one, Noah. Now you come to this city as well in order to make its residents eat humans and drink their blood so that they too might end up accursed and destroyed. For you assume that God will obliterate what he has moulded. Enemy! Have you not heard that God said, "I will never again bring a flood on the earth?" If any punishment is prepared, it is for retaliation against you.'

Andrew and Matthias then rose up and prayed, and after the prayer Andrew put his hands on the faces of the blind men in the prison, and immediately they received their sight. He also put his hand on their hearts, and their minds regained human consciousness. Then Andrew said to them, 'Stand up, go to the lower parts of the city, and you will find along the road a large fig tree. Sit under the fig tree and eat its fruit until I come to you. Should I delay coming there, you will find enough food for yourselves, for the fruit of the fig tree will not fail. No matter how much you eat, it will bear more fruit and feed you, just as the Lord commanded.'

The Acts of Andrew and Matthias 20–1

---

is right, while three soldiers place Sostratus in a sack in a stream. (3) Andrew is left, his hands raised toward an arc of heaven from which rays descend. Two angels, one wingless, remove the sack from the stream. Two veiled women crouch by the stream. (4) Andrew is center. Two men kneel and lift their hands beseeching Andrew. Before the saint are two horned devils and the corpse of the youth [Text 6.M].

Page 18: (1) The father of the child holds his hands to his face, and the veiled mother places her hands over her head. The child lies in right foreground, attacked by two demons. (2) Andrew is left, with a beardless man to his left. The father kneels before Andrew. In the background is a boy, his hands raised, on a canopied bed; above

6.L

At Thessalonica was a rich noble youth, Exuos, who came without his parents' knowledge and asked to be shown the way of truth. He was taught, and believed, and followed Andrew, taking no care of his worldly estate. The parents heard that he was at Philippi and tried to bribe him with gifts to leave Andrew. He said, 'Would that you had not these riches, then you would know the true God, and escape his wrath.' Andrew, too, came down from the third storey and preached to them, but in vain: he retired and shut the doors of the house. They gathered a band and came to burn the house, saying, 'Death to the son who has forsaken his parents', and brought torches, reeds, and faggots, and set the house on fire. It blazed up. Exuos took a bottle of water and prayed, 'Lord Jesus Christ, in whose hand is the nature of all the elements, who moisten the dry and dry the moist, cool the hot and kindle the quenched, put out this fire that your servants may not grow evil, but be more enkindled unto faith.' He sprinkled the flames and they died. 'He is become a sorcerer', said the parents, and got ladders, to climb up and kill them, but God blinded them. They remained obstinate, but one Lysimachus, a citizen, said, 'Why persevere? God is fighting for these. Desist, lest heavenly fire consume you.' They were touched, and said, 'This is the true God.' It was now night, but a light shone out, and they received sight. They went up and fell before Andrew and asked pardon, and their repentance made Lysimachus say, 'Truly Christ whom Andrew preaches is the Son of God.' All were converted except the youth's parents, who cursed him and went home again, leaving all their money to public uses. Fifty days after they suddenly died, and the citizens, who loved the youth, returned the property to him. He did not leave Andrew, but spent his income on the poor.

The Acts of Andrew from Gregory of Tours, *Epitome* 12

the bed in the corner is an arc of heaven, with rays coming forth. (3) (Gregory, *Epitome* 24) The story of the shipwreck. The vessel is shown above four drowning youths. Andrew leans over the head of one of the drowned, whom the apostle is resuscitating [Text 6.N].

Page 19: (*Acts of Andrew*; *Epitome* 36ff.) (1) Andrew baptizes Maximilla of Patras. Maximilla of Patras is in a font. (2) Andrew preaches against idolatry. Aegeates (Egeas) is present. (3) Andrew is imprisoned. (4) Andrew is beaten by soldiers who are flaying him.

Page 20: (*Acts of Andrew* 54–63; *Epitome* 36) (1) Andrew, Martyrdom. Andrew, nimbed, is kneeling before a cross. (2) Andrew is crucified. (3) Andrew is laid in his sarcophagus. (4) Andrew saves a cleric from a demon who has taken the form of a beautiful woman. (The miracle is a posthumous act of the apostle.)

6.M

A Christian lad named Sostratus came to Andrew privately and told him 'My mother cherishes a guilty passion for me: I have repulsed her, and she has gone to the proconsul to throw the guilt on me. I would rather die than expose her.' The officers came to fetch the boy, and Andrew prayed and went with him. The mother accused him. The proconsul bade him defend himself. He was silent, and so continued, until the proconsul retired to take counsel. The mother began to weep. Andrew said, 'Unhappy woman, you do not fear to cast your own guilt on your son.' She said to the proconsul, 'Ever since my son entertained his wicked wish he has been in constant company with this man.' The proconsul was enraged, ordered the lad to be sewn into the leather bag of parricides and drowned in the river, and Andrew to be imprisoned until his punishment should be devised. Andrew prayed, there was an earthquake, the proconsul fell from his seat, every one was prostrated, and the mother withered up and died. The proconsul fell at Andrew's feet praying for mercy. The earthquake and thunder ceased, and he healed those who had been hurt. The proconsul and his house were baptized.

The Acts of Andrew from
Gregory of Tours, *Epitome* 4

6.N

They sat down, with others, on the sand and Andrew taught. A corpse was thrown up by the sea near them. 'We must learn', said Andrew, 'what the enemy has done to him.' So he raise him, gave him a garment, and bade him tell his story. He said, 'I am the son of Sostratus, of Macedonia, lately come from Italy. On returning home I heard of a new teaching and set forth to find out about it. On the way here we were wrecked and all drowned.' And after some thought, he realized that Andrew was the man he sought, and fell at his feet and said, 'I know that you are the servant of the true God. I beseech you for my companions, that they also may be raised and know him.' Then Andrew instructed him, and thereafter prayed God to show the bodies of the other drowned men: thirty-nine were washed ashore, and all there prayed for them to be raised. Philopator, the youth, said, 'My father sent me here with a great sum. Now he is blaspheming God and his teaching. Let it not be so.' Andrew ordered the bodies to be collected, and said, 'Whom will you have raised first?' He said, 'Varus my foster-brother.' So he was first raised and then the other thirty-eight. Andrew prayed over each, and then told the brethren each to take the hand of one and say, 'Jesus Christ the son of the living God raises you.'

The Acts of Andrew from Gregory of Tours, *Epitome* 24

Another Andrew cycle is in the fresco decorations of the Cathedral at Parma (fifteenth century).[78] This series lays emphasis upon the contentions between the apostle and Aegeates (Egeas), whose wife, Maximilla, the apostle turns to celibacy (*Acts of Andrew*). This image represents the main contention in depictions of the apostle's struggle with Christianity's opponents, the contest which leads to Andrew's martyrdom. The Parma cycle also contains an image of the story of the old man, Nicolaus, who frequents a brothel and goes to Andrew for a cure for his lechery (Gregory, *Epitome* 28) [Text 6.O]. He receives the word from Andrew, after the apostle fasts and prays, that he has received grace. In addition, there are the stories of the drowned sailors (Gregory, *Epitome* 24).

In the series of frescoes in the Crypt of the Church of S. Lorenzo (thirteenth to fifteenth centuries?) in Sanseverino, the martyrdom of the Saint is followed by the story of Aegeates' punishment for his crucifying Andrew. After protests from the people about the execution of the apostle, the proconsul is strangled by a demon.[79] According to Gregory's *Epitome* 35–6, Aegeates is stunned by a speech that Andrew

---

6.O

An old man, Nicolaus, came with clothes rent and said, 'I am seventy-four years old and have always been a libertine. Three days ago I heard of your miracles and teaching. I thought I would turn over a new leaf, and then again that I would not. In this doubt, I took a Gospel and prayed God to make me forget my old devices. A few days after, I forgot the Gospel I had about me, and went to the brothel. The woman said, "Depart, old man, depart: you are an angel of God, do not touch me or approach me, for I see in you a great mystery." Then I remembered the Gospel, and am come to you for help and pardon.' Andrew discoursed for a long time against incontinence, and prayed from the sixth to the ninth hour. He rose and washed his face and said, 'I will not eat till I know if God will have mercy on this man.' A second day he fasted, but had no revelation until the fifth day, when he wept vehemently and said, 'Lord, we obtain mercy for the dead, and now this man that desires to know your greatness, why should he not return and you heal him?' A voice from heaven said, 'You have prevailed for the old man; but just as you are worn with fasting, let him also fast, that he may be saved.' And he called him and preached abstinence. On the sixth day he asked the brethren all to pray for Nicolaus, and they did. Andrew then took food and permitted the rest to eat. Nicolaus went home, gave away all his goods, and lived for six months on dry bread and water. Then he died. Andrew was not there, but in the place where he was he heard a voice, 'Andrew, Nicolaus for whom you interceded, is become mine.' And he told the brethren that Nicolaus was dead, and prayed that he might rest in peace.

The Acts of Andrew from Gregory of Tours, *Epitome* 28

6.P

After this a youth who followed the apostle sent for his mother to meet Andrew. She came, and after being instructed, begged him to come to their house, which was devastated by a great serpent. As Andrew approached, it hissed loudly and with raised head came to meet him; it was fifty cubits long: everyone fell down in fear. Andrew said, 'Hide your head, foul one, which you raised in the beginning for the hurt of mankind, and obey the servants of God, and die.' The serpent roared, and coiled about a great oak near by and vomited poison and blood and died.

The Acts of Andrew from
Gregory of Tours, *Epitome* 19

gives from the cross, Maximilla leaves him, he becomes despondent and kills himself (dying childless) by jumping from 'a high place.'

One of the earliest of the Andrew cycles is at Notre Dame de Chartres. According to a description in Houvet, the Andrew cycle begins at panel 16 of window XXXIII (according to the enumeration of Delaporte and Houvet, see note 36, above), center apsidal chapel.[80] (Window 16–17) Andrew heals a blind man (this may be Matthias). (18) He raises a dead man. (19) Gregory, *Epitome* 19. He kills a serpent [Text 6.P]. (20) A child dies from a serpent's bite; Andrew commands a woman to raise the child. (21) He tells of a dream announcing his death. (22) At a panel on the bottom of the window, Andrew declares innocent a man accused of a crime. (23) Andrew announces his death to his disciples. (24) Andrew's last Mass. (25) The proconsul Aegeates is seated on his throne, making judgment. (26) Andrew in prison. (27) Andrew appears before his accuser. (28) Andrew kneels before his cross. This clearly represents Andrew's address to the cross in the *Passion of Andrew* 54 [Text 6.Q]. (30) The people reproach Aegeates for his cruelty. (31) Andrew debates with Aegeates. (32) Andrew dead on the cross; two angels take his soul to heaven. (33) The punishment of Aegeates. (34–36) Christ with angels.

A particularly popular narrative image in the iconic story is that of the demons who become savage dogs and are quelled by Andrew (Gregory, *Epitome* 6) [Text 6.R]. The iconic version of the story is on a fresco panel which is now in the Kress Collection in New York; the panel is likely fifteenth-century and is attributed to Carlo Braccesco.[81] This scene appears in the frescoes at Parma and in a window of the Cathedral of Saint-Pierre, Troyes, Chapel of S. Nicolas, Bay IV. The window has an extensive set of scenes featuring Andrew.[82]

As we would expect, the most prolific of the stories about Andrew is his martyrdom. At San Marco, the scene is just above that of the Martyrdom of Thomas. Andrew is dressed in a loin-cloth and is clearly addressing the crowd and Aegeates. The image is one of the baroque reworkings of the medieval mosaics. The distinctive X-shaped cross (*crux decussata*) which is one of the identifying features of Andrew's martyrdom became, according to Demus, only a staple of Andrew's crucifixion in the late middle

6.Q

He left everyone, approached the cross, and spoke to it in a loud voice: 'Greetings, O cross! Greetings indeed! I know well that, though you have been weary for a long time, planted and awaiting me, now at last you can rest. I come to you, whom I have known. I recognize your mystery, why you were planted. So then, cross that is pure, radiant, full of life and light, receive me, I who have been weary for so long.'

The blessed one said these things standing on the ground looking intently at the cross. When he came to it, he commanded the brethren to summon the executioners, who were standing far away, to carry out their orders. When they came, they tied up only his feet and armpits, without nailing up his hands or feet nor severing his knees because of what the proconsul had commanded them, for Aegeates intended to torment him by being hung and being eaten by dogs if he were still alive at night.

The Acts of Andrew 54

6.R

After this he went to Nicaea where were seven devils living among the tombs by the wayside, who at noon stoned passers-by and had killed many. And all the city came out to meet Andrew with olive branches, crying, 'Our salvation is in you, O man of God.' When they had told him all, he said, 'If you believe in Christ you shall be freed.' They cried, 'We will.' He thanked God and commanded the demons to appear; they came in the form of dogs. Said he, 'These are your enemies: if you profess your belief that I can drive them out in Jesus' name, I will do so.' They cried out, 'We believe that Jesus Christ whom you preach is the Son of God.' Then he bade the demons go into dry and barren places and hurt no man till the last day. They roared and vanished. The apostle baptized the people and made Callistus bishop.

The Acts of Andrew from
Gregory of Tours, *Epitome* 6

ages.[83] The rhetorical version of Andrew's execution at the hands of an enraged Aegeates specifically states that Andrew was first scourged and badly wounded. Aegeates then had him tied to a pole[84] in order that the apostle's death would be more painful. It is from this pole or cross that Andrew addresses the cross and Aegeates in one of the most dramatic scenes in the story. In the *Très Riches Heures*, fol. 201ro, the scene is recreated [Figure 6.18]. Andrew is on the left, elevated on the X-shaped cross, tied to its beams. The proconsul is on a white horse, among the crowd, listening to Andrew's homily.

Figure 6.18 The Martyrdom of Andrew (above); Andrew is dragged and beaten. Manuscript illumination, fifteenth century. Musée Condé, Chantilly, France, *Très Riches Heures* du Duc de Berry, fol. 201ro. Photograph: Giraudon/Art Resource, NY.

The cycles at Sanseverino, Parma, and in the Vatican Passional depict a posthumous Andrew legend for which we have no early text. But the story is worth noting. It concerns a cleric who is approached at supper by a beautiful woman – a demon in disguise – who is bent upon the seduction of the bishop. Andrew appears and, in the nick of time, rescues the bishop from the seductive demon. This scene also appears in a thirteenth-century painting in the Musée d'arts décoratifs, Paris.

The fourteenth-century cycle of frescoes at Stein an der Donau deals mainly with Matthias. (1) Matthias is shown, nimbed and named; he is beardless. A group of figures is to the right of the apostle, who stands with a scroll in his hand. Matthias points to a hole into which figures are falling. One of the men standing on Matthias' right holds a sword. (2) Christ visits Matthias in prison, and he heals the apostle's blindness. Soldiers with swords are present in the prison cell. (3) The martyrdom of Matthias. The apostle is hit with an axe.[85]

Judas Thomas (the Twin)

In company with Peter, Judas Thomas (Judas the Twin) is better known by his 'nickname' than by his given name. As is the case in San Marco's mosaics, the emphasis of the Thomas cycles is upon his contentions which lead to his martyrdom. There is a Thomas window (thirteenth century) in the Church Notre Dame de Chartres which replicates the iconic version of the *Acts of Thomas* as it was received in the middle ages. The window's narrative begins with the most well-known attribute of Thomas and a staple scene in Thomas cycles – he doubts (John 20:24–9). It then continues the series with Thomas' 'acts,' beginning with the call of Thomas to his mission; Christ sells him into slavery in India, thus creating both a rhetorical and visual pun upon the apostle's being the *doulos* of Christ (as well as his twin). The series in the windows at Chartres follows this pattern: (1) Thomas, nimbed, kneeling, on left, touches a cross-nimbed Christ's side. (2) (*Acts of Thomas* 1–3) Jesus announces to Thomas that Thomas must go to India. Christ is right, cross-nimbed. Thomas is left, nimbed. (3) Christ sells Thomas into slavery, to Abban (Abbanes) a merchant of King Gundaphorus. (4) Thomas embarks for India with his new master, Abban. (5) (*Acts of Thomas* 4–8) The episode of the Wedding Feast. The travellers arrive at a town where the king celebrates the marriage of his daughter. (6) Thomas is invited to the feast where the servant hits the apostle. (7) The servant is eaten by a lion. (8) Thomas is presented by Abban as an architect to the king Gundaphorus. (9) (*Acts of Thomas* 17–24) The king is astonished by the plan of a palace (actually a heavenly palace) that Thomas presents to him; he rewards Thomas with a great deal of money to construct his palace. (10) The king goes on a journey. (11) While the king is absent, Thomas employs the monies to build churches and to give to the poor. (13) The king returns and puts Thomas in jail, intending to burn him alive. (14) The death of the king's brother, Gad, delays the project. (15–16) Four days later, the dead brother comes to life, goes to find his brother, and tells him that he has seen the heavenly palace. (17) Thomas, set free, preaches and converts the realm of Gundaphorus. (18) In another place, he refuses to worship false idols and the king, Misdaeus, forces Thomas to walk on red-hot stones. (19) He is put in a hot furnace, but refuses to recant his faith. (20) Thomas before an idol. (21) Thomas exorcises the demon of the idol. (22) The priest of the idol hits Thomas. (23) Thomas' sepulchre.

6.S

And as the apostle Thomas looked to the ground, one of the cupbearers stretched forth his hand and struck him. And the apostle, having raised his eyes, looked at the man who had struck him, saying, 'My God will forgive you for this wrong in the world to come, but in this world he will show his wonders, and I shall soon see that hand that struck me dragged along by dogs.'. . .

And when the flute-girl had finished her flute-playing, she sat down opposite Thomas and looked steadily at him. But he looked at no one at all neither did he pay attention to any one, but kept his eyes only on the ground, waiting until he could depart. And the cupbearer that struck him came down to the fountain to draw water. And there happened to be a lion there which killed him and left him lying in the place, after tearing his limbs asunder. And dogs immediately seized his limbs, among them a black dog, which grasped his right hand in his mouth and brought it to the place of the banquet.

When they all saw it they were frightened and inquired who was absent. And when it became known that it was the hand of the cupbearer that struck the apostle, the flute-girl broke her flute and threw it away, and went and sat at the feet of the apostle, saying, 'This man is either God or God's apostle. For I heard him say in Hebrew to the cupbearer, "I shall soon see the hand that struck me dragged about by dogs." This you have now seen. For just as he said, so also it has come to pass.'

The Acts of Thomas 6, 9

The iconic series of the *Acts of Thomas*, as is the case with many of the iconic versions of the apocryphal acts, has lost a great deal of the theological flavor of the earliest rhetorical versions; it has been catholicized, so to speak. The often-called 'gnostic flavor' of the *Acts of John* has evaporated in the high middle ages, but not, of course, its ascetic emphasis. So has the influence of the theology which one finds in the Wedding Hymn and the Hymn of the Pearl in the *Acts of Thomas*.[86] The wedding scene is one of the most depicted scenes of the *Acts of Thomas*, but the emphasis in the iconic form is now upon Thomas' contention with the servant at the wedding feast. The servant strikes Thomas, goes to fetch water, and is torn apart by lions. A dog then brings back the servant's arm and presents it to Thomas at the dinner table [Text 6.S]. This scene occurs in a number of venues: a fourteenth-century fresco at the Church of S. Croce, Sassoferrato; at the Cathedral of Bourges, window, outer ambulatory (in company with Thomas and King Gundaphorus and, in an insert, Thomas' arrival at India in the prow of a ship). At the wedding feast scene in a window at S. Gatien's, Tours, Thomas stands addressing the bridegroom. This is a scene which comes as close to the rhetorical version's emphasis upon the meaning of the wedding event as we have found. The oldest version of the wedding scene appears to be a metal

6.T

Thomas was suddenly brought to the Mount of Olives and saw the holy body being taken up, and cried out to Mary, 'Make your servant glad by your mercy, for now you go to heaven.' And the girdle with which the apostles had girt the body was thrown down to him; he took it and went to the valley of Josaphat. When he had greeted the apostles, Peter said, 'You were always unbelieving, and so the Lord has not suffered you to be at his mother's burial.' He smote his breast and said, 'I know it and I ask pardon of you all', and they all prayed for him. Then he said, 'Where have you laid her body?', and they pointed to the sepulchre. But he said, 'The holy body is not there.' Peter said, 'Formerly you would not believe in the resurrection of the Lord before you touched him: how should you believe us?' Thomas went on saying, 'It is not here.' Then in anger they went and took away the stone, and the body was not there; and they did not know what to say, being vanquished by Thomas's words. Then Thomas told them how he had been saying mass in India (and he still had on his priestly vestments), and how he had been brought to the Mount of Olives and seen the ascension of Mary and she had given him her girdle; and he showed it. They all rejoiced and asked his pardon, and he blessed them and said, 'Behold how good and pleasant a thing it is, brethren, to dwell together in unity.'

Joseph of Arimathea, *The Assumption of the Virgin* 17–21

vessel in the museum of the Franciscan Convent in Jerusalem, although the scenes are difficult to identify.

In addition to the wedding feast at the Church of S. Croce in Sassoferrato, there are scenes of Thomas' preaching before Mygdonia, and his baptizing of Vazan. There is also a scene of the apostle's martyrdom, after Thomas causes pagan idols and a temple to fall to the ground. The Pamplona Bibles contain a scene of Thomas' martyrdom; see Fig. 6.21.

Over half of the rhetorical *Acts of Thomas* is taken up with the story of Misdaeus and his wife Mygdonia, and Vazan. It is a section in which Mygdonia is the *Acts of Thomas'* equivalent of Thecla – but without the charm of the folk-tale aspects of the *Acts of Paul and Thecla*. The iconic version picks up the story, but without the rhetorical version's emphasis upon Mygdonia's turning from her husband to live a life of chastity and the *Acts of Thomas'* heavy emphasis upon chastity. At Chartres and Bourges, Thomas is shown preaching to Mygdonia. At Bourges, however, Mygdonia kneels, wimpled, before Thomas, while the King observes from his throne and a servant appears to be telling the King about Mygdonia's defection.

One Thomas scene is associated with the stories of the Life of the Virgin. In the Kaiser Friedrich Museum, Berlin, is a fourteenth-century Italian painting, attributed to Maso di Banco, in which the Virgin, during her assumption, gives her girdle to Thomas. The story is in the *Golden Legend* and *Transitus Mariae* of Pseudo-Joseph of Arimathea[87] [Text 6.T]. Thomas has arrived late at the Dormition, and, as she ascends, the Virgin gives him her girdle. According to Kaftal, the girdle is preserved in the Duomo at Prato.

James Minor (the Less)

In addition to the images of James Minor at San Marco (see p. 178–9, above), there is an early Byzantine version of James the Less' martyrdom in a Vatican Menologion (Biblioteca Vaticana, cod. gr. 1613, p. 131). It is an abbreviated version which shows only the clubbing. A Western version, which is likely the earliest extant version of the martyrdom is in the Regensburg Martyrologium, Clm. 13074 fol. 81–82 (*c.* 1170 CE).[88]

James and the Nag Hammadi *Apocryphon of James* (Codex I, 2)

The discovery of the Nag Hammadi library in Egypt has brought to the study of early Christian apocrypha a new dimension and field of study. There is a fifth-century ivory in the Bavarian National Museum, Munich [see Figure 4.36], which may parallel one of the scenes in a document of the Nag Hammadi codices, *The Apocryphon of James*. This apocryphon is a secret letter from a James, who is usually identified as James, the brother of Jesus, although the manuscript does not identify the author precisely.[89] In the document James describes that he and Peter were the only two disciples to witness Christ's ascension. The ivory contains two scenes. One is the women at the empty tomb, the early church's common symbol for the resurrection, the other is the ascension. In the ascension scene Jesus, on the top of a mountain, reaches up toward a Hand of God in an arc of heaven. There are only two disciples, Peter and James, present. Weitzmann suggests that this scene is an iconic parallel of the *Apocryphon of James*.[90] The scene is remarkable in that it shows only the two disciples present at the ascension. It differs markedly from other early ascension scenes in this respect; the usual iconography features the twelve (often with the Virgin present) observing Jesus' rising in a mandorla to the heavens. In addition, the juxtaposition of the empty tomb and the ascension is unusual. In the *Gospel of Peter* 13, the ascension of Jesus occurs immediately after the resurrection. The iconography of the Munich ivory suggests the same theological position.[91]

Philip

Philip's portrait occurs in a number of early churches, although one cannot find a text in Christian apocrypha which parallels the iconography in portraits. An unusual portrait of Philip is on a bread stamp of the late sixth or early seventh century. The apostle stands facing frontally, holding a scroll. The stamp is inscribed in reverse. It appears to have been used to imprint the bread offered to the faithful at the celebration of the saint's day.[92] The bust of the apostle is in the Church of Panagia Kanakaria, apse, arch soffit, among busts of other apostles and saints. The art work in the church is variously dated from the fifth through the seventh centuries.[93]

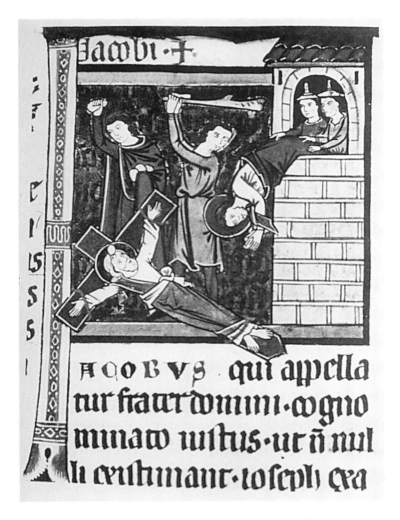

Figure 6.19 Martyrdoms of Philip and James. Manuscript illumination, thirteenth century.
Keble College Library, Oxford, Legendarium, fol. 73vo. Photograph: by permission of
the Warden and Fellows of Keble College Library, Oxford.

Depictions of Philip's deeds are few. The two most frequent are his martyrdom
and his confrontation with the dragon of Mars. He is often depicted with James Minor.
This is the case at San Marco and in a fourteenth-century Breviary in the Vatican
(Urb. lat. 603, fol. 382vo). In the Breviary, as at San Marco, Philip stands with his
hand raised toward a dragon. A second image pictures James Minor clubbed. A picture
in a twelfth-century Passional in Stuttgart (Landesbibliothek, Bibl. fols. 57, 56, 58.
Passional, I, fol. 49vo) depicts his confrontation with the dragon. The scene is in an
historiated initial P which is formed by the dragon. Philip is raising victims of the
serpent.[94] A thirteenth-century miniature at Keble College, Oxford (Legendarium, fol.
73vo) [Figure 6.19] shows Philip lying on the ground, tied to a cross. He is looking

up at James who is being pushed from a window. Two men, one with a club and the other with a rock are about to strike the apostle.[95]

Bartholomew

The preaching of Bartholomew among the mosaics at San Marco is in 'Upper India,' according to the inscription over the image. His martyrdom is depicted at San Marco as the famous flaying. Michelangelo portrays this form of martyrdom on the ceiling of the Sistine Chapel, and the scene appears as early as the eleventh century on the altarpiece from the Monastery of Stavelot, which is now in Brussels (Musée royal des beaux-arts, portable altar; inv. nr. 1580). An attempt to find a parallel text for this scene as the final martyrdom of the apostle is somewhat problematic. Many of the various rescensions of the tale speak of the flaying, but they continue with a number of different endings of the apostle: crucifixion (*Acts of Philip* 137 (Elliott, p. 518)), beheading (*Passion of Bartholomew* (Elliott, p. 520; see Migne, PL CX, col. 1164; CXX III, col. 185; CXXIV col. 394)), drowning, in which Bartholomew is put in a sack weighted with rocks and thrown into the sea (see an Ethiopic version in, E. A. Wallis Budge, *The Contendings of the Apostles* (London, 1901) pp. 108–10), or his being clubbed to death. An ancient Breviary sees the flaying as his last martyrdom.[96] According to Demus, the flaying is found only in Western versions.[97]

There are scenes of each of these martyrdoms. Arguably the most famous image of Bartholomew's flaying is in the Sistine Chapel. He holds his skin over his head, '[a]voiding the rays of the last judgment.'[98] A fourteenth-century polyptych in the Church of S. Bartolomeo del Fossato in Genoa combines the various martyrdoms into a sequence, in which, after the flaying, he continues to preach and is finally dispatched by beheading.[99] A scene of the apostle preaching, with his skin draped over the pulpit, is in the Church of S. Gottardo, in Cannobio, along with his performing exorcisms (one of the daughter of the king, Polymius), driving a demon from a temple, and his contention with pagan authorities.[100] Bartholomew confronts two demons in a scene from the Pamplona Bibles in Fig. 6.21.

In a thirteenth-century window of the upper basilica of S. Francis at Assisi, there are the following scenes: (1) Bartholomew, portrait, with two angels above his head. (2) Bartholomew healing a demoniac. Two men hold the demoniac, a devil escapes from his mouth. Bartholomew is on the right, pearl nimbed, with an attendant. (3) Bartholomew is summoned by the king. Two men on the left stand before Bartholomew, who is pearl nimbed. (4) A servant holds the arms of king Polymius' daughter. A devil escapes from her mouth. Bartholomew is right, nimbed, holding a scroll, and the king, Polymius of India, holds a sceptre. (5) Polymius is crowned, holding a sceptre and globe; Bartholomew is nimbed, holding a scroll. Both are before a building. (6) Bartholomew, nimbed, is beaten with clubs by the two executioners.

One group of stories about Bartholomew is difficult to trace back beyond medieval texts; the tales involve the birth of the apostle. These appear in a fourteenth-century painting, an altarpiece, which is now in the Galleria Nazionale delle Marche in Urbino.[101] It tells of the stories surrounding the birth of the apostle: (1) The birth of Bartholomew; his father, the King, is away with his army. The apostle's mother lies in a house, left, in a bed, cradling the infant. Several attendants. Outside, center and right, a messenger is sent with the news. He meets a devil. The messenger falls asleep and the devil steals the Queen's letter and substitutes a bogus letter. The false letter says the mother and child are ill, demon possessed, and should be burned. (2) The King receives the letter with puzzlement. He gives the messenger a note to the Queen announcing the King's victory in battle and his immediate return. On the way back, the messenger falls asleep and is given another false letter which gives the order to kill the Queen and Bartholomew. (3) Bartholomew exorcises King Polemius' daughter. (4) Bartholomew topples idols. (5) Bartholomew is flayed, while he is tied to a post.

Matthew

Matthew, as is the case with the other gospel-writing apostles, Mark and John, is often portrayed seated at a desk, with a pen in hand (Ayvali Kilise, Cappadocia, ninth century): The scene is in a 'Mission of Apostles' format. Three apostles, Matthew, John, Paul (left to right), nimbed and named, sit in thrones, in identical poses, each with an open codex on his left thigh. The book is inscribed with apostle's name (on verso) and opening of his writing on the recto. The names of the apostles are inscribed above their heads. An angel, nimbed, descends head-first (from upper right) over Paul's head; the angel carries a large medallion or plate.[102]

In thirteenth-century mosaics in San Marco, Venice, south aisle, Matthew is (1) baptizing King Egippus (Phulbanos ?). Matthew is right, white bearded, nimbed. He half bends over, to the left, his left hand is on the king's head. The king is crowned, nude, in a basin. Matthew's right hand is raised in blessing. To the left, under a canopy stand two female and three male figures. The scene is inscribed. (2) To the right of the Baptism scene is an image of Matthew's Martyrdom. Matthew is on the right, before an altar upon which is a book. He faces right. A man to Matthew's left is thrusting a sword into the apostle's neck. Two men again to the left; one is royal, the other a soldier.[103] These scenes appear to be parallel to an Ethiopic version of Matthew's deeds.[104]

In two scenes on the same page from the Pamplona Bibles (Bibliothèque de la Ville, 108, Pamplona Bibles, fol. 210vo) [Figure 6.20] we have a depiction of Matthew's martyrdom by beheading. In the upper zone, Matthew confronts magicians. Matthew, bearded and nimbed, on the left with his right hand raised, discourses with two male figures on the right. The lower zone is of Matthew's martyrdom. A crowned figure sits enthroned on the left. Matthew, kneeling falls forward beneath a chopping block. The apostle's head, bearded, not nimbed, lies under the block.[105]

Simon and Jude

The mosaics of San Marco which recall the acts and martyrdom of Simon and Jude are mirror images. This arrangement is natural; the *Passion of Simon and Jude*, found in Ps-Abdias, links the two. They fight as a team against the magicians in Persia and this contention leads to their martyrdom. Other collections of the martyrdoms of apostles arrange Simon and Jude so that they are together, if not mirrored images. In the twelfth-century Pamplona Bibles (Bibliothèque de la Ville, 108, Pamplona Bible, fol. 211vo)[106] [Figure 6.22] the two saints lie, their bodies crossed; they are pierced by four lances wielded by four men in a zone above them. The lances are thrust

Figure 6.20 Matthew argues with two magicians; Matthew is beheaded. Manuscript illumination, twelfth century. Bibliothèque municipale d'Amiens, ms. 108, Pamplona Bible, fol. 210vo. Photograph: Bibliothèque municipale d'Amiens.

Figure 6.21 Martyrdom of Thomas; Bartholomew confronts two demons. Manuscript illumination, twelfth century. Bibliothèque municipale d'Amiens, ms. 108, Pamplona Bible, fol. 209vo. Photograph: Bibliothèque municipale d'Amiens.

Figure 6.22 Martyrdoms of Simon and Jude. Manuscript illumination, twelfth century. Bibliothèque municipale d'Amiens, ms. 108, Pamplona Bible, fol. 211ro. Photograph: Bibliothèque municipale d'Amiens.

diagonally so that their shafts are also crossed. The composition of the scene is designed to tie together the two martyrs. Another twelfth-century piece, a portable altar from the Monastery of Stavelot, but now in the Musée royal des beaux-arts, Brussels (inv. nr. 1580), depicts the martyrdoms of all the apostles. Again, Simon and Jude are linked. Their martyrdoms are on an end of the altar, each saint in his own zone, but the zones are linked by a figure of Christ in an arc of heaven at the top of the border which divides the two side-by-side zones. Rays of light from the arch extend into each image. In this case, Simon is speared by three executioners and Jude is both struck by a sword and speared.

An earlier image of the martyrdoms of Simon and Jude differs from the twelfth-century presentations. A ninth-century (c. 880) homily of Gregory Nazianzus (Bibliothèque nationale, gr. 510, fol. 32vo) devotes the whole folio to a twelve-zone martyrology of the apostles. In this case, in the third rank of images, central zone, is the burial of Jude, with a priest leaning over him, carrying a censer. Simon, in the zone to the left, is shown crucified.

Demus lists other images of Simon and Jude; they are not numerous. In addition to gr. 510 in Paris, he mentions a Jerusalem Menologion (Saba 208, fol. 91vo) in which Simon is crucified. The Regensburg martyrology (Munich, Clm. 13074) shows the two beheaded before the king.[107]

Mark

Although apocryphal deeds of Mark are not well known, they do exist. De Santos Otero traces the earliest materials about Mark back to as early as the fourth century. There is a reference in Eusebius (*Historia Ecclesiastica* II. 16) of Mark's missionary work in Egypt, and one by Paulinus of Nola (353–431) which tells of Mark's conflict in Alexandria with the cult of Sarapis.[108] These elements appear in *The Martyrdom of the Holy Apostle and Evangelist Mark* which seems to have appeared in the seventh century and a later *Acts of Mark* (or *Life of Mark*).[109]

There are early images of Mark as an evangelist, that is, writing his gospel. As early as any is the frontispiece to the Gospel According to Mark in the *Rossano Gospels*, fol. 121ro Mark sits in an armchair; he is bearded and nimbed, busily writing on a scroll. The pen is in his right hand. Standing to the right, half-facing the evangelist, is a female figure in a blue cloak and veil. She is nimbed and with her right hand touches the scroll at the point where Mark is writing. In this image the female figure is not named; on the basis of other such figures in which the female is named 'Sophia,' we can assume that Sophia is intended here. The frame of the image is a geometrically abstract arch between two rounded columns. The composition 'ultimately goes back to that of an ancient poet or philosopher inspired by a Muse.'[110]

One of the earliest narrative images of Mark's acts is part of a series of five Mark-reliefs in ivory in the Castello Sforzesco, Milan [Figure 6.23].[111] This set is, in turn, one of fourteen in the Castello Sforzesco. The image is of Mark's healing of Anianos, a shoemaker of Alexandria who injured himself repairing Mark's sandals. S. Mark is suspended in front of a background of architecture; he is facing half-left, nimbed, bearded, a book with a cross on its cover in his left hand. His right hand reaches out to hold the hand of Anianos, whose left hand is wounded. According to the story, Anianos was converted and became the successor to Mark as bishop of Alexandria.

Figure 6.23
Mark heals Anianos. Ivory plaque, eighth century. Castello Sforzesco, Milan, Civiche raccolte d'arte applicata ed incisioni, Ivory 3. Photograph: Civiche raccolte d'arte applicata ed incisioni, Castello Sforzesco, Milan.

The ivories are objects of contention in art historical circles. They were first considered to be from a *cathedra* of the saint, a chair which was made in Alexandria in about 600 CE and presented to the cathedral of Grado (the place, where legend has it, that Peter first set foot in Italy). Vikan reports that there are some fourteen ivory reliefs which Graeven counted from the 'Chair of Grado.'[112] One, a very fine ivory, is of the Annunciation to the Virgin (seventh or eighth century), another is of the Nativity of Christ (seventh or eighth century).[113] It is very doubtful that these ivories were of a set or that the 'Chair of Grado' existed.

One would expect San Marco in Venice to feature the traditions about Mark the Evangelist, who, according to legend, was commissioned by Peter to write the Gospel According to Mark. San Marco does have a series of mosaics on the life of Mark, and on a large altarpiece in the cathedral, called the Pala d'Oro, there are also Marcan scenes. San Marco holds two Marcan cycles. The first, in the Chapel of S. Peter has been badly restored.[114] It deals with Mark's mission in Alexandria. The second is in the Chapel of S. Clemente (off the south choir), and it is devoted to the bringing of the relics of Mark to Venice. This second series 'illustrates a textual source that originated in and for Venice; the tradition was either unknown or unaccepted outside the region.'[115]

The first series, that in the Cappella di San Pietro, appears to go back to the earliest stories of Mark's acts. Working from drawings of the San Pietro mosaics before their final 'restoration' (better, perhaps, disfiguration) Demus reconstructs the following episodes from the ancient stories of Mark:

1 Mark is consecrated by S. Peter.
2 Mark heals and baptizes a leper (Athaulf) in Aquileia (two images).
3 Peter consecrates Hermagoras as Bishop, when Mark brings the convert to Peter.
4 Hermagoras is shown baptizing converts.
5 Mark preaches.
6 Mark baptizes.
7 Mark sails for Alexandria.
8 Mark heals the shoemaker, Anianos. The shoemaker was repairing Mark's sandals and hurt himself. Mark heals him, baptizes him and makes him his successor. This scene, then, is the most enduring of the Marcan story.
9 The martyrdom of Mark in Alexandria. Mark is dragged by a noose around his neck through the streets and finally clubbed to death. The San Marco version is abbreviated.[116]
10 Mark's burial, which, in San Marco, is apparently symbolic of the more drawn-out martyrdom in the rhetorical version.

The second series of Marcan acts is in the Chapel of S. Clemente at San Marco. It narrates the Venetian enterprise to bring Mark's remains to Venice. Such ad hoc narratives are not unusual additions to the basic apostolic acts. The Marcan story at San Marco is as follows:

1 Mark's body is exhumed from its tomb.
2 The relics are carried away.
3 Muslims carefully examine the relics.
4 The vessel sails away from Alexandria.
5 Mark saves the ship from its foundering on a reef.
6 The ship arrives in Venice.
7 The relics are received in Venice by the doge, the clergy and the people.[117]

The series in the S. Clemente chapel is paralleled by legends which are local to Venice and which are not as ancient as the legends connected with the first series. We thus have at San Marco an extension of the original Marcan legends by the interests of Venice.

Undoubtedly one of the most familiar scenes from the legends of S. Mark is in the *Très Riches Heures* of the Duc de Berry, one of the most famous Books of Hours in Christian art. The image is of the martyrdom of the saint in Alexandria. He lies before an entrance to a church after he has been dragged through the streets and clubbed (fol. 19vo) [Figure 6.24].

Concluding remarks

When the pictorial versions of the apostle's deeds emerged in force in the twelfth century, it is likely that they had resided in the church's tradition from pre-Carolingian times in the West and in the pre-iconoclastic era in the East. The images reappeared when the popularity of certain apostles and strong theological trends which favored certain of the apostles met with the growing wealth and power of the medieval period. The combination produced manuscript illuminations and decorations for great churches, many of which were the product of a revived aesthetic impetus in post-iconoclastic Constantinople.[118] Just as is the relatively clear case with the cycles of John the Evangelist, we can apply this schema of the other apostles' iconic cycles. At San Marco, as Demus points out, scenes from the lives of the saints seem to have derived their order and form from sacramentaries and menologia.[119] In a manner similar to the way in which the Genesis scenes of San Marco migrated from the so-called 'Cotton Genesis' to the walls of the church, the cycles of the lives of the saints initially travelled from illuminated manuscripts to the windows and walls of the great churches of the period.

When we deal with the iconic lives of the saints in the Romanesque and Gothic periods, we get glimpses into early Christian art, but they are glimpses colored by the filters of the medieval church's particular theological interests. That so few of these manuscripts of the fourth through the eleventh centuries have survived (most, perhaps, meeting the fate of the Cotton Genesis, that is, an unfortunate fire) is one of the great aesthetic tragedies of our history. That many libraries have recently begun to catalog the illuminations on their manuscript holdings will undoubtedly strengthen our knowledge of early Christian pictorial ventures.

To the modern reader familiar with the rhetorical versions of the apostles, the iconic versions discussed in this chapter may appear to be drastically diminished in scope (with the possible exception of that of S. John), both in terms of their content and in their seeming failure to represent the varieties of theology which have made, in our modern world, an exciting part of the study of the Christian apocrypha. There are episodes which seem to beg for illumination which are either not extant or not yet discovered: Thomas' confrontation with the wild asses and Philip's story of the leopard and the kid, for example. One must remember, however, that the early Christian apocrypha as we have them in modern editions are modern constructions from varieties of manuscript traditions of each apocryphon; these manuscript traditions are witness to the tendency of the 'original' versions of the apocrypha to form extracts, to add traditions and to migrate to ecclesiastically useful forms such as liturgies, lectionaries, homilies and menologia. In the case of the acts of the apostles, it was undoubtedly ecclesiastical concerns with the martyrdom of the apostles which contributed to the eventual weeding out of such scenes. In addition, there were technical matters which brought about this limitation of scenes displayed. Among them

Figure 6.24 Martyrdom of Mark. Manuscript illumination, fifteenth century. Musée Condé, Chantilly, France, *Très Riches Heures* du Duc de Berry, fol. 19vo. Photograph: Giraudon/Art Resource, NY.

Figure 6.25 Martyrdoms of Paul, Peter, Andrew, John the Evangelist, James and Bartholomew. Manuscript illumination. Pierpont Morgan Library, New York, Liégeoise Psalter, ms. 183, fol. 12vo. Photograph: Pierpont Morgan Library.

was the matter of space in books and on church walls which contributed to the truncation of the stories. Such delimiting began early not only in the church but in the wider society when the scroll gave way to the codex.

Thus, one also misses the distinct theological flavors of the rhetorical acts of the apostles. To the modern viewer, the customary series of the apostle's calling, one or two aretalogical deeds and a martyrdom, no matter how the execution was administered, begin to blend together in the eyes of the beholder. An example of that filtered view is folio 12 verso of the Liégoise Psalter in the Pierpont Morgan Library (ms. 183) [Figure 6.25]. The martyrdoms of Paul, Peter, Bartholomew, John, James and Andrew surround New Testament scenes. Martyrdom comes close to its being a thing unto itself; the causes for which the martyrs died lose variety. This is likely especially true for those who do not know the stories in their rhetorical form. The viewer must, however, keep in mind the purpose of a Byzantine church's decoration, which was to cause the worshiper to enter into a multi-dimensional iconostasis. In like manner, the Western Churches carried on Pope Gregory's desire to place 'the gospel on the walls.' Immersed in scene after scene of contention and martyrdom, the medieval viewer would experience the images accompanied by the liturgies and homilies of the saint's day. In the Middle-Ages, the worshiper participated in these liturgies and homilies; each act of worship was illuminated by the glow of light reflected from a mosaic or transmitted through stained glass.

NOTES

INTRODUCTION

1 Jacobus de Voragine, *The Golden Legend*, ET by William Granger Ryan, Princeton, Princeton University Press, 1993.
2 E. Hennecke, *Neutestamentliche Apokryphen in deutscher Übersetzung*, Tübingen and Leipzig, Mohr, 1904; 1924.
3 Montague Rhodes James, *The Apocryphal New Testament*, Oxford, Clarendon Press, 1924.
4 'Hennecke' is now in a sixth edition edited by Wilhelm Schneemelcher, Tübingen, Mohr (Siebeck), 1990, 1997; James' edition has now been replaced by J. K. Elliott, *The Apocryphal New Testament*, Oxford, Clarendon Press, 1993.
5 F. Bovon and P. Geoltrain, *Écrits apocryphes chrétiens*, Paris, Gallimard, 1997 = *Bibliothèque de la Pléiade* 442.
6 A. de Santos Otero, *Los Evangelios Apócrifos*, Madrid, Biblioteca de Autores Cristianos, 1988.
7 L. Moraldi, *Apocrifi del Nuovo Testamento*, Turin, Unione Tipografico-Editrice Torinese, 1971, 2nd edn 1994.
8 M. Erbetta, *Gli apocrifi del Nuovo Testamento*, Casale Monferrato, Marietti, 1966–81.

1 TEXT, ART AND THE CHRISTIAN APOCRYPHA

1 D. L. Dungan, 'The New Testament Canon in Recent Study', *Interpretation*, 29, 1975, pp. 339–51. See also W. Schneemelcher in W. Schneemelcher, ed., *New Testament Apocrypha*, 2 vols., Philadelphia, Westminster Press, 1991, vol. I, pp. 9–49. H. von Campenhausen, *The Formation of the Christian Bible*, Philadelphia, Fortress Press, 1972.
2 Although not without objection from certain quarters. Most noteworthy is Papias' protest against the written gospel form: 'I did not suppose that the things from the books would aid me so much as the things from the living and continuing voice.' Papias is quoted by Eusebios, *Historia Ecclesiastica* III.39:1–7.
3 See the discussions by A. B. Lord, *The Singer of Tales*, Harvard Studies in Comparative Literature 11, Cambridge, MA, Harvard University Press, 1960. W. J. Ong, *Orality and Literacy: The Technologizing of the Word*, London, Methuen, 1982. W. Kelber, *The Oral and the Written Gospel: The Hermeneutics of Speaking and Writing in the Synoptic Tradition, Mark, Paul, and Q*, Philadelphia, Fortress Press, 1983.
4 What follows is adapted from a previously published article: David R. Cartlidge, 'Which Path at the Crossroads? Early Christian Art as a Hermeneutical and Theological Challenge', *Common Life in the Early Church. Essays Honoring Graydon F. Snyder*, ed. Julian V. Hills, Harrisburg, PA, Trinity Press International, 1998, pp. 357–72.
5 Especially Tertullian, *de pudicitia* VII.x.12; Clement of Alexandria, *Paedagogus* III.12.1. These texts and others are discussed in full in Sister Charles Murray, 'Art and the Early Church', *Journal of Theological Studies*, N.S. XXVIII, 1977, pp. 319ff.
6 W. Lowrie, *Art in the Early Church*, New York, Pantheon Books, 1947, p. 29. C. Murray, 'Art and the Early Church', p. 318.

7 For a sampling of such discussions see, in addition to Lowrie, D. R. Cartlidge, 'Which Path at the Crossroads? Early Christian Art as a Hermeneutical and Theological Challenge', pp. 357–72; R. M. Jensen, *Understanding Christian Art*, London and New York, Routledge, 2000, pp. 8–31. G. F. Snyder, *Ante Pacem: Archaeological Evidence of Church Life Before Constantine*, Macon, GA, Mercer University Press, 1985, pp. 1–11. In addition to Snyder's discussion, Sister Charles Murray has summed up the controversy, with considerable bibliography. Murray, 'Art and the Early Church', pp. 303–45. The texts are collected in Murray and in C. Mango, *The Art of the Byzantine Empire 312–1453*, Sources and Documents, The History of Art Series, Englewood Cliffs, NJ, Prentice-Hall, 1972.

8 H. L. Kessler, 'Pictorial Narrative and Church Mission in Sixth-Century Gaul', *Pictorial Narrative in Antiquity and the Middle Ages*, Studies in the History of Art, Washington, DC, 1985, pp. 75–91.

9 A. Grabar, *Christian Iconography: A Study of Its Origins*, A. W. Mellon Lectures in the Fine Arts, Bollingen Series XXXV.10, 1961, Princeton, NJ, Princeton University Press, 1968, p. 24.

10 Snyder, *Ante Pacem*, pp. 1–11. Murray, 'Art and the Early Church', p. 303–45. Jensen, *Understanding Christian Art*, pp. 13–15.

11 Murray, 'Art and the Early Church', pp. 303–19.

12 H. L. Kessler and M. S. Simpson, eds., *Pictorial Narrative in Antiquity and the Middle Ages*, Studies in the History of Art, vol. 16, Washington, National Gallery of Art, 1985. K. Weitzmann, *Illustrations in Roll and Codex: A Study of the Origin and Method of Text Illustration*, Studies in Manuscript Illustration, Princeton, NJ, Princeton University Press, 1948; second edition, 1970. E. Kitzinger, 'The Role of Miniature Painting in Mural Decoration', K. Weitzmann, *et al.*, eds., *The Place of Book Illumination in Byzantine Art and in the Art of Byzantium and the Medieval West: Selected Studies (32–41)*, The Art Museum, Princeton University, Princeton, NJ, Princeton University Press, 1975, pp. 99ff.

13 K. Schubert, 'Jewish Pictorial Traditions in Early Christian Art' in H. Schreckenberg and K. Schubert, *Jewish Historiography and Iconography in Early and Medieval Christianity*, Assen/Maastricht/Minneapolis, Fortress Press, 1992, pp. 141ff.

14 W. Tronzo, *The Via Latina Catacomb: Imitation and Discontinuity in Fourth-Century Roman Painting*, University Park and London, Pennsylvania State University Press, 1986. E. Dinkler, 'Abbreviated Representations' in K. Weitzmann, ed., *The Age of Spirituality*, The Metropolitan Museum of Art, Princeton, NJ, Princeton University Press, 1978, p. 401.

15 R. Stark, *The Rise of Christianity: A Sociologist Reconsiders History*, Princeton, NJ, Princeton University Press, 1996, pp. 5–7.

16 The earliest complete Christian work we have is Papyrus Bodmer V, a manuscript of the *Protevangelium Jacobi*, if de Strycker's dating is correct. See É. de Strycker, *La forme la plus ancienne du Protévangile de Jacques: Recherches sur le Papyrus Bodmer 5*, *Subsidia Hagiographica*, 33, Brussels, Société des Bollandistes, 1961. R. Hock, *The Infancy Gospels of James and Thomas*, The Scholars Bible, Santa Rosa, CA, Polebridge Press, 1995, pp. 11–12.

17 'The root cause was not, as is often claimed, the Old Testament commandment against graven images but rather a state of mind which equated image-making with pagan cult practices and the entire pagan way of life.' E. Kitzinger, *Byzantine Art in the Making: Main Lines of Stylistic Development in Mediterranean Art, 3rd–7th Century*, Cambridge, MA, Harvard University Press, 1977, p. 29. Kitzinger employs this against Murray. Kitzinger, 'Christian Imagery: Growth and Impact' in *The Age of Spirituality: A Symposium*, K. Weitzmann, ed., Metropolitan Museum of Art, Princeton, NJ, Princeton University Press, 1980, p. 142.

18 The sarcophagus is in the Museo Pio Cristiano, inv. 181, known as the Via Salaria sarcophagus. Kitzinger, 'Christian Imagery: Growth and Impact', p. 142. Cf. J. N. Carder in Weitzmann, ed., *Age of Spirituality*, p. 518, nr. 462.

19 P. C. Finney, *The Invisible God: The Earliest Christians on Art*, New York, Oxford, Oxford University Press, 1994.

20 Finney, *Invisible God*, pp. 116ff.

21 Finney, *Invisible God*, p. 125

22 Eusebios, *Epistle to Constantia Augusta* (Migne, *Patrologia Graeca*, 20, 1545ff.), quoted in Mango, *The Art of the Byzantine Empire 312–1453*, pp. 16–18.

23 Lowrie, *Art in the Early Church*, p. 30.

24 *Stromateis* VI. 16. 147. Murray, 'Art and the Early Church', pp. 320–1.

25 P. J. Achtemeier, 'Omne Verbum Sonat: The New Testament and the Oral Environment of Late Western Antiquity', *Journal of Biblical Literature*, 109, 1990, pp. 3–27.

26 E. Panofsky, 'Iconography and Iconology: An Introduction to the Study of Renaissance Art,' reprinted in E. Panofsky, *Meaning in the Visual Arts*, Collected papers, Garden City, NY, Doubleday Anchor Books, 1939, pp. 26–54 (originally published in E. Panofsky, *Studies in Iconology*, Oxford University Press, 1939).

27 B. Cassiday, 'Introduction: Iconography, Texts and Audiences' in *Iconography at the Crossroads*, B. Cassiday, ed., Index of Christian Art, Occasional Papers II, Princeton, NJ, Princeton University Press, 1993, p. 6. Cassiday's article is an excellent introduction to current discussions in iconography.

28 L. Steinberg, *The Sexuality of Christ in Renaissance Art and in Modern Oblivion*, New York, Pantheon, 1983, second edition, 1996, p. 220.

29 C. Bynum, 'The Body of Christ in the Later Middle Ages: A Reply to Leo Steinberg' in *Fragmentation and Redemption: Essays on Gender and the Human Body in Medieval Religion*, New York, 1992, pp. 79–117.

30 T. F. Mathews, *The Clash of Gods: A Reinterpretation of Early Christian Art*, Princeton, NJ, Princeton University Press, 1993, p. 141. Emphasis mine.

31 Cartlidge, 'Which Path at the Crossroads? Early Christian Art as a Hermeneutical and Theological Challenge', pp. 357–72. Jensen, 'Giving Texts Vision and Images Voice', pp. 344–56.

32 Jensen, 'Giving Texts Vision and Images Voice', pp. 344–56.

33 Cassiday, 'Introduction: Iconography, Texts and Audiences', p. 9.

34 Jensen, 'Giving Texts Vision and Images Voice', pp. 344–56. Snyder, *Ante Pacem*, pp. 1–11. Cartlidge, 'Which Path at the Crossroads? Early Christian Art as a Hermeneutical and Theological Challenge', pp. 357–72.

35 Mathews, *The Clash of Gods*, p. 11.

36 Also known as *New Testament Apocrypha*.

37 See *The Lost Books of the Bible and the Forgotten Books of Eden*, Collins-World, 1977, especially the introduction by Dr Frank Crane. The book contains a selection of well-known materials including the Apostolic Fathers, the *Odes of Solomon* and the *Protevangelium Jacobi*. This mystery-religion approach to the extra-canonical Christian writings continues in spite of the fact that English translations and commentary upon the texts are readily available in public and academic libraries, as well as in bookstores catering to mass-market publications.

38 A. della Croce, *Canonical Histories and Apocryphal Legends Relating to the New Testament, Represented in Drawings with a Latin Text. A Photo-Lith Reproduction from an Ambrosian MS. Executed for James Gibson-Craig, Esq.*, preface and notes by A. M. Ceriani, Milan, J. B. Pogliani, 1873. Emphasis mine. Two of the most well known extant monographs on the apocrypha and art continue this trend: J. Weis-Liebersdorf, *Christus- und Apostelbilder. Einfluss der Apokryphen auf die ältesten Kunsttypen*, Freiburg im Breisgau, Herder, 1902. U. Fabricius, *Die Legende im Bild des 1 Jahrtausends der Kirche*, Kassel, Oncken, 1957. Fabricius' title speaks for itself; Weis-Liebersdorf consistently refers to the apocryphal materials as 'legends.'

39 J. K. Elliott, *The Apocryphal New Testament: A Collection of Apocryphal Christian Literature in an English Translation Based on M.R. James*, Oxford, The Clarendon Press, 1993, pp. 350–89. W. Schneemelcher, ed., *New Testament Apocrypha*, vol. II, pp. 213–70.

40 The hymn, 'Good Christian Men, Rejoice!' (*In dulci jubilo*), translated by John M. Neale, 1873.

41 However, this gospel appears to have begun as an expansion of *Protevangelium Jacobi* and of *The Gospel of the Nativity of Mary*. Elliott, *The Apocryphal New Testament* 84–6. Schneemelcher, ed., *New Testament Apocrypha*, vol. I, pp. 456–9.

42 G. Schiller, *Ikonographie der christlichen Kunst*, 5 vols., Gütersloh, Gerd Mohn, 1966–91, vol. 1, fig. 143.

43 *The New Yorker*, December 15, 1997, p. 107.

2 MARY

1 The *Protevangelium* and *The Gospel of the Birth of Mary*, along with the early traditions of the first section of *Pseudo-Matthew* are not about Christ's infancy; they are, as the true title of *Protevangelium* states, 'the story of Mary.'

2 These texts are available in English translations, with critical notes, and with a bibliography to direct the reader to other versions of the gospels, in J. K. Elliott, *The Apocryphal New Testament: A Collection of Apocryphal Christian Literature in an English Translation Based on M.R. James*, Oxford, The Clarendon Press, 1993. W. Schneemelcher, ed., *New Testament Apocrypha*, 2 vols., Philadelphia, Westminster Press, 1991, vol. 1. See also J. Gijsel and R. Beyers, *Libri de Nativitate Mariae*, 2 vols., Corpus Christianorum Series Apocryphorum 9 and 10, Turnhout, Brepols, 1997.

3 J. Pelikan, *Mary Through the Centuries: Her Place in the History of Culture*, New Haven and London, Yale University Press, 1996, p. 2.

4 Pelikan, *Mary Through the Centuries*, p. 8.

5 The Nativity of Christ will be discussed in the next chapter.

6 See note 16, Chapter 1, above. Both Origen (*Commentarii in Matthaeum* 10.17) and Clement of Alexandria (*Stromateis* 7.16.93) know the *Protevangelium*. See R. F. Hock, *The Infancy Gospels of James and Thomas*, The Scholars Bible, Santa Rosa, CA, Polebridge Press, 1995, p. 11. In addition, Justin Martyr knows of the Nativity of Christ in a cave: *Dialogus cum Trypho* 78.

7 Elliott, *The Apocryphal New Testament*, p. 50. Hock, *The Infancy Gospels of James and Thomas*, pp. 23–5.

8 Elliott, *The Apocryphal New Testament*, p. 50.

9 Elliott, *ibid.*, and Hock, *ibid.*

10 (1) Joachim expelled from the temple; (2) Joachim in the wilderness, among his shepherds; (3) The annunciation to Anna; (4) Joachim offers a sacrifice in the wilderness; (5) Joachim's dream (announcing Anna's pregnancy); (6) Joachim and Anna meet at the Golden Gate; (7) The birth of the Virgin; (8) The presentation of the Virgin to the temple; (9) The ceremony of the rods to choose a husband for the Virgin; (10) Prayer over the rods; (11) The handing over of the Virgin to Joseph who holds a flowering rod, over which hovers a dove. (12) Either the marriage procession of the Virgin, or Mary in a procession of temple virgins. E. Baccheschi, *The Complete Paintings of Giotto*, Classics of the World's Great Art, New York, Harry N. Abrams, 1969, pp. 99–100, nrs. 53–64.

11 Baccheschi, *The Complete Paintings of Giotto*, p. 100, fig. 64.

12 P. Weiss, *Die Mosaiken Des Chora-Klosters in Istanbul*, Stuttgart and Zürich, Belser Verlag, 1997, pp. 57–86, Abb. 20–42.

13 (1) Joachim's offering refused; (2) Joachim and Anna return home after the expulsion from the temple; (3) Joachim laments in the wilderness; (4) The annunciation to Anna; (5) The annunciation to Joachim; (6) Joachim and Anna meet at the gate. (7) The birth of the Virgin; (8) The Virgin's first steps. (9) The Virgin is blessed by the priests at a feast. (10) The caresses; (11) The presentation of the Virgin to the temple; (12) The Virgin is fed by an angel in the temple; (13) The Virgin is instructed in the temple; (14) The Virgin receives the purple wool. (15) The prayer over the rods to choose a husband for the Virgin. (16) The handing over of the Virgin to Joseph; (17) Joseph takes Mary home. (18) Joseph leaves on a journey. Jacqueline Lafontaine-Dosogne, 'Iconography of the Cycle of the Life of the Virgin' in *Kariye Djami*, 4 vols., Bollinger Series LXX, ed. P. A. Underwood, New York, Pantheon Books, 1966, vol. 4, pp. 163–93. For the discussions of the several images of this cycle, see J. Lafontaine-Dosogne, *Iconographie de l'enfance de la Vierge dans l'Empire byzantin et en Occident*, 2 vols., Académie royale de Belgique, Classe des Beaux-Arts, Brussels, Palais des Académies, réédition anastatique avec compléments, 1992, vol. 1.

14 K. Weitzmann, *The Icon: Holy Images – Sixth to Fourteenth Century*, New York, George Braziller, 1978, p. 23.

15 See note 12, above.

16 In addition to Lafontaine-Dosogne, most of these images are listed and shown in G. Schiller, *Ikonographie der christlichen Kunst*, 5 vols., Gütersloh, Gerd Mohn, 1966–91. The first two volumes of Schiller's work have been translated into English. G. Schiller, *Iconography of Christian*

Art, 2 vols., translation of first two volumes of German edition, Janet Seligman, trans., Greenwich, CT and London, New York Graphic Society Ltd. and Lund Humphries, 1971; 1972. The numbering of plates and figures is the same in both the English and German editions.

17 Lafontaine-Dosogne, *Iconographie de l'enfance de la Vierge*, vol. II, p. 59.

18 Lafontaine-Dosogne, *Iconographie de l'enfance de la Vierge*, vol. II, has all the images from the *Wernherlied*.

19 Lafontaine-Dosogne, *Iconographie de l'enfance de la Vierge* vol. II, *passim*. N. Thierry, 'L'illustrations des apocryphes dans les églises du Cappadoces', *Apocrypha: Le champ des apocryphes*, 2, 1991, pp. 217–47.

20 Lafontaine-Dosogne, *Iconographie de l'enfance de la Vierge*, vol. I, pp. 196ff.

21 Lafontaine-Dosogne, *Iconographie de l'enfance de la Vierge*, vol. I, pp. 197–9.

22 O. Demus, *The Mosaic Decoration of San Marco, Venice*, Herbert W. Kessler, ed., Chicago, The University of Chicago Press, 1988, p. 127.

23 Demus, *The Mosaic Decoration of San Marco, Venice*, p. 129.

24 Demus, *The Mosaic Decoration of San Marco, Venice*, p. 138, fig. 49.

25 The list from Demus, *The Mosaic Decoration of San Marco, Venice*, p. 139.

26 Demus, *The Mosaic Decoration of San Marco, Venice*, p. 141. See also Lafontaine-Dosogne, *Iconographie de l'enfance de la Vierge*, vol. I, pp. 35, 70–2, pls. I–III.

27 Lafontaine-Dosogne, *Iconographie de l'enfance de la Vierge*, vol. I, p. 35.

28 N. Thierry, 'L'iconographie cappadocienne de l'affront à Anne d'après le *Protévangile de Jacques*', *Apocrypha*, 7, 1996, pp. 261–72, fig. 5.

29 C. Kraeling, 'The Christian Building: The Excavations at Dura-Europos. Final Report, 8, Pt. 3' in *The Excavations at Dura-Europa Conducted by Yale University and the French Academy of Inscriptions and Letters*, C. B. Welles, ed., New Haven, Yale University Press, 1961–7, 1968, pls. XLIV–VI. Schiller, *Ikonographie der christlichen Kunst*, vol. 3, fig. 1.

30 E. Dinkler, 'Die ersten Petrusdarstellungen. ein archäologischer Beitrag zur Geschichte des Petrusprimates', *Marburger Jahrbuch für Kunstwissenschaft*, 11, 1939, p. 12.

31 A. Grabar, *Early Christian Art: From the Rise of Christianity to the Death of Theodosius*, New York, Odyssey Press, 1968, pp. 68–71, fig. 59.

32 Schiller, *Ikonographie der christlichen Kunst*, vol. 3, fig. 1.

33 A. Ferrua, S.I., *Le pittura della nuova catacomba di Via Latina*, Pontificio Istituto di Archeologia cristiana, Vatican City, 1960, p. 55, Tav. XCVIII. W. Tronzo, *The Via Latina Catacomb: Imitation and Discontinuity in Fourth-Century Roman Painting*, University Park and London, Pennsylvania State University Press, 1986, p. 28.

34 U. Fabricius, *Die Legende im Bild des 1 Jahrtausends der Kirche*, Kassel, Oncken, 1957, pp. 34–5. C. Nauerth and R. Warns, *Thekla, ihre Bilder in der frühchristlichen Kunst*, Göttingen Orientforschungen II, Studien zur spätantiken und frühchristlichen Kunst 3, Wiesbaden, Otto Harrassowitz, 1981, *c.* 3, figs. 5–7.

35 Fabricius, *Die Legende im Bild des 1 Jahrtausends der Kirche*, pp. 34–5.

36 Lafontaine-Dosogne, *Iconographie de l'enfance de la Vierge*, vol. II, pp. 22, 37.

37 *Ibid.*, vol. I, p. 22, see n. 2.

38 For the symbolism of the Virgin *orans*, see A. Grabar, *Christian Iconography: A Study of Its Origins*, Bollingen Series XXXV.10, A. W. Mellon Lectures in the Fine Arts, 1961, Princeton, NJ, Princeton University Press, 1968, pp. 74–9.

39 Lafontaine-Dosogne, *Iconographie de l'enfance de la Vierge*, vol. I, 22, fig. 48. Fabricius, *Die Legende im Bild des 1 Jahrtausends der Kirche*, Taf. VIII, 1. J. Hubert, J. Porche and W. Volbach, *Europe of the Invasions*, The Arts of Mankind, André Malraux and André Parrot, eds., New York, George Braziller, 1969, fig. 19.

40 St Petersburg, The Hermitage, Omega 300, 301; Manchester, John Rylands Library, ivories 6; Berlin, Staatliche Museen Preussischer Kulturbesitz, Frühchristlich-Byzantinische Sammlung 2976. K. Weitzmann, ed., *Age of Spirituality*, catalog of the exhibition at The Metropolitan Museum of Art, New York, Metropolitan Museum of Art and Princeton University Press, 1979, pp. 509–11, nrs. 457–61.

41 N. Thierry, 'L'iconographie cappadocienne de l'affront à Anne d'après le *Protévangile de Jacques*', *Apocrypha* 7, 1996, p. 265, fig. 2.

42 Thierry, 'L'iconographie cappadocienne de l'affront à Anne d'après le *Protévangile de Jacques*', p. 261 and figures on pp. 271–2.

43 Hock, *The Infancy Gospels of James and Thomas*, pp. 15–16.

44 M. Geerard, *Clavis Apocryphorum Novi Testamenti*, Corpus Christianorum, Turnhout, Brepols, 1992.

45 M. Clayton, *The Apocryphal Gospels of Mary in Anglo-Saxon England*, Cambridge, Cambridge University Press, 1998, p. 106.

46 J. Lafontaine-Dosogne, 'Peintures mediévale dans le temple dit de la Fortune Virile à Rome', *Études de philologie, d'archéologie et d'histoire anciennes publiées par l'Institut historique belge de Rome* 6, Brussels, 1959, pp. 29–35.

47 Clayton, *The Apocryphal Gospels of Mary in Anglo-Saxon England*, p. 107.

48 Clayton, *The Apocryphal Gospels of Mary in Anglo-Saxon England*, pp. 104–5 and n. 10. See also B. Kurth, 'The Iconography of the Wirksworth Slab', *The Burlington Magazine*, 86, 1945, pp. 114–21. and R. W. P. Cockerton, 'The Wirksworth Slab', *Derbyshire Archaeological Journal*, 82, 1962, pp. 1–20.

49 Kurth, 'The Iconography of the Wirksworth Slab', figs. 1 and C.

50 R. Deshman, *The Benedictional of Aethelwold*, Studies in Manuscript Illumination 9, Princeton, NJ, Princeton University Press, 1995, pl. 31. Schiller, *Ikonographie der christlichen Kunst*, vol. 4.2, fig. 604.

3 IMAGES OF THE CHRIST

1 J. K. Elliott, *The Apocryphal New Testament: A Collection of Apocryphal Christian Literature in an English Translation Based on M. R. James*, Oxford, The Clarendon Press, 1993, p. 541.

2 M. R. James, *The Apocryphal New Testament*, Oxford, The Clarendon Press, 1924, p. 477.

3 Others are in the Mingana collection of Near Eastern medieval texts at the Selly Oak Colleges, Birmingham, England. See Elliott, *The Apocryphal New Testament*, p. 541.

4 E. von Dobschütz, *Christusbilder: Untersuchungen zur christlichen Legende*, Texte und Untersuchungen zur Geschichte der altchristichen Literatur, vol. 18, O. von Gebhart and A. Harnack, eds., Leipzig, J. C. Hinrichs, 1899, p. 171*. Elliott, *The Apocryphal New Testament*, p. 538. H. J. W. Drijvers in W. Schneemelcher, ed., *New Testament Apocrypha*, 2 vols., Philadelphia, Westminster Press, 1991, vol. I, pp. 492–500. See the recent discussion in N. MacGregor with E. Langmuir, *Seeing Salvation*, London and New Haven, CT, BBC Worldwide Ltd. and Yale University Press, 2000, ch. 6.

5 von Dobschütz, *Christusbilder*, pp. 160ff. and 39**ff; K. Weitzmann, 'The Mandylion and Constantine Porphyrogennetos', *Studies in Classical and Byzantine Manuscript Illumination*, H. L. Kessler, ed., Chicago and London, University of Chicago Press, 1971, p. 231 (originally published in *Cahiers archéologiques*, XI, 1960, pp. 163–84).

6 Weitzmann, 'The Mandylion and Constantine Porphyrogennetos', pp. 224–46 and MacGregor and Langmuir, *Seeing Salvation*, ch. 6.

7 See his reconstruction on p. 230, fig. 215 of 'The Mandylion and Constantine Porphyrogennetos'.

8 For discussion of the Veronica legend and those associated with it, see E. von Dobschütz, *Christusbilder*, c. VI and pp. 273* ff.

9 P. J. Achtemeier, 'Toward the Isolation of Pre-Marcan Miracle Catenae', *Journal of Biblical Literature*, 87, 1968, pp. 404–17. P. J. Achtemeier, 'The Origin and Function of the Pre-Marcan Miracle Catenae', *Journal of Biblical Literature*, 90, 1971, pp. 198–221.

10 Achtemeier, 'Omne Verbum Sonat: The New Testament and the Oral Environment of Late Western Antiquity', *Journal of Biblical Literature*, 109, 1990, pp. 3–27.

11 T. F. Mathews, *The Clash of Gods: A Reinterpretation of Early Christian Art*, Princeton, NJ, Princeton University Press, 1993, c. 5.

12 P. R. L. Brown, 'Art and Society in Late Antiquity' in *The Age of Spirituality: A Symposium*, K. Weitzmann, ed., New York, Metropolitan Museum of Art/Princeton University Press, 1980, p. 501.

13 Augustine, *de Trinitate* VIII.4.7

14 Origen, *Contra Celsum*, ed. and trans. H. Chadwick, Cambridge, Cambridge University Press, 1965, pp. 388–91.

15 Chapter 1, n. 35.

16 N. MacGregor, in *The Daily Telegraph* (arts and books), Saturday February 19, 2000. See also MacGregor with Langmuir, *Seeing Salvation*, p. 79.

17 The literature on the image of the Good Shepherd in the early church is prolific. See R. M. Jensen, *Understanding Early Christian Art*, London and New York, Routledge, 2000, pp. 51ff. G. F. Snyder, *Ante Pacem: Archaeological Evidence of Church Life Before Constantine*, Macon, GA, Mercer University Press, 1985, pp. 22–4 for discussion and bibliography.

18 E. Dinkler, 'Abbreviated Representations', in Weitzmann, ed., *Age of Spirituality*, Catalog of the exhibition at The Metropolitan Museum of Art, New York, Metropolitan Museum of Art and Princeton University Press, 1979, p. 396.

19 See Jensen, *Understanding Early Christian Art*, pp. 37–61 for discussions of the literature and various interpretations of the Good Shepherd, especially in the church fathers.

20 Elliott, *The Apocryphal New Testament*, p. 368.

21 P. C. Finney, *The Invisible God: The Earliest Christians on Art*, New York and Oxford, Oxford University Press, 1994, pp. 277–80.

22 Finney, *The Invisible God*, pp. 116–32, discusses such purchases and the prevalence of Good Shepherd oil lamps in both Christian and pagan usage.

23 M. Bal and N. Bryson, 'Semiotics and Art History', *The Art Bulletin*, LXXIII/2, June 1991, p. 207.

24 *de pudicitia* 10.

25 Sister Charles Murray, 'Art and the Early Church', *Journal of Theological Studies*, N.S. XXVIII, 1977, pp. 303–45, especially p. 322.

26 E. Kitzinger, 'The Cleveland Marbles,' *Atti del IX congresso internazionale di archaeologia cristiana*, 2 vols., Studi di antichità cristiana 32; Città del Vaticano, Roma, Pontificio istituto di archaeologia cristiana, 1978. Weitzmann, ed., *Age of Spirituality*, pp. 406f., nr. 364.

27 F. Mancinelli, *Catacombs and Basilicas: The Early Christians in Rome*, Florence, Scala Books, 1981, fig. 52. P. du Bourguet, *Early Christian Art*, New York, William Morrow and Company, 1971, p. 57.

28 E. Kitzinger, *Byzantine Art in the Making: Main Lines of Stylistic Development in Mediterranean Art, 3rd–7th Century*, Cambridge, MA, Harvard University Press, 1977, pp. 53–4, pl. I. G. Bovini, *Ravenna*, New York, Harry N. Abrams, 1969, pl. 9, 10.

29 For Christ as Orpheus, see Jensen, *Understanding Early Christian Art*, pp. 58ff., for further discussion and bibliography.

30 Jensen, *Understanding Early Christian Art*, pp. 39–40.

31 'Arizona's Sistine Chapel', *Newsweek*, November 27, 1995, p. 88A; 'New Face for a Desert Mission', *National Geographic*, vol. 188, nr. 6, December, 1995, pp. 52ff., photo, p. 55.

32 On hair-style, see Mathews, *The Clash of Gods*, pp. 123–8. Mathews also supplies a bibliography of this element of Jesus' appearance.

33 Mathews, *The Clash of Gods*. See P. Brown, 'Review of Thomas Mathews, *The Clash of Gods*', *Art Bulletin*, LXXVII/3, September 1995, pp. 499–502.

34 J. Weis-Liebersdorf, *Christus- und Apostelbilder. Einfluss der Apokryphen auf die ältesten Kunsttypen*, Freiburg im Breisgau, Herder, 1902. U. Fabricius, *Die Legende im Bild des 1 Jahrtausends der Kirche*, Kassel, Oncken, 1957, are exceptions to this statement as is Mathews, *The Clash of Gods*, ch. 5.

35 Note the change in gender: *aliae* to *alii*. See Weis-Liebersdorf, *Christus- und Apostelbilder*, p. 32, n. 4.

36 R. Lipsius and M. Bonnet, eds., *Acta Apostolorum Apocrypha*, 2 vols., Darmstadt, Wissenschaftliche Buchgesellschaft, 1959, original publication, 1891, vol. II.1, p. 217.

37 Weis-Liebersdorf, *Christus- und Apostelbilder*. Fabricius, *Die Legende im Bild des 1 Jahrtausends der Kirche*.

38 For a review of this discussion see Mathews, *The Clash of Gods*, c. 1. Mathews, unfortunately, falls into more *argumenta ad hominem* than many readers find comfortable.

39 D. Raoul-Rochette, *Discours sur l'origine, le développement et le caractère des types imitatifs qui constituent l'art du christianisme*, Paris, 1834. A discussion of the history of the interpretation of Jesus-types in the early church is in Weis-Liebersdorf, *Christus- und Apostelbilder*, c. 2.

40 On this see Snyder, *Ante Pacem*, pp. 1–11. Murray, 'Art and the Early Church', pp. 303–45.

41 Weis-Liebersdorf, *Christus- und Apostelbilder*, c. 2.

42 Mathews, *The Clash of Gods*, p. 179.

43 Brown, 'Art and Society in Late Antiquity', p. 18.

44 Eusebios, *Historia Ecclesiastica* VII, 18.4.

45 Snyder, *Ante Pacem*, 18.

46 Elliott, *The Apocryphal New Testament*, pp. 285ff.

47 M. Gough, *The Origins of Christian Art*, New York, Praeger, 1971, p. 137, fig. 126. Weis-Liebersdorf, *Christus- und Apostelbilder*, pp. 34–5, fig. 18.

48 F. W. Deichmann, G. Bovini and H. Brandenburg, *Repertorium der christliche-antiken Sarkophage, I: Rom und Ostia*, 2 vols., Deutsches archäologisches Institut, Wiesbaden, Steiner, 1967, nr. 134, tf. 32, 134.

49 W. F. Volbach, *Elfenbeinarbeiten der spätantike und des frühen Mittelalters*, Verlag des römisch-germanischen Zentralmuseums, Mainz, 1952, 1976 3rd edn, p. 91. R. Garrucci, *Storia dell'arte cristiana nei primi otto secoli della chiesa*, Rome, 1876–81, vol. VI, taf. 467, 2.

50 F. Mancinelli, *Catacombs and Basilicas: The Early Christians in Rome*, fig. 24. G. F. Snyder, *Ante Pacem*, pl. 31. P. du Bourguet, *Early Christian Art*, William Morrow and Company, New York, 1971, fig. p. 117. J. Beckwith, *Early Christian and Byzantine Art*, New Haven and London, Yale University Press, 1970, pl. 1.

51 Weitzmann, ed., *Age of Spirituality*, no. 342; D. Levi, *Antioch Mosaic Pavements*, Princeton, Princeton University Press, 1947, vol. I, pp. 226–57, pls. CLX–CLXII.

52 A. N. Wilder, *The Language of the Gospel: Early Christian Rhetoric*, Cambridge, MA, SCM Press/Harper & Row, 1964, pp. 115–18. Jensen, *Understanding Christian Art*, pp. 42–4.

53 The following discussion owes much to Mathews, *The Clash of Gods*, c. 5.

54 W. A. Meeks, 'The Image of the Androgyne: Some Uses of a Symbol in Earliest Christianity', *History of Religions*, 13/3, February 1974, pp. 165–208. The topic of the sexuality of Jesus has appeared in 'no fewer than five publications' between 1965 and 1978. 'Each of these was a work of thoughtful, sometimes passionate scholarship . . .,' L. Steinberg, *The Sexuality of Christ in Renaissance Art and in Modern Oblivion*, New York, Pantheon, 1983, second edition, 1996, p. 326. The authors include Tom Driver, Rosemary Reuther, Stephen Sapp, William Phipps and Malcolm Boyd. To this list one must add Elaine Pagels, *The Gnostic Gospels*, New York, Random House, 1979.

55 Steinberg, *The Sexuality of Christ*, pp. 326ff.; Mathews, *The Clash of Gods*, c. 5.

56 Steinberg, *The Sexuality of Christ*, p. 298. The quotation is from a former director of the London National Gallery – Michael Levey.

57 W. Lowrie, *Art in the Early Church*, New York, Pantheon Books, 1947, p. 32.

58 A. Grabar, *The Golden Age of Justinian*, New York, Odyssey Press, 1967, fig. 286; Mathews, *The Clash of Gods*, c. 5, fig. 100.

59 Mathews, *The Clash of Gods*, pp. 140ff., fig. 109.

60 Mathews, *The Clash of Gods*, fig. 98.

61 Fabricius, *Die Legende im Bild des 1 Jahrtausends der Kirche*, pp. 79–82; Mathews, *The Clash of Gods*, figs. 102–4; Bovini, *Ravenna*, pp. 46f., figs. 17, 18.

62 Mathews, *The Clash of Gods*, p. 115.

63 Mathews, *The Clash of Gods*, p. 116.

64 Mathews, *The Clash of Gods*, p. 115. For a discussion of the chapel and its history, see R. E. Hoddinott, *Early Byzantine Churches in Macedonia and Southern Serbia*, New York, St. Martin's Press, 1963, pp. 68f., 173f.

65 Mathews, *The Clash of Gods*, p. 116.

66 L. James, review of Mathews, *The Clash of Gods*, *Burlington Magazine*, 136, 1994, p. 458f.

67 W. E. Kleinbauer, 'Review of Thomas Mathews, *The Clash of Gods*', *Speculum*, 70, p. 941 (Emphasis mine).

68 'In a vision . . . Christ came to me in the form of a woman in a bright garment, endowed me with wisdom.' Translation of Epiphanius, *Panarion* 49, from R. Kraemer, ed., *Maenads, Martyrs, Matrons, Monastics*, Philadelphia, Fortress Press, 1988, p. 226.

69 Page numbers refer to J. M. Robinson, gen. ed., *The Nag Hammadi Library in English*, San

Francisco, Harper and Row, 1988, third edition. These materials are also collected in Pagels, *The Gnostic Gospels*, pp. 57f., and W. A. Meeks, 'The Image of the Androgyne', pp. 165–208.

70 See logia 4, 22, 23, 75, 106. (Cf. Gospel of the Egyptians.)

71 M. Eliade, *Patterns in Comparative Religion*, New York, World Publishing Company, 1963, pp. 419–25.

72 Paris, Bibliothèque nationale, gr. 74, fol. 167ro. K. Weitzmann, *The Monastery of Saint Catherine at Mount Sinai, The Icons, Volume I, From the Sixth to the Tenth Century*, Princeton, Princeton University Press, 1976, p. 41.

73 Bibliothèque nationale, Cabinet des Médailles. W. F. Volbach, *Elfenbeinarbeiten der Spätantike und des frühen Mittelalters*, Verlag des römisch-germanischen Zentralmuseums, Mainz, 1952, 3rd edn. 1976, pp 71–2, nr. 145, taf. 47. D. T. Rice, *The Art of Byzantium*, London, Hirmer, 1959, p. 9, fig. 19. J. Natanson, *Early Christian Ivories*, London, Alec Tiranti, 1953, fig. 50. Mathews, *The Clash of Gods*, p. 140, fig. 108.

74 Bovini, *Ravenna*, p. 78f., fig. 36, 40, 47, 48, 56, 57; Schiller, *Ikonographie*, vol. 1, figs. 428–37; vol. 2, fig. 67, 141, 158–9, 185, 196–7, 208, 274; G. Kaftal, *Iconography of the Saints in North East Italy*, Florence, Casa Editrice le Lettere, 1978, col. 38, fig. 51.

4 THE LIFE AND MISSION OF JESUS

1 A. della Croce, *Canonical Histories and Apocryphal Legends Relating to the New Testament, Represented in Drawings with a Latin Text. A Photo-Lith Reproduction from an Ambrosian MS. Executed for James Gibson-Craig, Esq.*, Milan, J. B. Pogliani, 1873.

2 K. Weitzmann, 'The Selection of Texts for Cyclic Illustration in Byzantine Manuscripts' in *Byzantine Books and Bookmen*, papers delivered at a colloquium at Dumbarton Oaks (1971), Center for Byzantine Studies, Washington, DC, J. J. Augustin, 1975, pp. 77–8.

3 Weitzmann, 'The Selection of Texts for Cyclic Illustration', p. 78. A. Baumstark, 'Ein apokryphes Herrenleben in mesopotamischen Federzeichnungen von Jahre 1299', *Oriens Christianus*, N.S. 1, 1911, pp. 249ff.

4 Weitzmann, 'The Selection of Texts for Cyclic Illustration', pp. 78–9.

5 D. R. Cartlidge, 'The Christian Apocrypha: Preserved in Art', *Bible Review*, XIII/2, June 1997, pp. 24–31, 56, fig. on the issue's cover.

6 For the *Protevangelium* as an encomium bios, see R. F. Hock, *The Infancy Gospels of James and Thomas*, The Scholars Bible, Santa Rosa, CA, Polebridge Press, 1995, pp. 4–20. For the literary form and function of the *Infancy Gospel of Thomas*, see Hock, pp. 92–9. For both of these 'gospels' see J. K. Elliott, *The Apocryphal New Testament*, Oxford, The Clarendon Press, 1993, pp. 48ff.; 68ff. See also O. Cullmann in W. Schneemelcher, ed., *New Testament Apocrypha*, 2 vols., Philadelphia, Westminster Press, 1991, vol. I, pp. 424–5.

7 D. R. Cartlidge and D. L. Dungan, *Documents for the Study of the Gospels*, Philadelphia, Fortress Press, 1994, pp. 284–9.

8 Cartlidge and Dungan, *Documents for the Study of the Gospels*, p. 290.

9 B. Cassiday, 'Introduction: Iconography, Texts and Audiences' in *Iconography at the Crossroads*, B. Cassiday, ed., Index of Christian Art, Occasional Papers II, Princeton, NJ, Princeton University Press, 1993, p. 7.

10 J. Lafontaine-Dosogne has written about the cycle of the Infancy of Christ in 'Iconography of the Cycle of the Infancy of Christ' in *Kariye Djami*, 4 vols., Bollinger Series LXX, P. A. Underwood, ed., New York, Pantheon Books, 1966, vol. 4, pp. 197–241.

11 M. Geerard, *Clavis Apocryphorum Novi Testamenti*, Corpus Christianorum, Turnhout, Brepols, 1992, pp. 25–42.

12 Weitzmann, 'The Selection of Texts for Cyclic Illustration', pp. 69–109.

13 U. Fabricius, *Die Legende im Bild des 1 Jahrtausends der Kirche*, Kassel, Oncken, 1957, pp. 37–9. G. Schiller, *Iconography of Christian Art*, 2 vols., translation of first two volumes of German edn.; Janet Seligman, trans., Greenwich, CT and London, New York Graphic Society and Lund Humphries, 1971; 1972, vol. 1, fig. 57. E. S. Malbon, *The Iconography of the Sarcophagus of Junius Bassus*, Princeton, NJ, Princeton University Press, 1990, fig. 4.

14 W. F. Volbach, *Early Christian Art*, London, Hirmer, 1961, fig. 101. W. F. Volbach, *Elfenbeinarbeiten der Spätantike und des frühen Mittelalters*, Verlag des römisch-germanischen Zentralmuseums, Mainz, 1952, 1976 (3rd edn.), nr. 119, Taf. 37. K. Weitzmann, ed., *Age of Spirituality*, catalog of the exhibition at The Metropolitan Museum of Art, New York, Metropolitan Museum of Art and Princeton University Press, 1979, p. 453, fig. 53. Schiller, *Iconography of Christian Art*, vol. 1, fig. 53. Fabricius, *Die Legende im Bild des 1 Jahrtausends der Kirche*, p. 36, Taf. XX, 3.

15 Schiller, *Iconography of Christian Art*, vol. 1, fig. 317. A. Goldschmidt, *Die Elfenbeinskulpturen aus der Zeit der karolingischen und sächsischen Kaiser*, Denkmäler der deutschen Kunst, Berlin and Oxford, Bruno Cassirer, 1969, vol. I, Taf. XLI, nr. 95b, c; Taf. XLIII, nr. 95g, h, i.

16 Lafontaine-Dosogne, 'Iconography of the Cycle of the Life of the Virgin', vol. I, nr. 98; vol. II, pl. 146ff. P. Weiss, *Die Mosaiken des Chora-Klosters in Istanbul*, Stuttgart and Zürich, Belser Verlag, 1997, pp. 87–96, Abb. 43–59. Weiss' volume contains excellent full-color plates of the series.

17 Fabricius, *Die Legende im Bild des 1 Jahrtausends der Kirche*, p. 48, Taf. X, 1. Volbach, *Elfenbeinarbeiten der Spätantike und des frühen Mittelalters*, p. 85, nr. 188, Abb. 1.

18 I. Rodnikova, *Pskov Icons: 13th–16th Centuries*, Leningrad, Aurora Art Publishers, 1991, cat. nr. 48.

19 W. M. Voelkle and R. S. Wieck, *The Bernard H. Breslauer Collection of Manuscript Illuminations*, Exhibition Catalog, New York, Pierpont Morgan Library, 1992, cat. nr. 65.

20 Leo Steinberg attributes the invention of the term to David Robb. L. Steinberg, *The Sexuality of Christ in Renaissance Art and in Modern Oblivion*, New York, Pantheon, second edition, 1983, p. 337. For a number of such images, see Schiller, *Iconography of Christian Art*, vol. 1, figs. 99–115.

21 O. Demus, *Byzantine Art and the West*, The Wrightman Lectures, Institute of Fine Arts, New York University, New York, New York University Press, 1970, p. 180, fig. 198.

22 J. Lafontaine-Dosogne, *Iconographie de l'enfance de la Vierge dans l'Empire byzantin et en Occident*, Brussels, Académie Royale de Belgique, vol. I, pls. I–III (the ciborium columns); fig. 99 (San Marco mosaics).

23 G. Schiller, *Ikonographie der christlichen Kunst*, 5 vols, Gütersloh, Gerd Mohn, 1966–91, vol. 4.2. figs. 468a–d, 532, 533, 567a–f, 585a–d, for the illustrations in the *Wernherlied*.

24 Weitzmann, ed., *Age of Spirituality*, p. 512, nr. 461. Volbach, *Elfenbeinarbeiten der Spätantike und des frühen Mittelalters*, nr. 128.

25 Schiller, *Iconography of Christian Art*, vol. 1, fig. 138. Fabricius, *Die Legende im Bild des 1 Jahrtausends der Kirche*, Taf. X, 2.

26 M. Restle, *Byzantine Wall Painting in Asia Minor*, 3 vols., Recklinghausen, Aurel Bongers, 1967.

27 della Croce, *Canonical Histories . . .*, fol. 1vo.

28 D. R. Cartlidge, 'The Christian Apocrypha: Preserved in Art', *Bible Review*, XIII/2, June, 1997, fig. p. 55–6.

29 Fabricius, *Die Legende im Bild des 1 Jahrtausends der Kirche*, p. 57, Taf. XIII, 4. Weitzmann, ed., *Age of Spirituality*, p. 499, nr. 449. Volbach, *Elfenbeinarbeiten der Spätantike und des frühen Mittelalters*, p. 80, nr. 169, Taf. 86.

30 One, from Cologne, is now in the Kunsthistorische Museum, Vienna. See Fabricius, *Die Legende im Bild des 1 Jahrtausends der Kirche*, p. 57, Taf. XIII, 3. The other is in Berlin, Staatliche Museen, Frühchr.-Byz. 585. See Fabricius, *Die Legende im Bild des 1 Jahrtausends der Kirche*, Taf. XIII, 1. Volbach, *Elfenbeinarbeiten der Spätantike und des frühen Mittelalters*, nr. 174, Taf. 88. Weitzmann, ed., *Age of Spirituality*, p. 497, nr. 447.

31 Lafontaine-Dosogne, *Iconographie de l'enfance de la Vierge dans l'Empire byzantin et en Occident*, vol. I, 35, 70–2, pls. I–III. O. Demus, *The Church of San Marco in Venice: History, Architecture, Sculpture*, Dumbarton Oaks Studies VI, Washington, DC, Dumbarton Oaks, 1960, pp. 166f., figs. 50–5.

32 Elliott, *The Apocryphal New Testament*, p. 65, n. 29.

33 On these complications, see L. Réau, *Iconographie de l'Art chrétien*, 3 vols., Paris, Presses universitaires de France, 1955–59, vol. III, pp. 222–3.

34 K. Weitzmann, *The Fresco Cycle of S. Maria di Castelseprio*, Princeton Monographs in Art and Archeology, XXVI, Princeton, Princeton University Press, 1951, pp. 80f., 84f., fig. 73.

35 The prepuce is said to be venerated as a sacred relic, a unique souvenir of the earthly Jesus, in the parish church at Calcata, Viterbo.

36 E. Jastrzebowska, *Bild und Wort: Das Marienleben und die Kindheit Jesu in der christlichen Kunst vom 4. bis 8. Jh. und ihre apokryphen Quellen*, photocopy of an Habilitationsschrift, University of Warsaw, Institute of Archaeology, Warsaw, 1992.

37 S. M. Pelekanidis, P. C. Christou, C. Tsioumis and S. N. Kadas, *The Treasures of Mount Athos*, 3 vols., trans. Philip Sherrard, Athens, Ekdotike Athenon, 1974, vol. II, figs. 349–89, p. 378.

38 T. F. Mathews, *The Clash of Gods: A Reinterpretation of Early Christian Art*, Princeton, NJ, Princeton University Press, 1993, p. 139. A French translation of the Armenian gospel is by P. Peeters, *Évangiles apocryphes*, Rédactions syriaques, arabe, et arméniennes, vol. 2, L'Évangile de l'Enfance, Paris, Auguste Picard, 1914, pp. 143–4. See Mathews, p. 198, note 45.

39 Fabricius, *Die Legende im Bild des 1 Jahrtausends der Kirche*, Kassel, Oncken, 1957, p. 65, Taf. XIX, 2.

40 Cartlidge, 'The Christian Apocrypha: Preserved in Art', cover photograph. D. R. de Campos, *Art Treasures of the Vatican: Architecture, Painting, Sculpture*, Englewood Cliffs, NJ, Prentice-Hall, 1974, fig. 14. Fabricius, *Die Legende im Bild des 1 Jahrtausends der Kirche*, Taf. IX, 2.

41 O. Demus, *The Mosaics of Norman Sicily*, New York, The Philosophical Library, Inc., 1950, fig. 11b.

42 E. Kitzinger, *The Mosaics of St. Mary's of the Admiral in Palermo*, Dumbarton Oaks Studies XXVII, Washington, DC, Dumbarton Oaks Research Library, 1990, pl. XIV, XVII, cat. nr. 68. O. Demus, *The Mosaics of Norman Sicily*, fig. 50A, B.

43 Weitzmann, *The Fresco Cycle of S. Maria di Castelseprio*, pp. 79–80, fig. 74.

44 Weitzmann, *The Fresco Cycle of S. Maria di Castelseprio*, pp. 81f., fig. 75.

45 Restle, *Byzantine Wall Painting in Asia Minor*, vol. 2, pl. 145.

46 Demus, *Byzantine Art and the West*, fig. 261.

47 Weiss, *Die Mosaiken des Chora-Klosters in Istanbul*, p. 95, Abb. 55.

48 Hock, *The Infancy Gospels of James and Thomas*, p. 9.

49 Schneemelcher, ed., *New Testament Apocrypha*, vol. I, p. 468.

50 G. Kaftal, *Iconography of the Saints in North East Italy*, Florence, Casa Editrice Le Lettere, 1978, col. 517, fig. 650.

51 Kaftal, *Iconography of the Saints in North East Italy*, fig. 649.

52 Fabricius, *Die Legende im Bild des 1 Jahrtausends der Kirche*, p. 70, Taf. XVIII, 1. Lafontaine-Dosogne, 'Iconography of the Cycle of the Infancy of Christ', vol. IV, fig. 57.

53 Fabricius, *Die Legende im Bild des 1 Jahrtausends der Kirche*, Taf. XVIII. H. A. Omont, *Miniatures des plus anciens manuscrits grecs de la Bibliothèque nationale du VIe au XIVe siècle*, Paris, 1929, Taf. XXXII. Weitzmann, *The Fresco Cycle of S. Maria di Castelseprio*, p. 59f., fig. 76. Lafontaine-Dosogne, 'Iconography of the Cycle of the Infancy of Christ', vol. IV, fig. 58.

54 A. Frolow, 'L'église rouge de Perustica' in *The Bulletin of the Byzantine Institute*, 5, 1946, pp. 31–5, T. X–XII.

55 Elliott, *The Apocryphal New Testament*, p. 69.

56 On the latter, see Mathews, *The Clash of Gods*, fig. 25. K. Vogler, *Die Ikonographie der Flucht nach Ägypten*, diss. Heidelberg, 1930.

57 Pelekanidis, Christou, Tsioumis and Kadas, *The Treasures of Mount Athos*, vol. I, fig. 251.

58 Weitzmann, *The Fresco Cycle of S. Maria di Castelseprio*, p. 77.

59 E. Murbach, *The Painted Romanesque Ceiling of St Martin in Zillis*, Peter Heman, ed. and photographer, New York, Praeger, 1967, p. 3.

60 This version of the 'Cherry Tree Carol' is admittedly from the author's childhood memories. As is the case with such folk-songs, both the text and the tune have more than one version. See P. Dearmer, R. Vaughan Williams and M. Shaw, *The Oxford Book of Carols*, London, New York, Toronto, Oxford University Press, 1964, nr. 66. who trace the version of the carol they print to the Coventry Mystery Plays, p. 146.

61 Cartlidge and Dungan, *Documents for the Study of the Gospels*, p. 87, n. 1.

62 Weitzmann, 'The Selection of Texts for Cyclic Illustration', p. 72.

63 Schiller, *Iconography of Christian Art*, vol. 1, fig. 321.

64 Schiller, *Iconography of Christian Art*, vol. 1, fig. 322.

65 Elliott, *The Apocryphal New Testament*, p. 68.

66 Cartlidge and Dungan, *Documents for the Study of the Gospels*, p. 87, n. 1.

67 Schiller, *Iconography of Christian Art*, vol. 1, fig. 329.

68 P. Dearmer, R. Vaughan Williams and M. Shaw, *The Oxford Book of Carols*, nr. 55.

69 For those in the British Museum, see M. R. James, 'Rare Medieval Tiles and their Story', *Burlington Magazine*, XLII, 1923, pp. 33–8, pls. 33, 34, 35. The Victoria and Albert Museum tiles' inventory number is C.470.1927. E. Beck, 'English Medieval Art at the Victoria and Albert Museum', *Burlington Magazine*, 56, 1930, p. xi, pl. 98.

70 M. R. James, 'Rare Medieval Tiles and Their Story,' p. 37.

71 Fabricius, *Die Legende im Bild des 1 Jahrtausends der Kirche*, pp. 72–4.

72 A. de Waal, 'Die apokryphen Evangelien in der altchristlichen Kunst', *Römische Quartalschrift für christliche Altertumskunde und Kirchengeschicte*, 1887, p. 173. Cf. also the Gospel of the Egyptians in Elliott, *Apocryphal New Testament*, p. 18.

73 M. Gough, *The Origins of Christian Art*, New York: Praeger Publishers, 1971, fig. 117.

74 R. Deshman, *The Benedictional of Aethelwold*, Studies in Manuscript Illumination 9, Princeton, NJ, Princeton University Press, 1995, p. 263.

75 See Chapter 3, above, for additional discussion of the Abgar legend in connection with the Mandylion.

76 Elliott, *The Apocryphal New Testament*, pp. 541–2. Schneemelcher, ed., *New Testament Apocrypha*, vol. I, pp. 492f.

77 Weitzmann, 'The Selection of Texts for Cyclic Illustration', pp. 77–8, figs. 10b, 11a, 11b. N. MacGregor with E. Langmuir, *Seeing Salvation*, London and New Haven, BBC Worldwide and Yale University, 2000, ch. 6.

78 See R. M. Jensen, *Understanding Early Christian Art*, London and New York, Routledge, 2000, *c.* 5.

79 Egeria, *Diary of a Pilgrimage*, Online. Available http://users.ox.ac.uk/~mikef/durham/egeria.html (accessed April 24, 2001). Posted by Michael Fraser, with both Latin text and English translation.

80 U. Fabricius, *Die Legende Im Bild Des 1 Jahrtausends der Kirche*, p. 84, Taf. XXV, a, b.

81 R. E. Brown, *The Gospel According to John*, Anchor Bible, 2 vols., New York, Doubleday, 1970, p. 902.

82 R. C. Trexler, 'Gendering Jesus Crucified' in *Iconography at the Crossroads*, ed. Brendan Cassiday, Index of Christian Art, Occasional Papers II, Princeton, NJ, Princeton University Press, 1993, pp. 113–14.

83 Jensen, *Understanding Early Christian Art*, *c.* 5. Trexler, 'Gendering Jesus Crucified', pp. 107–19.

84 Trexler, 'Gendering Jesus Crucified', p. 114.

85 K. Weitzmann, *The Monastery of Saint Catherine at Mount Sinai, The Icons, Volume I, From the Sixth to the Tenth Century*, Princeton, Princeton University Press, 1976, vol. I, p. 61, pls. XXV, LXXXIV–XC.

86 Weitzmann, *The Monastery of Saint Catherine at Mount Sinai*, p. 81, pls. XXXII and CV–CVI.

87 Volbach, *Elfenbeinarbeiten der Spätantike und des frühen Mittelalters*, nr. 116. E. Kitzinger, 'Christian Imagery: Growth and Impact', *The Age of Spirituality: A Symposium*, ed. Kurt Weitzmann, New York: Metropolitan Museum of Art/Princeton University Press, 1980, p. 146, fig. 6.

88 The parallels are not exact. On this and for an excellent discussion of the history of the image of the Anastasis see A. D. Kartsonis, *Anastasis: The Making of an Image*, Princeton, NJ, Princeton University Press, 1986, pp. 10–16. Kartsonis argues that the *Gospel of Nicodemus* was not 'the breeding ground for the Anastasis' (p. 16), a statement with which we do not disagree. Also relevant is A. von Erbach-Fürstenau, 'L'Evangelo di Nicodemo', *Archivo storico dell'arte*, 11/3, 1893, pp. 225–37, which gives illustrations of a *Gospel of Nicodemus* in Madrid, Biblioteca nacional, Vit. 23–8, vol. 2, fol. 162ro–200vo.

89 The dating of these columns is much discussed. The current belief is that they are medieval copies of early church originals. Weitzmann, 'The Selection of Texts for Cyclic Illustration', p. 77. O. Demus, 'A Renascence of Early Christian Art in Thirteenth Century Venice' in *Late Classical and Mediaeval Studies in Honor of A. M. Friend, Jr.*, Princeton, NJ, Princeton University Press, 1955, pp. 349ff. See also Kartsonis, *Anastasis: The Making of an Image*, p. 11.

90 Kartsonis, *Anastasis*, pp. 69–70.

91 Kartsonis, *Anastasis*, pp. 70, fig. 14a, b.
92 Kartsonis, *Anastasis*, pp. 70, fig. 15.
93 Kartsonis, *Anastasis*, pp. 8–9.
94 Schiller, *Ikonographie der christlichen Kunst*, vol. 3, fig. 131.

5 PAUL, THECLA AND PETER

1 N. P. Ševčenko in K. Weitzmann, ed., *Age of Spirituality*, Catalog of the exhibition at The Metropolitan Museum of Art, New York, Metropolitan Museum of Art and Princeton University Press, 1979, p. 569, nr. 506.
2 Ševčenko in Weitzmann, ed., *Age of Spirituality*, pp. 569–70, nr. 507.
3 Ševčenko in Weitzmann, ed., *Age of Spirituality*, pp. 570–1, nr. 508.
4 On the dating and authenticity of these medallions, see E. Dinkler, 'Die ersten Petrusdarstellungen. Ein archäologischer Beitrag zur Geschichte des Petrusprimates', *Marburger Jahrbuch für Kunstwissenschaft*, 11, 1939, p. 11, figs. 4 and 5.
5 G. F. Snyder, *Ante Pacem: Archaeological Evidence of Church Life Before Constantine*, Macon, GA, Mercer University Press, 1985, p. 141, pl. 49. F. Mancinelli, *Catacombs and Basilicas: The Early Christians in Rome*, Florence, Scala Books, 1981, fig. 34.
6 On this literature, see J. Irmscher and G. Strecker in W. Schneemelcher, ed., *New Testament Apocrypha*, 2 vols., Philadelphia, Westminster Press, 1991, vol. II, pp. 483ff. J. K. Elliott, *The Apocryphal New Testament: A Collection of Apocryphal Christian Literature in an English Translation Based on M. R. James*, Oxford, The Clarendon Press, 1993, pp. 431–8.
7 D. R. MacDonald, *The Legend and the Apostle: The Battle for Paul in Story and Canon*, Philadelphia, Westminster Press, 1983, *passim*.
8 G. Bovini, *Ravenna*, New York, Harry N. Abrams, 1969, p. 178, fig. 108. S. Kostof, *The Orthodox Baptistery of Ravenna*, New Haven and London, Yale University Press, 1965, pp. 70f., fig. 81.
9 Bovini, *Ravenna*, p. 178, fig. 108.
10 Bovini, *Ravenna*, p. 178, fig. 11.
11 Elliott, *The Apocryphal New Testament*, pp. 385–8; R. A. Lipsius and M. Bonnet, *Acta Apostolorum Apocrypha*, Darmstadt, Wissenschaftliche Buchgesellschaft, 1959, vol. I, pp. 104–17.
12 H. L. Kessler, 'The Meeting of Peter and Paul in Rome: An Emblematic Narrative of Spiritual Brotherhood', *Studies on Art and Archeology in Honor of Ernst Kitzinger on his Seventy-Fifth Birthday*, William Tronzo and Irving Lavin, eds., 41, 1987, pp. 265–75.
13 Kessler, 'The Meeting', fig. 3.
14 Kessler, 'The Meeting', p. 266. There is an eighteenth-century drawing of these frescoes reproduced in Weitzmann, ed., *Age of Spirituality*, p. 489, nr. 440, with commentary on their history by Kessler. The drawings are in the Vatican, Biblioteca Apostolica Vaticana, cod. Vat. lat. 9843.
15 Kessler, 'The Meeting', p. 266
16 Kessler, 'The Meeting', fig. 6.
17 Kessler, 'The Meeting', p. 268, fig. 6.
18 Kessler, 'The Meeting', p. 274, fig. 8.
19 O. Demus, *The Mosaics of Norman Sicily*, New York, The Philosophical Library, Inc., 1950, figs. 43A, 43B.
20 Kessler, 'The Meeting', p. 65.
21 Demus, *The Mosaics of Norman Sicily*, fig. 83. G. Kaftal, *Iconography of the Saints in Central and South Italian Schools of Painting*, Florence, Casa Editrice Le Lettere, 1986, col. 858, fig. 1020. Kessler, 'The Meeting', fig. 1.
22 Kessler, 'The Meeting', p. 65, n. 8.
23 Lipsius and Bonnet, eds., *Acta Apostolorum Apocrypha*, vol. I, pp. 118f.
24 Gaudentius, who was bishop of Brescia *c.* 400, in his Tractate XX, On Peter and Paul, emphasizes that '[Petrus et Paulus] in vera fraternitate coniunxerit.' See Kessler, 'The Meeting', p. 268.
25 E. Dinkler, 'Die ersten Petrusdarstellungen', pp. 1–80. G. Stuhlfauth, *Die apocryphen Petrusgeschichten in der altchristlichen Kunst*, Berlin, de Gruyter, 1925.

26 Stuhlfauth, *Die apocryphen Petrusgeschichten*, p.129.

27 Stuhlfauth, *Die apocryphen Petrusgeschichten*, pp. 11f.

28 A. Grabar, *Christian Iconography: A Study of Its Origins*, Bollingen Series XXXV.10, A. W. Mellon Lectures in the Fine Arts, 1961, Princeton, Princeton University Press, 1968, pp. 31–4.

29 On this see E. Kitzinger, *Byzantine Art in the Making: Main Lines of Stylistic Development in Mediterranean Art, 3rd–7th Century*, Cambridge, MA, Harvard University Press, 1977, p. 7, fig. 4.

30 Elliott, *The Apocryphal New Testament*, p. 385.

31 P. Zanker, *The Mask of Socrates: The Image of the Intellectual in Antiquity*, translation of *Maske des Sokrates*, trans. Alan Shapiro, Berkeley, University of California Press, 1995, p. 32.

32 Zanker, *The Mask of Socrates*, p. 34.

33 There is a bust in the Museo Nazionale in Naples: Zanker, *The Mask of Socrates*, p. 12, figs. 5, 6; p. 34, fig. 21.

34 Zanker, *The Mask of Socrates*, fig. 23.

35 Cf. Plato, *Symposium* 222A–223A.

36 Dinkler, 'Die ersten Petrusdarstellungen', pp. 8–16.

37 On this see Dinkler, 'Die ersten Petrusdarstellungen', p. 8.

38 Stuhlfauth, *Die apocryphen Petrusgeschichten*, pp. 11f.; Dinkler, 'Die erste Petrusdarstellungen', p. 65.

39 C. R. Matthews, 'Nicephorus Callistus' Physical Description of Peter: An Original Component of the *Acts of Peter*?', *Apocrypha*, 7, 1996, pp. 134–45. The quotation from Nicephorus is on p. 136.

40 Matthews, 'Nicephorus Callistus', p. 143

41 Dinkler, 'Die ersten Petrusdarstellungen', pp. 10–11.

42 P. C. Finney, 'Images on Finger Rings and Early Christian Art', *Studies on Art and Archaeology in Honor of Ernst Kitzinger on His Seventy-fifth Birthday*, Dumbarton Oaks Papers, 31, 1987, pp. 181–6.

43 P. C. Finney, *The Invisible God*, New York, Oxford, 1994, discusses *passim* the probable methods by which the pre-Constantinian Christians bought their household items and their funereal decorations. Of particular note are pp. 152–4.

44 H. L. Kessler, 'Scenes from the Acts of the Apostles on Some Early Christian Ivories', *Gesta*, XVIII/1, 1979, pp. 109–19.

45 The sarcophagus of Junius Bassus is pictured in virtually every book on early Christian art. It can also be viewed on the World Wide Web at the Vatican's web-site linked to HTTP http://www.christusrex.org

46 E. S. Malbon, *The Iconography of the Sarcophagus of Junius Bassus*, Princeton, NJ, Princeton University Press, 1990, pp. 2–3.

47 U. Fabricius, *Die Legende im Bild des 1 Jahrtausends der Kirche*, Kassel, Oncken, 1957, Taf. p. 121.

48 F. W. Deichmann, G. Bovini and H. Brandenburg, *Repertorium der christliche-antiken Sarkophage, I: Rom und Ostia*, 2 vols., Deutsches archäologisches Institut, Wiesbaden, Steiner, 1967, vol. I, nr. 667, Taf. 101, 667.

49 J. Wilpert, *I sarcofagi cristiani antichi*, 3 vols., Monumenti dell'antichità cristiana publicati per cura del Pontificio Istituto di archeologia cristiana, Rome, Città del Vaticano, 1929–36, vol. I, pl. CXLII (1).

50 Stuhlfauth, *Die apocryphen Petrusgeschichten*, p. 109, fig. 28. A. Saggiorato, *I Sarcofagi paleocristiani con scene di passione*, Studi di antichità cristiana, Bologna, Casa Patron, 1968, nr. 17.

51 Malbon, *The Iconography of the Sarcophagus of Junius Bassus*, fig. 9. Deichmann, Bovini and Brandenburg, *Repertorium der christliche-antiken Sarkophage*, nr. 61, Taf. 19, 61. Saggiorato, *I sarcofagi paleocristiani*, nr. 22, fig. 23.

52 E. Dinkler, 'Abbreviated Representations' in *Age of Spirituality*, K. Weitzmann, ed., Princeton, NJ, Princeton University Press, 1978, pp. 396f.

53 M. P. Lillich, *The Stained Glass of Saint-Père de Chartres*, Middletown, CT, Wesleyan University Press, 1978, pl. 59. É. Houvet, *Monographie de la Cathédrale de Chartres*, Chartres, E. Chambrin, pp. 25–6.

54 G. Kaftal, *Iconography of the Saints in North East Italy*, Florence, Casa Editrice Le Lettere, 1978, col. 835, fig. 1094.

55 L. Bellosi, *Giotto*, Florence, Sogema Marzari Schio, 1984, p. 68, fig. 142. E. Baccheschi, *The Complete Paintings of Giotto*, Classics of the World's Greatest Art, New York, Harry N. Abrams, 1969, p. 120, fig. 151A. J. Burckhardt, *The Altarpiece in Renaissance Italy*, Cambridge and New York, Cambridge University Press, 1988, pl. 33.

56 O. Demus, *The Mosaic Decoration of San Marco, Venice*, ed. Herbert W. Kessler, Chicago, The University of Chicago Press, 1988, pp. 220–1, fig. 42.

57 C. Nauerth and R. Warns, *Thekla, ihre Bilder in der frühchristlichen Kunst*, Göttingen Orientforschungen II. Studien zur spätantiken und frühchristlichen Kunst 3., Wiesbaden, Otto Harrassowitz, 1981. Weitzmann, ed., *Age of Spirituality*, pp. 507f., nr. 455. W. Volbach, *Elfenbeinarbeiten der spätantike und des frühen Mittelalters*, Mainz, Verlag des römisch-germanischen Zentralmuseums, 1952, 1976 (3rd edition), nr. 117, pl. 61 J. Natanson, *Early Christian Ivories*, London, Alec Tiranti, 1953, p. 13, nr. 16. H. L. Kessler, 'Scenes from the Acts of the Apostles on Some Early Christian Ivories', pp. 111–12, fig. 3.

58 L. Kötzsche in Weitzmann, ed., *Age of Spirituality*, p. 508.

59 Iconographers tend to follow the nomenclature used by text-bound church historians: if the scene is paralleled by a canonical source, it is a narrative; if it is associated with an apocryphal source, it is a legend.

60 Kessler, 'Scenes from the Acts of the Apostles', p. 113

61 Kessler, 'Scenes from the Acts of the Apostles', p. 113, nn. 45, 46.

62 Snyder, *Ante Pacem*, p. 18, pl. 5.

63 Nauerth and Warns, *Thekla, c.* 13, fig. 30. Deichmann, Bovini and Brandenburg, *Repertorium der christliche-antiken Sarkophage*, nr. 832. Snyder, *Ante Pacem*, p. 18, pl. 5.

64 MacDonald, *The Legend and the Apostle, c.* 3–4.

65 Nauerth and Warns, *Thekla, c.* 10, figs. 20, 21. A. Grabar, 'Un Reliquaire provenant d'Isaurie', *Cahiers archéologiques*, XIII, 1962, pp. 49f and fig. 4.

66 Nauerth and Warns, *Thekla, c.* 10, figs. 20, 21.

67 R. Pervo, *Profit with Delight*, Philadelphia, Fortress Press, 1987.

68 D. R. MacDonald and A. D. Scrimgeour, 'Pseudo-Chrysostom's Panegyric to Thecla: The Heroine of the Acts of Paul in Homily and Art', *Semeia*, 38, 1986, p. 151. See also MacDonald, *The Legend and the Apostle.*

69 Egeria, *Diary c.* 23. See Chapter 4, above, and note 79.

70 G. Dagron, *Vie et miracles de Sainte Thècle*, Greek and French texts, *Subsidia Hagiographica*, 62, Société des Bollandistes, 1978.

71 MacDonald, *The Legend and the Apostle.* Elliott, *The Apocryphal New Testament*, pp. 350–61. Schneemelcher, ed., *New Testament Apocrypha*, vol. II, pp. 213–37. See for discussion and bibliography.

72 MacDonald and Scrimgeour, 'Pseudo-Chrysostom's Panegyric to Thecla: The Heroine of the Acts of Paul in Homily and Art', pp. 151–2.

73 R. Warns, 'Weitere Darstellungen der Heiligen Thekla', *Studien zur frühchristlichen Kunst*, Guntram Koch, ed., II, Göttinger Orientforschungen, Wiesbaden, Harrassowitz, 1986, pp. 85f., Taf. 22.

74 Nauerth and Warns, *Thekla, c.* 2a, fig. 3. A. Grabar, *Martyrium: Recherches sur le culte des reliques et l'art chrétien antique*, vol. I, Architecture; Vol. II, Iconographie, Paris, Collège de France, 1943 (vol. I); 1946 (vol. II), pl. XXXV, 1, 2. A. Fakhry, *The Necropolis of El-Bagawat in the Kharga Oasis*, Service des antiquités de l'Égypte, Cairo, Government Press, 1951, fig. 6.

75 Fakhry, *The Necropolis*, fig. 74; Nauerth and Warns, *Thekla*, p. 11, n. 7.

76 Nauerth and Warns, *Thekla, c.* 8, fig. 2.

77 Nauerth and Warns, *Thekla, c.* 12b, fig. 24. Brooklyn Museum, *Pagan and Christian Egypt. Art from the First to the Tenth Century A.D.*, exhibition catalog, Brooklyn, The Brooklyn Museum, 1941, nr. 50.

78 Nauerth and Warns, *Thekla, c.* 12b, fig. 24.

79 Migne, *Patrologia Graeca*, 50, col. 745–8.

80 Nauerth and Warns, *Thekla, c.* 3, figs. 5, 6, 7. Fakhry, *The Necropolis*, pl. I, 21, 24.

81 F. Bucher, *The Pamplona Bibles; a Facsimile Compiled from Two Picture Bibles with Martyrologies Commissioned by King Sanco el Fuerte of Navarra (1194–1234): Amiens Manuscript Latin 108 and Harburg MS. 1, 2, Lat.*, New Haven, Yale University Press, 1970, vol. I, p. 284.

82 Nauerth and Warns, *Thekla, c.* 5, fig. 14. N. P. Ševčenko in Weitzmann, ed., *Age of Spirituality*, p. 574, nr. 513.

83 Nauerth and Warns, *Thekla, c.* 4, figs. 10, 11. Weitzmann, ed., *Age of Spirituality*, pp. 576ff., nr. 516. F. Cabrol, H. Leclerq and H.-I. Marrou, *Dictionnaire d'archéologie chrétienne et de liturgie*, 15 vols., Paris, Letouzey and Ané, 1908–53, vol. I, cols. 1729–30, fig. 452.

84 E. Willis, 'The Development of the Iconography of Saint Thecla from the 4th Century to the 20th Century CE', unpublished paper presented at the Society of Biblical Literature, Annual Meeting, 1994, p. 3.

85 K. Weitzmann, *The Monastery of Saint Catherine at Mount Sinai, The Icons, Volume I, From the Sixth to the Tenth Century*, Princeton, Princeton University Press, 1976, pp. 44–5, pls. LXVI–LXVIII. G. and M. Sotiriou, *Icones de Mont Sinai*, Athens, 1956 (vol. I), 1958 (vol. II), vol. II, pls. 21, 23, 24, 28, 35.

86 Warns, 'Weitere Darstellungen der Heiligen Thekla', p. 95, Taf. 26, 1. G. Millet, *La peinture de moyen Âge en Yougoslavie (Serbie, Macédoine et Monténégro)*, Paris, E. Baccard, 1962, vol. III, pl. 110, (1).

87 R. Warns, 'Weitere Darstellungen der Heiligen Thekla', p. 86, Taf. 25.

88 E. J. Goodspeed, *Modern Apocrypha*, Beacon Press, Boston, 1956. P. Beskow, *Strange Tales About Jesus*, Philadelphia, Fortress Press, 1983.

89 Warns, 'Weitere Darstellungen der Heiligen Thekla', pp. 75–137.

90 B. Kleinschmidt, *Die Basilika San Francesco in Assisi*, 3 vols., Berlin, Verlag für Kunstwissenschaft, 1915–1928, vol. I, fig. 257.

91 E. Kloss, *Die schlesische Buchmalerei des Mittelalters*, Berlin, Deutscher Verein für Kunstwissenschaft, 1942, fig. 76.

92 L. Rodley, *Cave Monasteries of Byzantine Cappadocia*, Cambridge, Cambridge University Press, 1985, p. 190. N. Thierry, 'Les enseignements historiques de l'archéologie cappadocienne', *Travaux et Mémoires* 8, 1981, pp. 501–19.

93 For the full discussion and for an extensive bibliography on this painting, see the Washington National Gallery's commentary available on their website http:// www.nga.gov

94 Willis, 'The Development of the Iconography of Saint Thecla', *passim.*

95 According to Elizabeth Willis who reported Colescott's statement to this author.

96 Dinkler, 'Die ersten Petrusdarstellungen', p. 15.

97 Dinkler, 'Abbreviated Representations', pp. 399–400. See also Dinkler, 'Die ersten Petrusdarstellungen', pp. 48–55.

98 Dinkler, 'Abbreviated Representations', fig. 56. See also Dinkler, 'Die ersten Petrusdarstellungen,' pp. 17ff.

99 Lipsius and Bonnet, eds., *Acta Apostolorum Apocrypha*, vol. I, pp. 6f. Usually Stuhlfauth is credited with the connection between this text and the scene of Peter's striking the rock. Stuhlfauth, *Die apocryphen Petrusgeschichten*, pp. 58–60.

100 Fabricius, *Die Legende im Bild des 1 Jahrtausends der Kirche*, p. 221. Dinkler lists 32 scenes of the 'Quellwunder.' Dinkler, 'Die ersten Petrusdarstellungen', p. 22.

101 According to Stuhlfauth, *Die apokryphen Petrusgeschichten*, pp. 50–1, Erich Becker lists a much larger number; he includes scenes later than those studied by Dinkler: 199 images – 71 frescoes in Rome, 1 in Naples, 99 on sarcophagi, 28 on other art-objects (12 goldglass, 5 leaded glass, 5 bronze, 1 wood carving, 2 ivory pieces, 2 mosaics and 1 grave plaque). There are sixty-four dated fresco images in the following centuries: second century (5); third century (13); fourth century (46). Becker's dating appears to lean toward the early side. Stuhlfauth refers the reader to E. Becker, 'Das Quellwunder des Moses in der altchristlichen Kunst', *Zur Kunstgeschichte des Auslandes*, 72, Strassburg, 1909.

102 Fabricius, *Die Legende im Bild des 1 Jahrtausends der Kirche*, Taf. p. 121. Stuhlfauth, *Die apocryphen Petrusgeschichten in der altchristlichen Kunst*, pp. 72–126. Dinkler, 'Die ersten Petrusdarstellungen', pp. 60–2.

103 See the discussion and bibliography in Finney, *The Invisible God*, pp. 284–5, fig. 7.4. A. Bank, *Byzantine Art in the Collections of the Soviet Museums*, Leningrad, Aurora Art Publishers, 1985, pls. 26–9. P. Levi, *Heythrop Journal*, 4, 1963, pp. 55–60.

104 Stuhlfauth, *Die apocryphen Petrusgeschichten*, p. 29.

105 R. Garrucci, *Storia dell'arte cristiana nei primi otto secoli della chiesa*, Rome, 1876–81, pp. 310–2.
106 L. von Sybel, *Christliche Antike. Einführung in die altchristiche Kunst*, 3 vols., Marburg, N. G. Elwert, 1909, vol. II, p. 148.
107 A. de Waal, 'Die biblischen Totenerweckungen an den altchristlichen Grabstätten', *Römische Quartalschrift für christliche Altertumskunde und Kirchengeschicte*, 20, 1906, p. 46.
108 P. Styger, 'Neue Untersuchungen über die altchristlichen Petrusdarstellungen', *Römische Quartalschrift für christliche Altertumskunde und Kirchengeschicte*, 27, 1923, pp. 70f.
109 Stuhlfauth, *Die apocryphen Petrusgeschichten*, pp. 31ff., Abb. 9.
110 Stuhlfauth, *Die apokryphen Petrusgeschichten*, pp. 34–5.
111 Fabricius, *Die Legende im Bild des 1 Jahrtausends der Kirche*, pp. 92–3, Taf. XXVII, 2.
112 E. Le Blant, *Les sarcophages chrétiens de la Gaule*, Paris, 1886, fig. p. 114.
113 Stuhlfauth, *Die apocryphen Petrusgeschichten*, p. 3, fig. 3. Fabricius, *Die Legende im Bild des 1 Jahrtausends der Kirche*, p. 95.
114 T. Klauser and F. D. Deichmann, *Frühchristliche Sarkophage in Bild und Wort*, Olten (Schweiz), Urs Graf-Verlag, 1966, pp. 37–8, Taf. 25. See also Wilpert, *I sarcofagi cristiani antichi*. vol. I, pl. CL (2).
115 Stuhlfauth, *Die apocryphen Petrusgeschichten in der altchristlichen Kunst*, pp. 72–126.
116 Snyder, *Ante Pacem*, p. 41, pl. 14.
117 W. F. Volbach, *Early Christian Art*, London, Hirmer, 1961, pl. 40. Weitzmann, ed., *Age of Spirituality*, p. 405, nr. 361. Klauser and Deichmann, *Frühchristliche Sarkophage in Bild und Wort*, p. 23, Taf. 1, 1. Fabricius, *Die Legende im Bild des 1 Jahrtausends der Kirche*, p. 98, Taf. XXIX.
118 Stuhlfauth, *Die apocryphen Petrusgeschichten*, p. 106, Abb. 6.
119 J. Weis-Liebersdorf, *Christus- und Apostelbilder. Einfluss der Apokryphen auf die ältesten Kunsttypen*, Freiburg im Breisgau, Herder, 1902, pp. 69–70, fig. 71.
120 Klauser and Deichman, *Frühchristliche Sarkophage*, Taf. 35, 2.
121 Finney, *The Invisible God*, pp. 281–3.

6 APOSTLES AND EVANGELISTS

1 U. Fabricius, *Die Legende im Bild des 1 Jahrtausends der Kirche*, Kassel, Oncken Verlag, 1957, p. 124.
2 K. Weitzmann, 'The Selection of Texts for Cyclic Illustration in Byzantine Manuscripts' in *Byzantine Books and Bookmen*, Washington, Dumbarton Oaks, 1975, p. 70. Weitzmann's article gives a survey of the favorite subject matter of such early book illumination in the East. The aesthetic domination of Constantinople throughout Europe up through the early middle ages, often by way of Italy and Gaul, assured that the Western church was also involved in the fruits of Eastern iconography. See also J. J. G. Alexander, *Medieval Illuminators and Their Methods of Work*, New Haven, Yale University Press, 1992, p. 53. A helpful history of book illumination is in W. Cahn, *Romanesque Bible Illumination*, Ithaca, NY, Cornell University Press, 1982, pp. 1–55, see especially pp. 15–16.
3 Weitzmann, 'The Selection of Texts', pp. 77–80.
4 The earliest are the Sinope Codex, the Rossano Gospels, the Rabbula Gospel, and the Augustine Gospels, all of the sixth century. But these codices all give evidence that they have a tradition of both monumental and book miniature art behind them. See C. Nordenfalk, *Studies in the History of Book Illumination*, London, Pindar Press, 1992, p. 2.
5 Weitzmann, 'The Selection of Texts', pp. 78–80.
6 J. (Jacobus) de Voragine, *The Golden Legend: Readings on the Saints*, 2 vols., trans. William Granger Ryan, Princeton, NJ, Princeton University Press, 1993, vol. 1, p. xiv.
7 O. Demus, *The Mosaic Decoration of San Marco, Venice*, ed. Herbert W. Kessler, Chicago, The University of Chicago Press, 1988, p. 24. K. Künstle, *Ikonographie der christlichen Kunst*, Freiburg im Breisgau, Herder, 1926–8, vol. II, p. 96.
8 A. Grabar, *Christian Iconography: A Study of Its Origins*, Bollingen Series XXXV.10, A. W. Mellon Lectures in the Fine Arts, 1961, Princeton, Princeton University Press, 1968, p. 33.

9 J. K. Elliott, *The Apocryphal New Testament: A Collection of Apocryphal Christian Literature in an English Translation Based on M. R. James*, Oxford, The Clarendon Press, 1993, p. 518. R. Lipsius and M. Bonnet, eds., *Acta Apostolorum Apocrypha*, 2 vols., Darmstadt, Wissenschaftliche Buchgesellschaft, 1959 (original 1891) vol. II.1, p. 131.

10 K. Künstle, *Ikonographie der christlichen Kunst* vol. II, pp. 96–7. J. K. Elliott, *The Apocryphal New Testament*, p. 520.

11 J. Beckwith, *Early Christian and Byzantine Art*, New Haven and London, Yale University Press, 1979, p. 122, fig. 98.

12 E. Kitzinger, *Byzantine Art in the Making: Main Lines of Stylistic Development in Mediterranean Art, 3rd–7th Century*, Cambridge, MA, Harvard University Press, 1977, p. 119, fig. 216. G. Kaftal, *Iconography of the Saints in Central and South Italian Schools of Painting*, Florence, Casa Editrice Le Lettere, 1986, fig. col. 68.

13 Elliott, *The Apocryphal New Testament* p. 314, n. 3.

14 Cf. K. Schäferdiek in Schneemelcher, ed., *New Testament Apocrypha*, Philadelphia, Westminster Press, 1991, vol. II, p. 176.

15 W. Wright, *The Apocryphal Acts of the Apostles: Edited from Syriac Manuscripts in the British Museum and Other Libraries with English Translation and Notes*, Amsterdam, Philo Press, 1968 (reprint, orginal, 1871), p. 10.

16 Künstle, *Ikonographie der christlichen Kunst*, II, pp. 93–101.

17 Demus, *The Mosaics of San Marco in Venice*, 2 vols., Chicago, University of Chicago Press, 1984, vol. I, p. 219.

18 Demus, *The Mosaics of San Marco in Venice*, vol. I, p. 219.

19 Elliott, *The Apocryphal New Testament*, p. 527.

20 Demus, *The Mosaics of San Marco in Venice*, vol. I, p. 222

21 Demus, *The Mosaics of San Marco in Venice*, vol. I, pp. 220–30.

22 Demus, *The Mosaics of San Marco in Venice*, vol. I, pp. 79–80. Emphasis mine.

23 Demus, *The Mosaics of San Marco in Venice*, vol. I, pp. 79–80.

24 Elliott, *The Apocryphal New Testament*, p. 342.

25 Aristodemus is named in the *Acts of John* 25 (Elliott, *The Apocryphal New Testament*, p. 313) but as one of the faithful. In the narrative of the destruction of the temple (*Acts of John* 37ff.) the high priest of the temple is not named.

26 Demus, *The Mosaics of San Marco in Venice* I, 85, pl. 2. P. J. Nordhagen, 'The Mosaics of John VII (705–707 A.D.). The Mosaic Fragments and Their Technique', *Acta ad Archaeologiam et Artium Historiam Pertinentia, Institutum Romanum Norvegiae* 2, 1965, pp. 121ff.

27 Demus, *The Mosaic Decoration of San Marco*, p. 92.

28 Demus, *The Mosaic Decoration of San Marco*, p. 20.

29 E. Junod and J.-D. Kaestli, eds., *Acta Iohannis*, 2 vols., Corpus Christianorum: Series Apocryphorum 1, Turnhout, Brepols, 1983, vol. 2, pp. 706–08.

30 H. W. Janson, *History of Art*, Englewood Cliffs, NJ, Prentice-Hall, 1991, fourth edition, fig. 447 (Colorplate 20 in the first edition); J. Beckwith, *Early Medieval Art*, World of Art, New York, Thames and Hudson, 1992 (reprint of 1969 edition), fig. 182.

31 Stained glass in Sainte-Chapelle, Paris; Bourges; Lyons; Rheims; Troyes. Manuscript illumination in the Trinity College Apocalypse (R 16.2), the Paris Apocalypse (Bibliothèque nationale fr. 403); London Lambeth Palace cod. 20.

32 Künstle, *Ikonographie der christlichen Kunst*, vol. II, p. 334.

33 O. Pächt, 'The Illustrations of St Anselm's Prayers and Meditations', *Journal of the Warburg and Courtauld Institutes*, 19, 1956, p. 62. M. R. James, *The Apocalypse in Art: The Schweich Lectures in Biblical Archaeology, 1927*, The British Academy, London, Oxford University Press, 1931.

34 A. Grabar and C. Nordenfalk, *Early Medieval Painting from the Fourth to the Eleventh Century*, New York, Skira, 1957, p. 168.

35 O. Pächt, *Book Illumination in the Middle Ages: An Introduction*, Oxford, Oxford University Press, 1986, p. 162; A. Grabar and C. Nordenfalk, *Early Medieval Painting from the Fourth to the Eleventh Century*, p. 168.

36 Y. Delaporte and É. Houvet, *Les vitraux de la cathédrale de Chartres: histoire et description*, 4 vols., Chartres, É. Houvet, 1926, pp. 160–4, fig. 9, pls. X–XII.

37 J. Lafond, 'Les vitraux de la Cathédrale Saint-Étienne d'Auxerre', *Congrès archéologique de France*,

116, 1958, pp. 60–75. V. C. Raguin, *Stained Glass in Thirteenth-Century Burgundy*, Princeton, NJ, Princeton University Press, 1982, p. 134 and fig. 93.

38 Raguin, *Stained Glass in Thirteenth-Century Burgundy*, p. 134 and fig. 70.

39 Lafond, 'Les vitraux de la Cathédrale Saint-Étienne d'Auxerre', *Congrès archéologique de France*, 113, 1955, pp. 28–46. J. Lafond, 'Les vitraux de la Cathédrale Saint-Étienne d'Auxerre', *Congrès archéologique de France*, 116, 1958, pp. 60–75.

40 J. Lafontaine-Dosogne, 'Peintures médiévale dans le temple dit de la Fortune Virile à Rome', *Études de philologie, d'archéologie et d'histoire anciennes publiées par l'institut historique belge de Rome* 6, Brussels, 1959, pp. 29–35.

41 On this see E. Junod and J.-D. Kaestli, *L'histoire des actes apocryphes des apôtres du IIIe au IXe siècle: le cas des Actes de Jean*, Cahiers de la Revue de théologie et de philosophie 7, Lausanne, Neuchâtel, 1982.

42 Junod and Kaestli, eds., *Acta Iohannis*, vol. I, pp. 81–6.

43 D. R. Cartlidge, 'An Illustration in the Admont "Anselm" and Its Relevance to a Reconstruction of the Acts of John', *Semeia*, 80, 1997, pp. 277–90. Pächt, 'The Illustrations of St. Anselm's Prayers and Meditations', pp. 68–83.

44 H. Wentzel, 'Christus-Johannes-Gruppe', *Reallexikon zur deutschen Kunstgeschichte*, III, 1954, col. 658f. Wentzel, 'Unbekannte Christus-Johannes-Gruppen', *Zeitschrift für Kunstwissenschaft* 13/1–2, 1959, pp. 155–76.

45 M. Aubert, L. Grodecki, J. LaFond and J. Verrier, *Les vitraux de Notre-Dame et de la Sainte-Chapelle de Paris*, Corpus Vitrearum Medii Aevi, France, Vol. I, Paris, Caisse nationale des monuments historiques, 1959, pp. 345–6, pl. 101, (1) and (9).

46 Cartlidge, 'An Illustration in the Admont "Anselm"', p. 281.

47 O. M. Dalton, *Byzantine Art and Archaeology*, Oxford, Oxford University Press, 1911, pp. 392f.

48 Künstle, *Ikonographie der christlichen Kunst*, vol. II, 344f.; J. Wilpert, *Die römischen Mosaiken und Malereien der kirchlichen Bauten vom IV. bis zum XIII. Jahrhundert*, 4 vols., Freiburg im Breisgau, Herder, 1916, vol. 2, fig. 64.

49 Elliott, *The Apocryphal New Testament* p. 316, n. 4.

50 M. R. James, *The Trinity College Apocalypse*, Cambridge, Cambridge University Press, 1909, note on p. 236.

51 See Elliott, *The Apocryphal New Testament*, pp. 338ff.

52 Kaftal, *Iconography of the Saints in Central and South Italian Schools of Painting*, col. 618, fig. 714. K. Künstle, *Ikonographie der christlichen Kunst*, vol. II, p. 344, no fig.

53 Künstle, *Ikonographie der christlichen Kunst*, vol. II, p. 344.

54 Kaftal, *Iconography of the Saints in Central and South Italian Schools of Painting*, col. 618, fig. 714.

55 Wilpert, *Die römischen Mosaiken und Malereien*, vol. II, p. 212, fig. 64.

56 S. Waetzoldt, *Die Kopien des 17. Jahrhunderts nach Mosaiken und Wandmalereien in Rom*, Römisch Forschungen der Bibliotheca Hertziana, Band XVIII, Vienna-Munich, Schroll Verlag, 1964, cat. 81, fig. 87.

57 Elliott, *The Apocryphal New Testament*, p. 316 and note 4. K. Schäferdiek in Schneemelcher, *New Testament Apocrypha*, vol. II, pp. 178–9.

58 Elliott, *The Apocryphal New Testament*, pp. 338f.; see Elliott's note 27 on the numbering of Pseudo-Abdias' work.

59 See *Beatha Eoin Bruinne* II, 12–13 in W. Schneemelcher, *New Testament Apocrypha*, vol. II, pp. 211–12.

60 See Elliott, *The Apocryphal New Testament*, pp. 304–5.

61 R. Marks and N. Morgan, *The Golden Age of English Manuscript Painting: 1200–1500*, New York, George Braziller, 1981, pl. 10–11.

62 Kaftal, *Iconography of the Saints in Central and South Italian Schools of Painting*, col. 630, fig. 733. J. Wilpert, *Die römischen Mosaiken und Malereien*, p. 154, pl. 237 (1).

63 G. Kaftal, *Iconography of the Saints in North East Italy*, Florence, Casa Editrice Le Lettere, 1978, col. 392, fig. 245.

64 Musée d'arts décoratifs; vestment (orphrey; embroidery: 1081–84; 1772).

65 Elliott puts this story as chs. 56–7, but he also places chs. 37–86 between chs. 105 and 106. See Elliott, *The Apocryphal New Testament*, pp. 322–35.

66 N. Morgan, *Early Gothic Manuscripts (II) 1250–1285*, A Survey of Manuscripts Illuminated in

the British Isles, General Editor: J. J. G. Alexander, London, Harvey Miller/Oxford University Press, 1988, vol. II, pl. 133ff.

67 M. R. James, *The Apocalypse in Art: The Schweich Lectures in Biblical Archaeology, 1927*, The British Academy, London, Oxford University Press, 1931, pp. 1–112.

68 K. Weitzmann, *The Monastery of Saint Catherine at Mount Sinai, The Icons, Volume I, From the Sixth to the Tenth Century*, Princeton, Princeton University Press, 1976, pp. 24–5.

69 Cambridge University Library, St John's College, K.21. Miscellany, fol. 61vo. For the text, see Elliott, *The Apocryphal New Testament*, pp. 691ff.

70 M. P. Lillich, *The Stained Glass of Saint-Père de Chartres*, Middletown, CT, Wesleyan University Press, 1978, pp. 95–6, pls. 4 and 10.

71 M. Clayton, *The Apocryphal Gospels of Mary in Anglo-Saxon England*, Cambridge, Cambridge University Press, 1998, pp. 106–7. J. Lafontaine-Dosogne, 'Peintures médiévales dans le temple dit de la Fortune Virile à Rome', pp. 29–35.

72 F. Bucher, *The Pamplona Bibles; a Facsimile Compiled from Two Picture Bibles with Martyrologies Commissioned by King Sanco el Fuerte of Navarra (1194–1234): Amiens Manuscript Latin 108 and Harburg MS. 1, 2, Lat.*, New Haven, Yale University Press, 1970, fol. 208ro.

73 Kaftal, *Iconography of the Saints in North East Italy*, col. 453, figs. 564, 565.

74 Kaftal, *Iconography of the Saints in North East Italy*, col. 452, 454, figs. 562, 566.

75 Elliott, *The Apocryphal New Testament*, pp. 231–5.

76 Kaftal, *Iconography of the Saints in North East Italy*, cols. 38–46, figs. 50, 53, 54, 55.

77 According to the sources at the Index of Christian art, these images are published in *Oesterreichische Zeitschrift für Kunst und Denkmalpflege*, VI, 1952, figs. 131, 132, 133.

78 Kaftal, *Iconography of the Saints in Central and South Italian Schools of Painting*, col. 61–6, figs. 55–6, 58–62.

79 Kaftal, *Iconography of the Saints in Central and South Italian Schools of Painting*, col. 60–1.

80 É. Houvet, *Monographie de la Cathédrale de Chartres*, Chartres, E. Chambrin, 1927, p. 28.

81 Kaftal, *Iconography of the Saints in North East Italy*, col. 57, 59, figs. 69, 75. See also R. Longhi, *Carlo Braccesco*, Milan, Istituto nazionale di studi sul rinascimento, 1942, figs. 11–17.

82 J. Lafond, 'Les vitraux de la Cathédrale Saint-Pierre de Troyes', *Congrès archéologie de France*, 113, 1955, pp. 28–62.

83 Demus, *The Mosaics of San Marco in Venice*, vol. I, p. 227 and n. 31.

84 In the *Passion of Andrew*, see D. R. MacDonald, *The Acts of Andrew and The Acts of Andrew and Matthias in the City of the Cannibals*, Texts and Translations 33, Atlanta, GA, Scholars Press, 1990, pp. 394–5 and n. 76.

85 *Oesterreichische Zeitschrift für Kunst und Denkmalpflege*, VI, 1952, figs. 131, 132, 133 (see also note 77, above).

86 G. Bornkamm, *Mythos und Legende in den apokryphen Thomas-Akten*, Göttingen, Vandenhoeck & Ruprecht, 1933.

87 Kaftal, *Iconography of the Saints in Tuscan Painting*, Florence, Casa Editrice le Lettere, 1952, col. 970, fig. 1091.

88 A. Boeckler, *Die Regensburg-Prüfeninger Buchmalerei des XII. und XIII. Jahrhunderts*, Munich, A. Reusch, 1929, figs. 56, 57.

89 D. Kirchner in Schneemelcher, ed., *New Testament Apocrypha*, vol. I, p. 288. F. E. Williams in J. M. Robinson, ed., *The Nag Hammadi Library in English*, San Francisco, Harper and Row, 1988, p. 29; Elliott, *The Apocryphal New Testament*, pp. 673–81, trans. Ronald Cameron.

90 K. Weitzmann, ed., *Age of Spirituality*, catalog of the exhibition at The Metropolitan Museum of Art, New York, Metropolitan Museum of Art and Princeton University Press, 1979, p. 455, fig. 67. W. F. Volbach, *Early Christian Art*, New York and London, Abrams, 1961, pl. 93. Kitzinger, *Byzantine Art in the Making*, p. 39, fig. 76. W. F. Volbach, *Elfenbeinarbeiten der Spätantike und des frühen Mittelalters*, Verlag des römisch-germanischen Zentralmuseum, 1952, 1976 (3rd edn), Taf. 33, nr. 110. H. L. Kessler, 'Scenes from the Acts of the Apostles on Some Early Christian Ivories', *Gesta* XVIII/1, 1979, p. 110, fig. 1.

91 G. Schiller, *Ikonographie der christlichen Kunst*, 5 vols. plus index volume, Gütersloh, Gerd Mohn, 1966–91, vol. III, fig. 183.

92 N. P. Ševčenko in Weitzmann, ed., *Age of Spirituality*, p. 590, nr. 530.

93 Other portraits of Philip appear in the following locations:

Apse of the Church of the Transfiguration, Mount Sinai: 5th–8th centuries, mosaic.
Apse of the Cathedral Church at Parenzo, Italy: 6th century, mosaic.
Orthodox Baptistery, Ravenna, Italy: 5th century, mosaic.
Choir of San Vitale, Ravenna, Italy: 6th century, mosaic.
Palazzo Arcivescovile, Ravenna, Italy, Andrea Chapel: 6th century, mosaic.
Baptistery of San Giovanni in Laterano, Croce Chapel: 5th century, mosaic.
Apse of the Church of Agata in Subura, Rome: 5th century, mosaic.
Nave of the Church of Prisco, San Prisco, Italy: 5th–6th century, mosaic (destroyed).
Church of Notre Dame de la Dourade, Toulouse, 6th century, mosaic.
Wool hanging in Cleveland Museum of Art, Cleveland, Ohio, textile.

94 A. Boeckler, *Das stuttgarter Passionale*, Augsburg, Dr. Filser, 1923, fig. 51.
95 H. Swarzenski, *Die lateinischen illuminierten Handscriften des XIII. Jahrhunderts in den Ländern an Rhein, Main und Donau*, Berlin, 1936, pl. 63.
96 See Migne, *Patrologia Latina* III, col. 1291; XCIV, col. 1016
97 Demus, *The Mosaics of San Marco in Venice*, vol. I, p. 224.
98 D. R. de Campos, *Art Treasures of the Vatican*, Englewood Cliffs, NJ, Prentice-Hall, 1974, fig. 200.
99 Kaftal, *Iconography of the Saints in North East Italy*, figs. 142, 144, 146, 151, 153, 154.
100 Kaftal, *Iconography of the Saints in North East Italy*, figs. 156–62.
101 Kaftal, *Iconography of the Saints in Central and South Italian Schools of Painting*, figs. 173–7.
102 O. Demus, *Byzantine Art and the West*, The Wrightman Lectures, Institute of Fine Arts, New York University, New York, New York University Press, 1970, pp. 3–4, fig. 1.
103 Demus, *The Mosaics of San Marco in Venice* vol. I, figs. 360, 371, 372. Demus, *The Mosaic Decoration of San Marco*, pl. 28b.
104 E. A. Wallis Budge, *The Contendings of the Apostles*. 2 vols., London, Henry Frowde, 1901, pp. 135–6.
105 Bucher, *The Pamplona Bibles*, vol. 2, fig. 470.
106 Bucher, *The Pamplona Bibles*, vol. 2, pl. 471.
107 Demus, *The Mosaics of San Marco in Venice*, vol. I, p. 225.
108 A. de Santos Otero in W. Schneemelcher, ed., *New Testament Apocrypha*, vol. II, pp. 461–5.
109 de Santos Otero in W. Schneemelcher, ed., *New Testament Apocrypha*, vol. II, p. 464.
110 K. Weitzmann, *Late Antique and Early Christian Book Illumination*, New York, George Braziller, 1977, p. l.
111 Civiche raccolte d'arte applicata ed incisioni; Ivory 3. See G. Vikan in Weitzmann, ed., *Age of Spirituality*, pp. 508–9, nr. 456.
112 G. Vikan in Weitzmann, ed., *Age of Spirituality*, pp. 498–9, nr. 448. Vikan's article contains a brief history of the cathedra of Grado.
113 A. St. Clair in Weitzmann, ed., *Age of Spirituality*, p. 582, nr. 521.
114 Demus, *The Mosaics of San Marco in Venice*, vol. I, p. 57.
115 Demus, *The Mosaics of San Marco in Venice*, vol. I, p. 65.
116 Demus, *The Mosaics of San Marco in Venice*, vol. I, p. 64.
117 Demus, *The Mosaics of San Marco in Venice*, vol. I, pp. 65–71.
118 A case in point are the profusely decorated churches in Norman Sicily. See O. Demus, *The Mosaics of Norman Sicily*, Philosophical Library, New York, The Philosophical Library, Inc., 1950).
119 Demus, *The Mosaics of Norman Sicily*, pp. 79–80.

BIBLIOGRAPHY

Achtemeier, P. J., 'The Origin and Function of the Pre-Marcan Miracle Catenae', *Journal of Biblical Literature*, 90, 1971, pp. 198–221.

—— 'Toward the Isolation of a Pre-Marcan Miracle Catenae', *Journal of Biblical Literature*, 87, 1968, pp. 404–17.

—— 'Omne Verbum Sonat: The New Testament and the Oral Environment of Late Western Antiquity', *Journal of Biblical Literature*, 109, 1990, pp. 3–27.

Alexander, J. J. G., *Medieval Illuminators and Their Methods of Work*, New Haven, Yale University Press, 1992.

Aubert, M., Grodecki, L., LaFond, J. and Verrier, J., *Les vitraux de Notre-Dame et de la Sainte-Chapelle de Paris*, Corpus Vitrearum Medii Aevi, France, vol. I, Paris, Caisse nationale des monuments historiques, 1959.

Baccheschi, E., *The Complete Paintings of Giotto*, Classics of the World's Greatest Art, New York, Harry N. Abrams, 1969.

Bal, M. and Bryson, N., 'Semiotics and Art History', *The Art Bulletin*, LXXIII/2, June, 1991, pp. 174–208.

Bank, A., *Byzantine Art in the Collections of the Soviet Museums*, Leningrad, Aurora Art Publishers,1985.

Baumstark, A., 'Ein apokryphes Herrenleben in mesopotamischen Federzeichnungen von Jahre 1299', *Oriens Christianus*, N.S. 1, 1911, pp. 249ff.

Beck, E., 'English Medieval Art at the Victoria and Albert Museum', *Burlington Magazine*, 56, 1930, p. 292, p. xi, pl. 98.

Becker, E., 'Das Quellwunder des Moses in der altchristlichen Kunst' in *Zur Kunstgeschichte des Auslandes*, 72, Strassburg, 1909.

Beckwith, J., *Early Christian and Byzantine Art*, New Haven, CT, Yale University Press, 1979.

—— *Early Medieval Art*, World of Art, New York, Thames and Hudson, 1992 (reprint of 1969 edition).

Bellosi, L., *Giotto*, Florence, Sogema Marzari Schio, 1984.

Beskow, P., *Strange Tales About Jesus*, Philadelphia, Fortress Press, 1983.

Boeckler, A., *Das stuttgarter Passionale,* Augsburg, Dr. Filser, 1923.

—— *Die Regensburg-Prüfeninger Buchmalerei des XII. und XIII. Jahrhunderts*, Munich, A. Reusch, 1929.

Bornkamm, G., *Mythos und Legende in den apokryphen Thomas-Akten*, FRLANT, n.f. 31, Göttingen, Vandenhoeck & Ruprecht, 1933.

Bovini, G., *Ravenna*, New York, Harry N. Abrams, 1969.

Bovon, F. and Geoltrain, P., *Écrits apocryphes chrétiens*, Paris, Gallimard, 1997 = *Bibliothèque de la Pléiade* 442.

Brooklyn Museum, *Pagan and Christian Egypt. Art from the First to the Tenth Century A.D.*, exhibition catalog, Brooklyn, The Brooklyn Museum, 1941.

Brown, P. R. L., 'Art and Society in Late Antiquity' in *The Age of Spirituality: A Symposium*, Kurt Weitzmann, ed., New York, Metropolitan Museum of Art/Princeton University Press, 1980, pp. 17–27.

—— 'Review of Thomas Mathews, *The Clash of Gods*', *Art Bulletin*, LXXVII/3, September, 1995, pp. 499–502.

Brown, R. E., *The Gospel According to John*, 2 vols., The Anchor Bible, New York, Doubleday, 1970.

Bucher, F., *The Pamplona Bibles; a Facsimile Compiled from Two Picture Bibles with Martyrologies Commissioned by King Sanco el Fuerte of Navarra (1194–1234): Amiens Manuscript Latin 108 and Harburg MS. 1, 2, Lat.*, New Haven, CT, Yale University Press, 1970.

Budge, E. A. Wallis, *The Contendings of the Apostles*, 2 vols., London, Henry Frowde, 1901.

Burckhardt, J., *The Altarpiece in Renaissance Italy*, Cambridge and New York, Cambridge University Press, 1988.

Bynum, C., 'The Body of Christ in the Later Middle Ages: A Reply to Leo Steinberg' in *Fragmentation and Redemption: Essays on Gender and the Human Body in Medieval Religion*, New York, Zone Books, 1992, pp. 79–117.

Cabrol, F., Leclerq, H. and Marrou, H.-I., *Dictionnaire d'archéologie chrétienne et de liturgie*, 15 vols., Paris, Letouzey and Ané, 1908–53.

Cahn, W., *Romanesque Bible Illumination*, Ithaca, NY, Cornell University Press, 1982.

Cartlidge, D. R., 'An Illustration in the Admont "Anselm" and Its Relevance to a Reconstruction of the Acts of John', *Semeia*, 80, 1997, pp. 277–90.

—— 'The Christian Apocrypha: Preserved in Art', *Bible Review* XIII:2, June, 1997, pp. 24–31, 56.

—— 'Which Path at the Crossroads? Early Christian Art as a Hermeneutical and Theological Challenge' in Julian V. Hills, ed., *Common Life in the Early Church. Essays Honoring Graydon F. Snyder*, Harrisburg, PA, Trinity Press International, 1998, pp. 357–72.

Cartlidge, D. R. and Dungan, D. L., *Documents for the Study of the Gospels*, Philadelphia, Fortress Press, 1994.

Cassiday, B., 'Introduction: Iconography, Texts and Audiences' in *Iconography at the Crossroads*, Brendan Cassiday, ed., Index of Christian Art, Occasional Papers II, Princeton, NJ, Princeton University Press, 1993, pp. 3–15.

Clayton, M., *The Apocryphal Gospels of Mary in Anglo-Saxon England*, Cambridge, Cambridge University Press, 1998.

Cockerton, R. W. P., 'The Wirksworth Slab', *Derbyshire Archaeological Journal*, 82, 1962 pp. 1–20.

Dagron, G., *Vie et miracles de Sainte Thècle*, Greek and French texts, Société des Bollandistes, *Subsidia Hagiographica*, 62, 1978.

Dalton, O. M., *Byzantine Art and Archaeology*, Oxford, Oxford University Press, 1911.

Dearmer, P., Vaughan Williams, R. and Shaw, M., *The Oxford Book of Carols*, London, New York, Toronto, Oxford University Press, 1964.

de Campos, D. R., *Art Treasures of the Vatican: Architecture, Painting, Sculpture*, Englewood Cliffs, NJ, Prentice-Hall, 1974.

de Santos Otero, A., *Los Evangelios Apócrifos*, Madrid, Biblioteca de Autores Cristianos, sixth edition, 1988.

de Strycker, É., *La forme la plus ancienne du Protévangile de Jacques: Recherches sur le Papyrus Bodmer 5*, *Subsidia Hagiographica*, 33, Brussels, Société des Bollandistes, 1961.

de Voragine, Jacobus, *The Golden Legend: Readings on the Saints*, 2 vols., William Granger Ryan, trans., Princeton, NJ, Princeton University Press, 1993.

de Waal, A., 'Die apokryphen Evangelien in der altchristlichen Kunst', *Römische Quartalschrift für christliche Altertumskunde und Kirchengeschicte*, 1, 1887, pp. 173–96.

—— 'Die biblischen Totenerweckungen an den altchristlichen Grabstätten', *Römische Quartalschrift für christliche Altertumskunde und Kirchengeschichte*, 20, 1906, pp. 40ff.

della Croce, A., *Canonical Histories and Apocryphal Legends Relating to the New Testament, Represented in Drawings with a Latin Text. A Photo-Lith Reproduction from an Ambrosian MS. Executed for James Gibson-Craig, Esq.*, Milan, J. B. Pogliani, 1873.

du Bourguet, P., *Early Christian Art*, William Morrow and Company, New York, 1971.

Deichmann, F. W., Bovini, G. and Brandenburg, H., *Repertorium der christlich-antiken Sarkophage, I: Rom und Ostia*, 2 vols., Deutsches archäologisches Institut, Wiesbaden, Steiner, 1967.

Delaporte, Y. et Houvet, É., *Les vitraux de la cathédrale de Chartres: Histoire et description*, 4 vols., Chartres, 1926.

Demus, O. *The Mosaics of Norman Sicily*, New York, The Philosophical Library, 1950.

—— 'A Renascence of Early Christian Art in Thirteenth Century Venice' in *Late Classical and Mediaeval Studies in Honor of A. M. Friend, Jr.*, Princeton, NJ, Princeton University Press, 1955, pp. 349ff.

—— *The Church of San Marco in Venice: History, Architecture, Sculpture*, Dumbarton Oaks Studies VI, Washington, DC, Dumbarton Oaks, 1960.s

—— *Byzantine Art and the West*, The Wrightman Lectures, Institute of Fine Arts, New York, New York University Press, 1970.

—— *The Mosaic Decoration of San Marco, Venice*, Herbert W. Kessler, ed., Chicago, The University of Chicago Press, 1988.

—— *The Mosaics of San Marco in Venice*, 2 vols., Chicago, University of Chicago Press, 1984.

Deshman, R., *The Benedictional of Aethelwold*, Studies in Manuscript Illumination 9, Princeton, NJ, Princeton University Press, 1995.

Dinkler, E., 'Die ersten Petrusdarstellungen. Ein archäologischer Beitrag zur Geschichte des Petrusprimates', *Marburger Jahrbuch für Kunstwissenschaft*, 11, 1939, pp. 1–80.

—— 'Abbreviated Representations' in *The Age of Spirituality*, Kurt Weitzmann, ed., Metropolitan Museum of Art, Princeton, NJ, Princeton University Press, 1978, pp. 396f.

Dungan, D. L., 'The New Testament Canon in Recent Study', *Interpretation*, 29, 1975, pp. 339–51.

Egeria, *Diary of a Pilgrimage*, Online. Available http://users.ox.ac.uk/~mikef/durham/egeria.html (accessed April 24, 2001). Posted by Michael Fraser, with both Latin text and English translation.

Eliade, M., *Patterns in Comparative Religion*, New York, World Publishing Company, 1963.

Elliott, J. K., *The Apocryphal New Testament: A Collection of Apocryphal Christian Literature in an English Translation Based on M.R. James*, Oxford, The Clarendon Press, 1993.

Erbetta, M., *Gli apocrifi del Nuovo Testamento*, Casale Monferrato, Marietti, 1066–81.

Fabricius, U., *Die Legende im Bild des 1 Jahrtausends der Kirche*, Kassel, Oncken, 1957.

Fakhry, A., *The Necropolis of El-Bagawat in Kharga Oasis*, Service des antiquités de l'Égypte, Cairo, Government Press, 1951.

Ferrua, A., *Le pittura della nuova catacomba di Via Latina*, Pontificio Istituto di archeologia cristiana, Vatican City, 1960.

Finney, P. C., 'Images on Finger Rings and Early Christian Art', Studies on Art and Archaeology in Honor of Ernst Kitzinger on His Seventy-Fifth Birthday, William Tronzo and Irving Lavin, eds., *Dumbarton Oaks Papers* 31, Washington, DC, Dumbarton Oaks, 1987, pp. 181–6.

—— *The Invisible God: The Earliest Christians on Art*, New York and Oxford, Oxford University Press, 1994.

Frolow, A., 'L'église rouge de Perustica', *The Bulletin of the Byzantine Institute*, 5, 1946, pp. 31ff.

Garrucci, R., *Storia dell'arte cristiana nei primi otto secoli della chiesa*, Rome, 1876–81.

Geerard, M., *Clavis Apocryphorum Novi Testamenti*, Corpus Christianorum, Tournhout, Brepols, 1992.

Gijsel, J. and Beyers, R., *Libri de Nativitate Mariae*, 2 vols., Corpus Christianorum Series Apocryphorum 9 and 10, Turnhout, Brepols, 1997.

Goldschmidt, A., *Die Elfenbeinskulpturen aus der Zeit der karolingischen und sächsischen Kaiser*, Denkmäler der deutschen Kunst, Berlin and Oxford, Bruno Cassirer, 1969.

Goodspeed, E. J., *Modern Apocrypha*, Boston, Beacon Press, 1956.

Gough, M., *The Origins of Christian Art*, New York, Praeger, 1971.

Grabar, A., *Martyrium: Recherches sur le culte des reliques et l'art chrétien antique*, vol. I, Architecture; vol. II, Iconographie, Paris, Collège de France, 1943 (vol. I); 1946 (vol. II).

—— 'Un reliquaire provenant d'Isaurie', *Cahiers archéologiques*, XIII, 1962, pp. 49ff.

—— *The Golden Age of Justinian*, New York, Odyssey Press, 1967.

—— *Early Christian Art: From the Rise of Christianity to the Death of Theodosius*, New York, Odyssey Press, 1968.

—— *Christian Iconography: A Study of Its Origins*, Bollingen Series XXXV.10, A. W. Mellon Lectures in the Fine Arts, 1961, Princeton, Princeton University Press, 1968.

Grabar, A. and Nordenfalk, C., *Early Medieval Painting from the Fourth to the Eleventh Century*, New York, Skira, 1957.

Hennecke, E., *Neutestamentliche Apokryphen in deutscher Übersetzung*, Tübingen and Leipzig, Mohr, 1904, second edition, 1924.

Hock, R. F., *The Infancy Gospels of James and Thomas*, The Scholars Bible, Santa Rosa, CA, Polebridge Press, 1995.

Hoddinott, R. E., *Early Byzantine Churches in Macedonia and Southern Serbia*, New York, St Martin's Press, 1963.

Houvet, É., *Monographie de la cathédrale de Chartres*, Chartres, E. Chambrin, 1927.

Hubert, J., Porche, J. and Volbach, W. F., *Europe of the Invasions*, The Arts of Mankind, André Malraux and André Parrot, eds., New York, George Braziller, 1969.

James, L., review of Mathews, *Clash of the Gods*, *Burlington Magazine*, 136, 1994, pp. 458ff.

James, M. R., *The Trinity College Apocalypse*, Cambridge, Cambridge University Press, 1909.

—— 'Rare Medieval Tiles and their Story', *Burlington Magazine*, XLII, 1923, pp. 33–8, pls. 33, 34, 35.

—— *The Apocryphal New Testament*, Oxford, The Clarendon Press, 1924.

—— *The Apocalypse in Art: The Schweich Lectures in Biblical Archaeology*, 1927, The British Academy, London, Oxford University Press, 1931.

Janson, H. W., *History of Art*, Englewood Cliffs, NJ, Prentice-Hall, 1991, fourth edition.

Jastrzebowska, J., *Bild und Wort: Das Marienleben und die Kindheit Jesu in der christlichen Kunst vom 4. bis 8. Jh. und ihre apokryphen Quellen*, photocopy of a Habilitationsschrift, University of Warsaw, Institute of Archaeology, Warsaw, 1992.

Jensen, R. M., 'Giving Texts Vision and Images Voice: The Promise and Problems of Interdisciplinary Scholarship' in *Common Life in the Early Church. Essays Honoring Graydon F. Snyder*, Harrisburg, PA, Trinity Press International, 1998, pp. 344–56.

—— *Understanding Early Christian Art*, London and New York, Routledge, 2000.

Junod, E. and Kaestli, J.-D., *L'histoire des Actes apocryphes des apôtres du IIIe au IXe siècle: Le cas des Actes de Jean*, Cahiers de la revue de théologie et de philosophie 7, Lausanne, Neuchâtel, 1982.

—— eds., *Acta Iohannis*, 2 vols., Corpus Christianorum: Series Apocryphorum 1, Turnhout, Brepols, 1983.

Kaftal, G., *Iconography of the Saints in Tuscan Painting*, Florence, Casa Editrice Le Lettere, 1952.

—— *Iconography of the Saints in North East Italy*, Florence, Casa Editrice Le Lettere, 1978.

—— *Iconography of the Saints in Central and South Italian Schools of Painting*, Florence, Casa Editrice Le Lettere, 1986.

Kartsonis, A. D., *Anastasis: The Making of an Image*, Princeton, NJ, Princeton University Press, 1986.

Kelber, W., *The Oral and the Written Gospel: The Hermeneutics of Speaking and Writing in the Synoptic Tradition, Mark, Paul, and Q.*, Philadelphia, Fortress Press, 1983.

Kessler, H. L., 'Scenes from the Acts of the Apostles on Some Early Christian Ivories', *Gesta*, XVIII/1, 1979, pp. 109–19.

—— 'Pictorial Narrative and Church Mission in Sixth-Century Gaul' in *Pictorial Narrative in Antiquity and the Middle Ages*, Studies in the History of Art, Washington, DC, Dumbarton Oaks, 1985, pp. 75–91.

—— 'The Meeting of Peter and Paul in Rome: An Emblematic Narrative of Spiritual Brotherhood' in Studies on Art and Archeology in Honor of Ernst Kitzinger on His Seventy-Fifth Birthday, William Tronzo and Irving Lavin, eds., *Dumbarton Oaks Papers* 41, 1987, pp. 265–75.

Kessler, H. L. and Simpson, M. S., eds., *Pictorial Narrative in Antiquity and the Middle Ages*, Studies in the History of Art, vol. 16, Washington, National Gallery of Art, 1985.

Kitzinger, E., 'The Role of Miniature Painting in Mural Decoration', K. Weitzmann, *et al.*, eds., *The Place of Book Illumination in Byzantine Art and The Art of Byzantium and the Medieval West: Selected Studies (32–41)*, The Art Museum, Princeton University, Princeton, NJ, Princeton University Press 1975, pp. 99ff.

—— *Byzantine Art in the Making: Main Lines of Stylistic Development in Mediterranean Art, 3rd–7th Century*, Cambridge, MA, Harvard University Press, 1977.

—— 'The Cleveland Marbles', in *Atti del IX congresso internazionale di archeologia cristiana*, Studi di antichità cristiana 32, Città del Vaticano, Roma, Pontificio Istituto di archeologia cristiana, 1978.

—— 'Christian Imagery: Growth and Impact' in *The Age of Spirituality: A Symposium*, K. Weitzmann, ed., New York, Metropolitan Museum of Art/Princeton University Press, 1980, pp. 141–63.

—— *The Mosaics of St. Mary's of the Admiral in Palermo*, Dumbarton Oaks Studies XXVII, Washington, DC, Dumbarton Oaks Research Library, 1990.

Klauser, T. and Deichmann, F. W., *Frühchristliche Sarkophage in Bild und Wort*, T. Klauser (text), F. W. Deichmann (selection of examples), Halbjahrschrift antiker Kunst, Beiheft 3, Olten (Schweiz), Urs Graf-Verlag, 1966.

Kleinbauer, W. E., 'Review of Thomas Mathews, *The Clash of Gods*', *Speculum*, 70, 1995, pp. 937–41.

Kleinschmidt, B., *Die Basilika San Francesco in Assisi*, 3 vols., Berlin, Verlag für Kunstwissenschaft, 1915–28.

Kloss, E., *Die schlesische Buchmalerei des Mittelalters*, Berlin, Deutscher Verein für Kunstwissenschaft, 1942.

Kostof, S., *The Orthodox Baptistery of Ravenna*, New Haven and London, Yale University Press, 1965.

Kraeling, C. H., 'The Christian Building: The Excavations at Dura-Europos. Final Report, 8, Pt.2' in *The Excavations at Dura-Europos Conducted by Yale University and the French Academy of Inscriptions and Letters*, C. Bradford Welles, ed., New Haven, Yale University Press, 1961–7, 1968.

Kraemer, R., ed., *Maenads, Martyrs, Matrons, Monastics*, Philadelphia, Fortress Press, 1988.

Künstle, K., *Ikonographie der christlichen Kunst*, Freiburg im Breisgau, Herder, 1926–8.

Kurth, B., 'The Iconography of the Wirksworth Slab', *The Burlington Magazine*, 86, 1945, pp. 114–21.

Lafond, J., 'Les vitraux de la Cathédrale Saint-Pierre de Troyes', *Congrès archéologique de France*, 113, 1955, pp. 28–62.

—— 'Les vitraux de la Cathédrale Saint-Etienne d'Auxerre', *Congrès archéologique de France*, 116, 1958, pp. 60–75.

Lafontaine-Dosogne, J., 'Peintures médiévales dans le temple dit de la Fortune Virile a Rome' in *Études de philologie, d'archéologie et d'histoire anciennes publiées par l'Institut historique belge de Rome 6*, Brussels, 1959, pp. 29–35.

—— 'Iconography of the Cycle of the Life of the Virgin' in P. A. Underwood, ed., *Kariye Djami*, 4 volumes, Bollinger Series LXX, New York, Pantheon Books, 1966, vol. 4, pp. 163–93.

—— 'Iconography of the Cycle of the Infancy of Christ' in P. A. Underwood, ed., *Kariye Djami*, 4 volumes, Bollinger Series LXX, New York, Pantheon Books 1966, vol. 4, pp. 197–241.

—— *Iconographie de l'enfance de la Vierge dans l'Empire byzantin et en Occident*, 2 vols., Académie royale de Belgique, Brussels, Palais des Académies, réédition anastatique avec compléments, 1992.

Le Blant, E., *Les sarcophages chrétiens de la Gaule*, Paris, Impr. nationale, 1886.

Levi, D., *Antioch Mosaic Pavements*, Princeton, Princeton University Press, 1947.

Levi, P., *Heythrop Journal*, 4, 1963, pp. 55–60.

Lillich, M. P., *The Stained Glass of Saint-Père de Chartres*, Middletown, CT, Wesleyan University Press, 1978.

Lipsius, R.A. and Bonnet, M., eds., *Acta Apostolorum Apocrypha*, 2 vols., Darmstadt, Wissenschaftliche Buchgesellschaft, 1959, original publication, 1891.

Longhi, R., *Carlo Braccesco*, Milan, Istituto nazionale di studi sul rinascimento, 1942.

Lord, A. B., *The Singer of Tales*, Harvard Studies in Comparative Literature 11, Cambridge, MA, Harvard University Press, 1960.

Lost Books of the Bible and the Forgotten Books of Eden, The (combined volume – authors/editors unknown), Collins-World, 1977.

Lowrie, W., *Art in the Early Church*, New York, Pantheon Books, 1947.

MacDonald, D. R., *The Legend and the Apostle: The Battle for Paul in Story and Canon*, Philadelphia, Westminster Press, 1983.

—— *The Acts of Andrew and The Acts of Andrew and Matthias in the City of the Cannibals*, Texts and Translations 33, Atlanta, GA, Scholars Press, 1990.

MacDonald, D. R. and Scrimgeour, A. D., 'Pseudo-Chrysostom's Panegyric to Thecla: The Heroine of the Acts of Paul in Homily and Art', *Semeia*, 38, 1986, pp. 151–60.

MacGregor, N. with Langmuir, E., *Seeing Salvation*, London and New Haven, CT, BBC Worldwide and Yale University Press, 2000.

Malbon, E. S., *The Iconography of the Sarcophagus of Junius Bassus*, Princeton, NJ, Princeton University Press, 1990.

Mancinelli, F., *Catacombs and Basilicas: The Early Christians in Rome*, Florence, Scala Books, 1981.

Mango, C., *The Art of the Byzantine Empire 312–1453*, Sources and Documents: The History of Art Series, Englewood Cliffs, NJ, Prentice-Hall, 1972.

Marks, R. and Morgan, N. J., *The Golden Age of English Manuscript Painting: 1200–1500*, New York, George Braziller, 1981.

Mathews, T. F., *The Clash of Gods: A Reinterpretation of Early Christian Art*, Princeton, NJ, Princeton University Press, 1993.

Matthews, C. R., 'Nicephorus Callistus' Physical Description of Peter: An Original Component of the *Acts of Peter*?', *Apocrypha: Revue internationale des littératures apocryphes*', 7, 1996, pp. 134–45.

Meeks, W. A., 'The Image of the Androgyne: Some Uses of a Symbol in Earliest Christianity', *History of Religions*, 13:3, February 1974, pp. 165–208.

Millet, G., *La Peinture de moyen âge en Yougoslavie*, Paris, E. de Boccard, 1962.

Moraldi, L., *Apocrifi del Nuovo Testamento*, Turin, Unione Tipografico-Editrice Torinese, 1971, second edition, 1994.

Morgan, N. J., *Early Gothic Manuscripts (II) 1250–1285*, A Survey of Manuscripts Illuminated in the British Isles, J. J. G. Alexander, general editor, London: Harvey Miller, Oxford University Press, 1988.

Murbach, E., *The Painted Romanesque Ceiling of St Martin in Zillis*, Peter Heman, ed. and photographer, New York, Praeger, 1967.

Murray, (Sister) C., 'Art and the Early Church', *Journal of Theological Studies*, N.S. XXVIII, 1977, pp. 303–45.

Natanson, J., *Early Christian Ivories*, London, Alec Tiranti, 1953.

Nauerth, C. and Warns, N., *Thekla, ihre Bilder in der frühchristlichen Kunst*, Göttingen Orientforschungen II. Studien zur spätantiken und frühchristlichen Kunst 3, Wiesbaden, Otto Harrassowitz, 1981.

Nordenfalk, C., *Studies in the History of Book Illumination*, collected papers, London, Pindar Press, 1992.

Nordhagen, P. J., 'The Mosaics of John VII (705–707 A.D.). The Mosaic Fragments and Their Technique', *Acta ad Archaeologiam et Artium Historiam Pertinentia, Institutum Romanum Norvegiae*, 2, 1965, pp. 121ff.

Oesterreichische Zeitschrift für Kunst und Denkmalpflege, VI, 1952.

Omont, H. A., *Miniatures des plus anciens manuscrits grecs de la Bibliothèque nationale du VIe au XIVe siècle*, Paris, Champion, 1929.

Ong, W. J., *Orality and Literacy: The Technologizing of the Word*, London, Methuen, 1982.

Origen, *Contra Celsum*, Henry Chadwick, ed. and trans., Cambridge, Cambridge University Press, 1965.

Pächt, O., 'The Illustrations of St. Anselm's Prayers and Meditations', *Journal of the Warburg and Courtauld Institutes*, 19, 1956, pp. 68–83.

—— *Book Illumination in the Middle Ages: An Introduction*, Oxford, Oxford University Press, 1986.

Pagels, E., *The Gnostic Gospels*, New York, Random House, 1979.

Panofsky, E., 'Iconography and Iconology: An Introduction to the Study of Renaissance Art' in *Meaning in the Visual Arts*, collected papers, Garden City, NY, Doubleday Anchor Books, 1939, pp. 26–54 (originally published in E. Panofsky, *Studies in Iconology*, Oxford University Press, 1939).

Peeters, P., *Évangiles apocryphes*, vol. 2, L'Évangile de l'Enfance, Rédactions syriaque, arabe, et arméniennes, Paris, Auguste Picard, 1914.

Pelekanidis, S. M., Christou, P. C., Tsioumis, C. and Kadas, S. N., *The Treasures of Mount Athos*, 3 vols., Philip Sherrard, trans., Athens, Ekdotike Athenon, 1974.

Pelikan, J., *Mary Through the Centuries: Her Place in the History of Culture*, New Haven and London, Yale University Press, 1996.

Pervo, R., *Profit with Delight*, Philadelphia, Fortress Press, 1987.

Raguin, V. C., *Stained Glass in Thirteenth-Century Burgundy*, Princeton, NJ, Princeton University Press, 1982.

Raoul-Rochette, D., *Discours sur l'origine, le développement et le caractère des types imitatifs que constituent l'art du christianisme*, Paris, 1834.

Réau, L., *Iconographie de l'art chrétien*, 3 vols., Paris, Presses universitaires de France, 1955–9.

Restle, M., *Byzantine Wall Painting in Asia Minor*, 3 vols., Recklinghausen, Aurel Bongers, 1967.

Rice, D. T., *The Art of Byzantium*, London, Hirmer, 1959.

Robinson, J. M., gen. ed., *The Nag Hammadi Library in English*, 3rd edn, San Francisco, Harper & Row, 1988.

Rodley, L., *Cave Monasteries of Byzantine Cappadocia*, Cambridge, Cambridge University Press, 1985.

Rodnikova, I., *Pskov Icons: 13th–16th Centuries*, Leningrad, Aurora Art Publishers, 1991.

Saggiorato, A., *I sarcofagi paleocristiani con scene di passione*, Studi di antichità cristiana, Bologna, Casa Patron, 1968.

Schiller, G., *Ikonographie der christlichen Kunst*, 5 vols., Gütersloh, Gerd Mohn, 1966–91.

—— *Iconography of Christian Art*, 2 vols., translation of first two volumes of German edition, Janet Seligman, Greenwich, CT and London, New York Graphic Society Ltd and Lund Humphries, 1971; 1972.

Schneemelcher, W., ed., *New Testament Apocrypha*, 2 vols., Philadelphia, Westminster Press, 1991.

Schubert, K., 'Jewish Pictorial Traditions in Early Christian Art' in H. Schreckenberg and K. Schubert, *Jewish Historiography and Iconography in Early and Medieval Christianity*, Assen/Maastricht/Minneapolis, Fortress Press, 1992, pp. 141ff.

Snyder, G. F., *Ante Pacem: Archaeological Evidence of Church Life before Constantine*, Macon, GA, Mercer University Press, 1985.

Sotiriou, G. and M., *Icones de Mont Sinai*, 2 vols., Athens, 1956–8.

Stark, R., *The Rise of Christianity: A Sociologist Reconsiders History*, Princeton, NJ, Princeton University Press, 1996.

Steinberg, L., *The Sexuality of Christ in Renaissance Art and in Modern Oblivion*, New York, Pantheon, 1983, second edition, 1996.

Stuhlfauth, G., *Die apocryphen Petrusgeschichten in der altchristlichen Kunst*, Berlin, de Gruyter, 1925.

Styger, P., 'Neue Untersuchungen über die altchristlichen Petrusdarstellungen', *Römische Quartalschrift*, 27, 1923, pp. 70ff.

Swarzenski, H., *Die lateinischen illuminierten Handschriften des XIII Jahrhunderts in den Ländern an Rhein, Main und Donau*, Berlin, 1936.

Thierry, N., 'Les enseignements historiques de l'archéologie cappadocienne', *Travaux et Mémoires*, 8, 1981, pp. 501–19.

—— 'L'illustrations des apocryphes dans les églises du Cappadoces', *Apocrypha: le champ des apocryphes*, 2, 1991, pp. 217–47.

—— 'L'iconographie cappadocienne de l'affront à Anne d'après le *Protévangile de Jacques*', *Apocrypha*, 7, 1996, pp. 261–72.

Trexler, R. C., 'Gendering Jesus Crucified' in *Iconography at the Crossroads*, Brendan Cassiday, ed., Index of Christian Art: Occasional Papers II, Princeton, NJ, Princeton University Press, 1993, pp. 107–19.

Tronzo, W., *The Via Latina Catacomb: Imitation and Discontinuity in Fourth-Century Roman Painting*, University Park and London, Pennsylvania State University Press, 1986.

Voelkle, W. M. and Wieck, W. S., *The Bernard H. Breslauer Collection of Manuscript Illuminations*, Exhibition Catalog, New York, The Pierpont Morgan Library, 1992.

Volbach, W. F., *Elfenbeinarbeiten der spätantike und des frühen Mittelalters*, Mainz, Verlag des römisch-germanischen Zentralmuseums, 1952, 1976 (3rd edition).

—— *Early Christian Art*, London, Hirmer, 1961.

von Campenhausen, H., *The Formation of the Christian Bible*, Philadelphia, Fortress Press, 1972.

von Dobschütz, E., *Christusbilder: Untersuchungen zur christlichen Legende*, Texte und Untersuchungen zur Geschichte der altchristichen Literatur, vol. 18, Oscar von Gebhart and Adolf Harnack, eds., Leipzig, J. C. Hinrichs, 1899.

von Erbach-Fürstenau, A., 'L'Evangelo di Nicodemo', *Archivo storico dell'arte* 11/3, 1893, pp. 225–37.

von Sybel, L., *Christliche Antike, Einführung in die altchristiche Kunst*, 3 vols., Marburg, N. G. Elwert, 1906–9.

Waetzoldt, S., *Die Kopien des 17. Jahrhunderts nach Mosaiken und Wandmalereien in Rom*, Römisch Forschungen der Bibliotheca Hertziana, Band XVIII, Vienna-Munich, Schroll-Verlag, 1964.

Warns, R., 'Weitere Darstellungen der Heiligen Thekla' in *Studien zur frühchristlichen Kunst, II*, Guntram Koch, ed., Göttinger Orientforschungen, Wiesbaden, Harrassowitz, 1986, pp. 75–137.

Weis-Liebersdorf, J. E., *Christus- und Apostelbilder. Einfluss der Apokryphen auf die ältesten Kunsttypen*, Freiburg im Breisgau, Herder, 1902.

Weiss, P., *Die Mosaiken des Chora-Klosters in Istanbul*, Stuttgart and Zürich, Belser Verlag, 1997.

Weitzmann, K., ed., *The Fresco Cycle of S. Maria di Castelseprio*, Princeton Monographs in Art and Archeology, XXVI, Princeton, Princeton University Press, 1951.

—— *Illustrations in Roll and Codex: A Study of the Origin and Method of Text Illustration*, Studies in Manuscript Illustration, Princeton, NJ, Princeton University Press, 1948; second edition, 1970.

—— 'The Mandylion and Constantine Porphyrogennetos' in *Studies in Classical and Byzantine Manuscript Illumination*, Herbert L. Kessler, ed., Chicago and London, University of Chicago Press, 1971, pp. 224–46 (originally published in *Cahiers archéologiques*, XI, 1960, pp. 163–84).

—— 'The Selection of Texts for Cyclic Illustration in Byzantine Manuscripts' in *Byzantine Books and Bookmen*, papers delivered at a colloquium at Dumbarton Oaks (1971), Center for Byzantine Studies, Washington, DC, J. J. Augustin, 1975, pp. 69–109.

—— *The Monastery of Saint Catherine at Mount Sinai, The Icons, Volume I, From the Sixth to the Tenth Century*, Princeton, NJ, Princeton University Press, 1976.

—— *Late Antique and Early Christian Book Illumination*, New York, George Braziller, 1977.

—— *The Icon: Holy Images – Sixth to Fourteenth Century*, New York, George Braziller, 1978.

—— *Age of Spirituality*, catalog of the exhibition at the Metropolitan Museum of Art, New York, Metropolitan Museum of Art and Princeton University Press, 1979.

Wentzel, H., 'Christus-Johannes-Gruppe', *Reallexikon zur deutschen Kunstgeschichte*, III, 1954, col. 658f.

—— 'Unbekannte Christus-Johannes-Gruppen', *Zeitschrift für Kunstwissenschaft*, 13:1–2, 1959, pp. 155–76.

Wilder, A. N., *The Language of the Gospel: Early Christian Rhetoric*, Cambridge, Massachusetts, SCM Press/Harper & Row, 1964.

Willis, E., 'The Development of the Iconography of Saint Thecla from the 4th Century to the 20th Century CE', unpublished paper presented at the Society of Biblical Literature, Annual Meeting, 1994.

Wilpert, J., *Die römischen Mosaiken und Malereien der kirchlichen Bauten vom IV. bis zum XIII. Jahrhundert.* 4 vols., Freiburg im Breisgau, Herder, 1916.

—— *I sarcofagi cristiani antichi,* 3 vols., Monumenti dell'antichità cristiana pubblicati per cura del Pontificio Istituto di archeologia cristiana, Rome, Città del Vaticano, 1929–36.

Wright, W., *The Apocryphal Acts of the Apostles: edited from Syriac manuscripts in the British Museum and other libraries with English translations and notes*, Amsterdam, Philo Press, 1968 (reprint of the London 1871 edition).

Zanker, P., *The Mask of Socrates: The Image of the Intellectual in Antiquity*, translation of *Maske des Sokrates*, trans. Alan Shapiro, Berkeley, University of California Press, 1995.

INDEX OF EXTRACTS FROM
APOCRYPHAL TEXTS

This index lists those extracts from the Apocryphal New Testament located in inserts throughout the text. Relevant page numbers are given in *italics*.

GENERAL INDEX

Figures and apocryphal text inserts are in bold type.